D0768724

RETURN TO THE SHADOWS

ALSO BY ALISON PARGETER

The New Frontiers of Jihad: Radical Islam in Europe

The Muslim Brotherhood: From Opposition to Power

Libya: The Rise and Fall of Qaddafi

RETURN TO THE SHADOWS

The Muslim Brotherhood and An-Nahda since the Arab Spring

ALISON PARGETER

SAQI

Published 2016 by Saqi Books

ISBN 978-0-86356-144-3
eISBN 978-0-86356-154-2

A full CIP record for this book is available from the British Library.

Printed and bound by CPI Group (UK) Ltd, Croydon, CR0 4YY

Saqi Books
26 Westbourne Grove
London W2 5RH
www.saqibooks.com

CONTENTS

ACKNOWLEDGMENTS

This book was made possible by a research grant from the Smith Richardson Foundation. This generous support enabled me to build on my previous work on the Muslim Brotherhood and to examine the movement and its counterparts following the tumultuous events of the Arab Spring. In particular it enabled me to conduct primary research on the Muslim Brotherhood in Egypt and Libya, and on An-Nahda in Tunisia, through a number of research visits to the region and beyond. As a result, much of this book is based on interviews carried out with members of these movements, as well as with specialists and experts in the field. In particular I would like to thank Nadia Schadlow from the Smith Richardson Foundation for her continued support for my research on the Brotherhood. I also thank her for her patience. The research project was conceived at a time when the Brotherhood had recently come to power in Egypt but was delayed to accommodate the dramatically changing circumstances on the ground. I am very grateful to have been given the space to carry out this project at such an important time.

I would also like to thank the Airey Neave Trust and the Dulverton Trust, both of which also supported this project with research grants. They provided funding that enabled me to extend my research, and in particular to carry out additional field visits. This proved particularly invaluable given that key leaders from the Egyptian Brotherhood ended up being displaced across the region. My thanks also go to the Royal United Services Institute, and to Professor Michael Clarke in particular, for being willing to host this project and to support my research.

I would also like to thank Lynn Gaspard and Sarah Cleave at Saqi Books for supporting this book and for all their help and patience. I am also hugely grateful to Charles Peyton for copy-editing the text.

I am deeply indebted to all those individuals who were willing to be interviewed for this book, particularly those from the Muslim Brotherhood and from An-Nahda. In particular I would like to thank Osama Haddad and Mohamed Soudan from the Egyptian Brotherhood, Mohamed Abdulmalik and Alamin Belhaj from the Libyan Brotherhood, and Amer Larayedh, Said Ferjani and Walid Bannani from An-Nahda. I thank them for their frankness, kindness and generosity. Special thanks go to Professor Alaya Allani and Professor Mehdi Mabrouk for all their help, kindness and, most importantly, their insights, during my visits to Tunisia. I would also like to thank Shafiq Gabr for his interest in my work and his assistance in facilitating interviews in Egypt, as well as for his insights. Lastly, I would like to thank all those individuals whose names I cannot mention but whose assistance has been indispensable.

INTRODUCTION

As Mohamed Morsi stepped up to the presidency on 30 June 2012, the world, or at least the Middle East, appeared to have changed irreversibly. After more than eight decades in the shadows of semi-clandestinity, the Muslim Brotherhood, a Sunni fundamentalist movement long considered to be the vanguard of political Islamism, had finally come to the fore. More importantly, it had done so through the ballot box. Following the uprisings that erupted in Egypt on 25 January 2011, leading to President Hosni Mubarak's ousting the following month, the Brotherhood, by virtue of being the only organised force in the country, moved quickly to fill the vacuum that had opened up. The Brotherhood's Freedom and Justice Party (FJP) won the public's support in both parliamentary and presidential elections, and was poised to put its project into action. This was a deeply symbolic moment for the Brotherhood and for the Islamic movement more widely. As the pioneer of political Islam, the Brotherhood at last had the opportunity to demonstrate that an Islamist party could lead an Arab state in the contemporary era. More importantly, it had a chance to steer Egypt down a different path, breaking the hold of the military-backed regime that had ruled for generations, and to reconnect society to what the movement deemed to be its authentic self.

It had been a very long wait. Established in 1928 in Ismailia by schoolteacher Hassan Al-Banna, the Muslim Brotherhood had a history of patience and persecution. It started out as a socio-religious movement chiefly preoccupied with how to confront the challenges of modernisation, and what Al-Banna saw as the spiritual and moral decline of the Ummah (united Muslim nation). Drawing on the ideas of the reformist thinkers of the nineteenth century, Al-Banna believed that the only way to counter such challenges was to reform society by returning to the ideal Islamic society of the past. Al-Banna's was a project of salvation aimed at putting Islam at the centre of things.

As it developed, the Brotherhood became more directly involved in politics, soon emerging as the most powerful opposition force not only in Egypt but across the region, where branches of the movement had sprung up. Inevitably, therefore, it came to clash with the secular nationalist regimes of the day, and found itself subjected to heavy repression. Not that it had ever been a movement that claimed to want to rule. 'Participation not domination' was its famous mantra – a phrase that was to be repeated again and again by senior Brotherhood leaders during the course of 2011. In fact, the Brotherhood invested significant energy over the years trying to signal that it was not power-hungry, but could work within the existing framework of the state. This was part of its almost schizophrenic approach that mixed appeasement and compromise on the one hand with opposition politics on the other, the aim being to carve out as much space as possible in which it could operate.

Moreover, the Brotherhood was a movement characterised by gradualism, believing that reforming society began with reforming the individual. Its project was a long-term one – something that elicited the condemnation of more militant elements over the years who, impatient for action, broke away to form their own groups. While the Brotherhood's gradualist stance enabled it to outlive many of these more radical and hot-headed offshoots, by the eve of the 2011 uprisings its long years of waiting were taking their toll. Indeed, this large, unwieldy body was proving unable to break free from its own traditions in order to meet the challenges of operating as a modern body in a modern age. Its attempts at reforming itself in the 2000s had born little fruit and the movement appeared to be on the retreat from politics rather than the opposite.

It struggled too to move away from its own psychological impediments, which had arisen out of the long years of suffering, including a victimisation complex in which the Brotherhood believed itself to be targeted by everyone. Its inability to throw off these shackles meant that, when the revolution broke out in 2011, the Brotherhood appeared thoroughly anachronistic – as much a part of the old furniture as the regime it was meant to be opposing.

When Egyptians took to the streets in January 2011, inspired by protests in Tunisia that had led to the ouster of President Zine El Abidine Ben Ali, the Brotherhood looked to be out of the fray. But once it realised the significance of what was happening, the Brotherhood stepped forward and deployed what until then had been its largely dormant might to direct the revolution as it saw fit. When the opportunity to take power finally arose the Brotherhood was less hesitant, seizing it with both hands. It was as if, despite its protestations to the contrary, this was what it had been waiting for all those long years.

The Brotherhood's taking of power was all the more momentous because it seemed as though the whole region was about to 'go Islamic'. The An-Nahda party in Tunisia, which while not actually part of the global Muslim Brotherhood movement was born out of the same tradition and ideological stable, was poised to take power in Tunisia. The triumphant return of its leader, Sheikh Rachid Ghannouchi, to Tunis from exile in January 2011, received by crowds of rapturous supporters, spoke of the dawn of a new era in which the region would regain its authenticity and self-respect. Meanwhile the Libyan Brotherhood, which because of the intolerance of the regime of Muammar Qadhafi had been more in the shadows than its counterparts elsewhere, had finally been able to move into the open. Although it could not boast the same networks or support base, it still looked set to do well in the country's first democratic elections in decades, due to be held in June 2012.

For these Islamist movements, therefore, this was a moment of triumph like no other, and translated into a widespread belief that the long years of suffering finally had a meaning, and that the Islamist project was finally within reach. The sense of euphoria was evident, some members of the Brotherhood going as far as to raise the prospect of the re-emergence of the Ummah. In 2011, Ghannouchi declared: 'These [Arab Spring] countries are working to increase the overall level of relations with fraternal countries to a level greater than cooperation and interdependence and mutual interests, and to reach progressive levels of Maghreb, Arab, Gulf, and Islamic unity. There are organizations of unity that remind us that we are one Ummah.'[1] Indeed, the Arab Spring had heralded a dreamlike time in which, despite the challenges, anything seemed possible.

Just one year later, however, the scene could not have been more different. The Egyptian Brotherhood had been toppled by a temporary alliance between 'people power' and the military, bringing Morsi's rule to an end. Worse, the movement was left decimated as it entered what was to be one of the most extreme periods of repression in its history. Although An-Nahda, thanks largely to the acumen of its leader, saved itself from sharing the same fate, it was nevertheless put very much on the back foot. Forced out of power, and the object of intense hostility and criticism, it was left wondering what had gone so wrong. The Libyan Brotherhood, meanwhile, had been consumed by the catastrophe that was post-Qadhafi Libya. While it remained part of the ruling establishment, it struggled – along with the establishment itself – to assert any authority. In the end, therefore, all three movements found themselves pushed out of the centre ground. As Tarek Osman put it: 'political Islam in the region, despite a brief moment of ascendancy, has returned to its earlier status: marginalized, mistrusted, or persecuted'.[2]

What went wrong? And why did it happen so quickly? These questions have triggered a whole series of arguments about why the Brotherhood failed. But some commentators have gone further, asking whether Morsi's collapse represented a bigger, more existential crisis related to the end of political Islam itself. 'Islamism is no longer the answer', proclaimed the *Economist* on 20 December 2014,[3] while analyst Ali Alrajjal asserted: 'The fall of the Muslim

Brotherhood was accompanied by the fall of Islamism, as the movement went from empowerment and Brotherhoodization to bewilderment and exclusion, and from aspirations of power to the labyrinth of decay.'[4] In some ways, the collapse of the Brotherhood seemed to vindicate the advocates of post-Islamism, who had long argued that political Islam had failed.[5]

To equate the Brotherhood's fall with the end of political Islam, however, is premature at the very least. As Fawaz Gerges has argued, it is too soon to write an obituary for political Islam, not least because Morsi's downfall was in large part a product of the conditions he had inherited: a country in deep economic crisis, plagued by decades of corruption and mismanagement.[6] Furthermore, the Brotherhood also came to power at a time of sudden and chaotic transition, in an arena that had been static for generations. It would have taken a team of miracle workers to master what the Brotherhood faced. Likewise, Jocelyn Cesari has argued that to identify Morsi's fall with the end of political Islam is to 'limit Islamism to the Freedom and Justice Party, which was not even created until after the 2011 revolution'.[7] Indeed, while Islamism may have been struck down in Egypt, it continues to survive elsewhere. In Tunisia, for example, while An-Nahda may have been weakened, it is not out of the game, remaining a powerful force in both the political and social arenas. Moreover, as Cesari notes, 'Islamism is first and foremost a social movement.'[8] While politics has always played a key role, political Islam's strength has always been rooted in the fact that it is also a social and religious force, making it impossible to dislodge with the same ease with which a president can be overthrown. More importantly, perhaps, for all that the Arab Spring brought changes to the region, not the least of which is that it broke the fear of challenging the authority of the day, the underlying conditions in the region that gave birth to political Islam in the first place have not fundamentally altered, leaving ample space for political Islam to operate and evolve.

But if political Islam is not dead, it is nonetheless in crisis, and the Brotherhood brand has been dealt a heavy blow. There are many factors that contributed to the Brotherhood's cataclysmic fall, and these have been discussed at length by numerous scholars. Indeed, there is a broad consensus that the Brotherhood's failures are rooted more in the political than the religious domain, and are largely the result of its woeful lack of experience and understanding. As Khalil Anani has commented, the Brotherhood failed to 'effectively and positively handle power', while its organisational problems 'exposed its weakness and lack of political vision'.[9] Similarly, Ashraf El-Sherif has shown how the Brotherhood misread the situation, moving towards political domination too quickly and making a series of tactical mistakes in the process. He argues too that the Brotherhood was ideologically 'shallow and opportunistic', and 'too willing to sacrifice elements of its ideology for short-term political victories'.[10] Many have also pointed to the Brotherhood's failure to work in a consensual fashion, alienating other political forces to its own detriment. Eric Trager has described how the initial source of the Brotherhood's political strength – its organisational prowess and mobilising capabilities, which enabled its presidential candidate to be elected with a significant popular mandate despite his shortcomings – obviated the necessity for it to work with others, precipitating its own downfall.[11] As Hani Sabra has noted, the Brotherhood relied on a narrow majoritarianism, which it confused with democracy, and believed gave it a free hand to pursue its agenda.[12]

These observations all reflect the fact that the Brotherhood's failings were the result of a combination of many different factors, both objective and subjective, but largely related to the movement's fundamental inability to turn itself from a semi-clandestine opposition movement into a credible political actor capable of dealing with the challenges that were being thrown at it. Indeed, the Brotherhood proved utterly incapable of rising to the challenge of being a modern political power in a modern age.

However, the Brotherhood's failings were also a reflection of a deeper internal crisis. Despite being considered as the standard-bearer of political Islam, when it came to actually putting its project into practice, the Brotherhood proved that not only was it bereft of viable political strategies, it also struggled to translate its Islamic ideals into concrete policy solutions. As I will argue, political Islam – or at least the version of it articulated by the Brotherhood and its counterparts – turned out to be an empty vessel comprising little more than slogans and generalities that could not be translated into tangible or meaningful political outcomes. The result was not only that the Brotherhood appeared utterly lost the moment it arrived in power, but that it became locked into a cycle of reactive policymaking in which it veered from one stance to another as it sought to appease all constituencies. Indeed, its vision seemed to boil down to little more than a belief that, if more virtuous or 'reformed' individuals were at the helm, then somehow things would magically work out. The Brotherhood was thus ultimately brought down by its own intellectual shallowness, and the flimsiness of the core tenets to which it had anchored itself since its inception.

This was true not only of the Egyptian Brotherhood. While An-Nahda had always presented itself as occupying the most progressive end of the Islamist spectrum, when it came to power it also struggled to articulate what it really stood for. In addition, despite its more enlightened stance, An-Nahda made many of the same mistakes as its Egyptian counterpart. It rushed at power before it was ready, alienated others through its inability to work in a truly consensual fashion, and proved unable to turn itself into a truly national force. Although An-Nahda ultimately proved shrewder than the Egyptian Brotherhood, absorbing some of the lessons of Morsi's fall, it was forced in the process to compromise to the point where it seemed like an Islamist political party without Islam.

Meanwhile the Libyan Brotherhood, which has received very little attention, was hampered from the start by its own weaknesses, finding itself outflanked at almost every turn – including in the Islamist sphere, where it was dwarfed by more militant elements. But this did not prevent it from exhibiting some of the same weaknesses as its Egyptian and Tunisian counterparts. Having struggled to establish itself inside the country, it had been obliged to hitch its wagon to a bigger force. But in its desire for power, it chose the forces of revolution and radicalism, and ended up pigeonholing itself with some of the most extreme elements operating in the Libyan arena.

If An-Nahda's experience in power seemed to uphold the 'inclusion–moderation' hypothesis – which holds that that, through open and participatory politics, ideological parties shift towards the centre ground in order to capture the broadest cross-section of the electorate,[13] and around which much scholarly debate on Islamist movements has revolved – the experience of the Libyan Brotherhood shattered it completely. Indeed, while all three movements shared similar traits and failings, once the democratic space opened up, they responded very differently, highlighting the fact that such complex movements operating in complex environments cannot be captured by reductive theories.

This book explores the trajectory of these three Islamist movements during the Arab Spring and beyond. The culmination of a research project that entailed interviewing scores of leaders and members of the Brotherhood and An-Nahda during the turbulent times of 2013 and 2014, it examines how these most un-revolutionary of movements dealt with the uprisings in their own countries, and how they tried to transform themselves into mainstream political actors. It also looks at their experiences in power, and how and why they fell from grace so quickly, showing that their naivety and fundamental lack of vision was at the root of their downfall.

Chapter One focuses on the mother branch, exploring how the Egyptian Brotherhood turned from being reluctantly revolutionary to become a force that not only sustained the revolution, but that also reaped its benefits. Chapter Two examines the Brotherhood's first few months in power, showing how it sowed the seeds of its own downfall. Chapter Three looks at the Brotherhood's final months, examining how, despite all its attempts at mobilisation, it could not save itself. Chapters Four and Five focus on the Libyan Brotherhood, showing how it came from out of nowhere to position itself at the centre of the political arena, only to be tripped up by its own mistakes. Chapters Six and Seven deal with An-Nahda, looking at the rise to power of this most progressive of Islamist movements and how its absorption of the lessons of the Egyptian crisis, while perhaps saving its skin, nonetheless culminated in an identity crisis of its own. This book is a study of the rise and fall of political Islam as articulated by the reformist school of the Muslim Brotherhood beyond the Arab Spring, and argues that, while it promised to offer both authenticity (connecting society to its authentic self) and a unifying ideology, it provided neither, leaving fractured and polarised societies in its wake. While this process of fracturing had as much to do with the societies in which these movements operated as with the shortcomings of the movements themselves, the fact remains that the Brotherhood manifestly failed to transform itself into the modern and truly national force for which so many of those who had taken to the revolutionary streets had yearned.

PART ONE

EGYPT

ONE

THE RISE OF THE BROTHERHOOD

As thousands of young Egyptians poured into the streets on 25 January 2011 to protest against the Mubarak regime, the Egyptian Muslim Brotherhood was thrown into disarray. Despite the events that had unfolded in neighbouring Tunisia, unleashing an air of change across the region, the Brotherhood appeared almost as taken aback by this sudden show of people power as the regime itself. The Brotherhood may have been the country's oldest and longest-suffering opposition movement, but its leadership was cautious about rushing headlong into what was still a developing situation. Instead, it watched what was unfolding as it deliberated over what stance to take. This cautious approach was driven partly by a strong sense of self-preservation. Having suffered years of repression at the hands of successive regimes, the movement feared making any wrong move that might lead to a further truncation of the limited space for activity that it had so painstakingly carved out over the decades. Although still an outlawed movement whose members were regularly rounded up and imprisoned, the Brotherhood was able nonetheless to operate under the radar, carrying out its educational and charitable activities, and periodically dipping its toe into Egyptian politics. The movement was not about to squander such gains lightly.

More importantly, the Brotherhood had never been a revolutionary movement, either politically or ideologically. Its teachings advocated a gradualist approach that revolved around reforming society from the bottom up, with the aim of preparing it for the eventual establishment of an Islamic state. As former

Murshid, or Supreme Guide, Mehdi Akef proclaimed in May 2005, 'We are not people of revolution. Revolution is not part of our vocabulary.'[1] Having held to this principle since its founding in 1928, the Brotherhood was hardly going to rush headlong into protests calling for the overthrow of the regime – or at least not until it became clear where these protests might lead.

In addition, on the eve of the revolution the Brotherhood was already on the back foot, and seemed like a movement that had turned in on itself. The long years of sacrifice, which had yielded so little, were starting to take their toll, and the Brotherhood become embroiled in petty squabbles and turf wars. Furthermore, there was a growing feeling of disenchantment inside the movement. The Brotherhood's attempts during the 2000s to engage more directly in the political arena, through the development of a new reformist discourse aimed at winning over both a domestic and an international audience, had produced few tangible results, prompting increasing calls inside the movement for it to turn its back on politics and focus instead on its traditional activities of preaching and education. In many ways, it seemed as though the Brotherhood had resigned itself to the role of a semi-clandestine opposition movement that would never have the chance to put its Islamist project into practice.

The revolution thus acted as a wake-up call for the Brotherhood, jolting it out of its inertia. Despite its initial hesitation, once it became apparent that Egypt was on the brink of major change, the movement shed it cautious approach and threw itself fully behind the unfolding events. In the absence of any other opposition movement or force that could match the Brotherhood's size or weight, it was not long before it was propelled to the fore. Emboldened by events and by a sense of its own mobilising power – which until now had been something it could only guess at, given its status as an outlawed movement – this was a position it seemed to relish. Once it saw its chance, this 'non-revolutionary' movement swept up the revolution in its arms, carrying it as if it were its own. Thus, while it is true that the Brotherhood did not initiate the revolution, accusations such as those of the US secretary of state, John Kerry – who claimed that the Brotherhood had 'stolen' the revolution from the 'kids' in Tahrir Square[2] – were overheated. Once the Brotherhood committed itself to the revolution, it became its major driving force. Without the Brotherhood, it is far from clear whether the revolution would have got as far as it did.

The realisation that it was shouldering the revolution gave the Brotherhood a strong sense of entitlement, which was further enhanced by the movement's sense of its own destiny. Having suffered patiently for so many long years, the Brotherhood felt that its preordained time had finally come. As it internalised the revolution, therefore, it started to direct events according to its own agenda. Less than two weeks after the protests had begun, the Brotherhood opened negotiations with the very regime it was protesting against. Indeed, with its natural aversion to revolutionary action, the Brotherhood jumped at the first opportunity to strike some sort of deal with the regime, despite the fact that those protesting in the streets and squares – including some of its own youth factions – were averse to any kind of compromise with the forces of the past. The Brotherhood was so caught up with itself and its own agenda, however, that it forged ahead, even claiming that it was negotiating with the regime in the name of the 'the people'.

The Brotherhood continued along this track following Mubarak's departure, entering into a kind of informal alliance with the military in which these two old powers thrashed out the terms of the transition. In fact, the Brotherhood seemed more comfortable dealing with the familiar furniture of the old regime – however unpalatable it may have been – than with the unknowns of Tahrir Square. Once the Brotherhood realised its own power and strength, it was therefore willing to cut the revolution short in order to achieve its own objectives. Not that it abandoned the revolution entirely. Seeing no contradiction in planting one foot with the regime and the other with the revolution, the Brotherhood continued to mobilise those on the streets to pressurise or dictate its own terms whenever the need arose. The Brotherhood used the revolution, in short, as a tool to try to secure the post-revolutionary order it desired.

This strategy paid off. By the time of the parliamentary elections, held between 28 November 2011 and 11 January 2012, the Brotherhood had positioned itself to dominate the transition. It had mobilised its networks to fill the political space opened up by the fall of the Mubarak regime; steered and taken charge of the revolution, enabling it to claim revolutionary legitimacy; and moulded the transition to derive maximum benefit for itself. In addition, the Brotherhood enjoyed the extra legitimacy arising out of its long years of sacrifice and suffering. It was able to portray itself as a clean and untainted alternative to the deposed regime. More importantly for many Egyptians, it also additional legitimacy through its identification with Islam and for some of its supporters represented Islam itself. It was hardly surprising, therefore, that when the elections came around the Brotherhood stormed ahead, its coalition taking 47.2 per cent of the vote. The Brotherhood looked unstoppable.

This did not mean that the movement had abandoned its traditional caution. Aware of concerns expressed both internationally and at home, the Brotherhood was at pains from the start to dispel any impression that it was power-hungry. It issued repeated promises that it was not seeking to dominate, that it would not be running for the presidency, and that it sought to share power. It was keen to give assurances, too, that it was not intent on Islamicising the state, but simply sought to re-anchor Egypt to its Islamic roots and traditions. The Brotherhood was keen to present an image of itself as a modern political Islamist movement that could meet the challenges of contemporary governance.

Yet as the transition progressed, the Brotherhood struggled to live up to such a heavy responsibility. It quickly fell back on its old way of doing things, entering into marriages of convenience and manoeuvring its way through by making promises it could not keep. It became reactive, responding to events as they arose with no clear vision for how to deal with the transition, let alone the period of rule. The Brotherhood thus gave the impression from very early on that it could not be trusted, and that its only real aim was to get to the end of the transition and into power. But at this stage it hardly seemed to matter. After almost a century in semi-clandestine opposition, the Brotherhood was poised to take over and Egypt looked to be on the dawn of a whole new era.

Reluctant Revolutionaries

It was scarcely a surprise that, when the revolution unfolded, the Brotherhood felt its time had come. Waiting in the wings for over eight decades, the Brotherhood had endured a long and arduous struggle marked by more downs than ups, in which it had paid a heavy price. Although the movement had shown a remarkable capacity for survival, turning itself into the most potent opposition force in the process, it had never come close to power and was always relegated to the margins.

Established by schoolteacher Hassan Al-Banna in 1928, the Brotherhood emerged as a response partly to the colonial presence in Egypt, but also to the sense of crisis engendered by the end of the last caliphate: the Ottoman Empire. Al-Banna, who was deeply preoccupied by what he saw as the moral degeneration of society, drew on the works of late-nineteenth-century reformist scholars such as Rashid Rida and Muhammad Abdu, promoting a simple message holding that the only way the Islamic world could meet the challenges posed by modernisation and encroaching Westernisation was to return to the 'uncorrupted' values of the Islamic past. As Egyptian philosopher Hassan Hanafi commented, Al-Banna's ideas amounted to 'an Islam that is simple and clear ... His ideas were very clear, very pure, and there was no ideological complexity.'[3] Indeed, the Brotherhood's primary message was that Islam offered a comprehensive system of values and governance that would bring social and moral renewal – hence its famous motto: 'Islam is the solution'.

The Brotherhood had thus never been a visionary movement, seeking the establishment of an entirely new order. Rather, its conservative ideology sought to imbue the existing order with Islam, focusing on gradual change from the bottom up. To this end the Brotherhood concentrated its attentions on educating and improving the individual, and by extension the family, viewing this as the best means to prepare society for the eventual establishment of an Islamic state. By providing its members with a rigorous Islamic 'upbringing', and subsequently enlisting them in religious outreach, the Brotherhood could enlarge the circle of committed Muslims until it encompassed society as a whole.[4] Its approach is encapsulated in the words of one of its most prominent thinkers, Sayid Qutb, who replied when asked whether the Brotherhood wanted to kill President Gamal Abdul Nasser, 'Killing Abdul Nasser is a stupid aim that we do not seek to achieve. The aim of the Brotherhood is to educate Muslims in order that they don't give birth to the likes of Abdul Nasser.'[5]

Right from the start, then, the Brotherhood was always more of an organisational force than an intellectual one, reflecting the qualities of Al-Banna himself, who was described by his former secretary, Farid Abdel Khaliq, as someone who 'wasn't about absolute ideas. He was an organisational thinker ... He translated theoretical ideas into reality.'[6] The Brotherhood was therefore a movement held together by the glue of Islam that presented itself as the guardian of an authentic native tradition, rather than a movement of ideas – least of all revolutionary ones.

Al-Banna's message proved potent, and the movement soon gathered momentum, spreading quickly across Egypt and beyond. However, while it started out primarily as a social and cultural movement, the Brotherhood's increasing involvement in politics meant that it soon came into direct conflict with the state. Firstly, in 1948, the monarchy banned the movement after its secret wing was implicated in a series of acts of violence against both British colonising forces and a number of public figures. Secondly, opposition came from the modernising secular regime of President Abdul Nasser, who had come to power in a military coup in 1952. Nasser viewed the Brotherhood as a reactionary opposition force. After a failed assassination attempt against him, he clamped down hard on the movement, carrying out a series of mass arrests that almost wiped it out.

It was during this time that more radical ideas started to emerge inside the movement. This was largely through the works of Sayid Qutb, who penned a series of tracts from prison arguing that, in order to achieve the ideal state, or Al-Hakimiya ('God's rule on earth'), the minority who truly understood Allah should be allowed to apply his rules. Only this, he held, would rid society of Jahiliya (pre-Islamic ignorance), and restore a proper moral order. Qutb's hugely controversial depiction of Egyptian society as *jahili*, or non-Islamic, as well as his top-down approach to revolution, did not sit comfortably with the main body of the movement. Thus, while Qutb's ideas held an attraction for more radical elements in the Brotherhood (sometimes referred to as the 1965 group, or generation), they did not result in a more generalised shift away from the core principles upon which the movement had been founded.

The coming to power of President Anwar Sadat in 1970 heralded the start of a period of revival for the Brotherhood. Firstly, Sadat saw that he could use the Brotherhood as a useful counterweight to his leftist and Nasserist opponents, and he released Brotherhood members from prison. Although the movement was still banned and subjected to periodic crackdowns, it at least had some space to operate. More importantly, the Islamic revivalism that was taking hold across the region, especially in the wake of the Iranian Revolution of 1979, prompted a wave of Islamic enthusiasm that the Brotherhood could tap into directly. It was at this time that scores of young Islamist students joined the Brotherhood, breathing new life into what had been an ailing organisation.

By the time President Mubarak came to power, in 1981, the Brotherhood had therefore developed into a major opposition force. Mubarak's relations with the movement were marked by periods of extreme brutality alternating with periods of containment. As a result, the Brotherhood held the rather incongruous position of being a banned movement whose members were regularly rounded up and detained, but that was allowed to operate its charitable and welfare networks, to run its own mosques, businesses and associations, and during some periods to hold prominent positions in unions and professional bodies. The Brotherhood even had its own headquarters in Cairo, from where its leaders gave frequent interviews to the media. The Brotherhood was thus not only able to cultivate a popular base; it became a state within a state. In the process, it rooted itself firmly in Egyptian society.

It was during Mubarak's rule that the Brotherhood made a foray into the mainstream political arena. During the 1980s the Brotherhood was permitted to contest parliamentary elections, although its candidates were obliged to stand as independents or in alliance with other parties. The Brotherhood jumped at the opportunity despite its awareness that these elections represented little more than a cosmetic exercise for the regime. Indeed, the Brotherhood, which was always ready to adapt itself to the prevailing political climate, was desperate to carve out space for itself in whatever arena it could. But the Brotherhood's participation in these elections also reflected its long-held accommodationist mentality. The movement was always willing to work with and be co-opted by the regime of the day in the hope of preserving its presence on the ground, thereby ensuring it could continue to carry out its core business of reforming the individual. This accommodationist tendency sometimes took on an almost sycophantic hue. On 29 July 2005, Mehdi Akef told the *Akhr Saar* magazine: 'We support the nomination of Mubarak [for president] and I would like sit with him.'[7]

In the years before the revolution the Brotherhood extended its accommodationist stance towards the international community, investing significant efforts in making itself more acceptable to Western powers. These efforts were driven in large part by the international spotlight that had been shone on Islamist groups in the aftermath of the 911/ terrorist attacks against the United States. It was no coincidence that, in the 2000s, the Brotherhood had begun to develop a more reformist discourse, promoting itself as a moderate movement that could operate within a pluralistic and democratic context. As scholar Nathan Brown has argued, 'From its birth, Egypt's Muslim Brotherhood has confronted the challenge of crafting its message in a way that appeals to (and draws on) a religious framework but simultaneously attracts, appeases, or soothes the various external audiences.'[8] This is not to say that the Brotherhood toned down its anti-Western rhetoric when addressing its adherents. While the Brotherhood may have been appeasing and accommodating in the appropriate context, it continued to mobilise its supporters with a fiery discourse that lambasted the regime and the West with equal ferocity. While this dualist approach elicited accusations of doublespeak, for the movement this was simply its way of manoeuvring itself through extremely challenging circumstances in order to survive.

But the reality was that the Brotherhood had become locked over the years into a relationship of staid coexistence with the regime. As Brown has also remarked, 'Regimes run to stay in place; Islamist movements push and prod at the limits that are imposed but often spend just as much energy assuring the regime that they will live within those limits. The result combines stability with the appearance of dynamism.'[9] It also produces politics without substance, and Egypt had become locked into a stultifying kind of pseudo-politics, the regime and the Brotherhood appearing as anachronistic as each other.

This sense of stagnation was taking its toll on the Brotherhood, which in the years prior to the uprisings had been undergoing a kind of internal crisis. Some of the splits that had developed inside the movement over the years were catapulted into the public domain. Most notably, the division between those of a more reformist bent and the old-style conservatives spilled over into the media. While these divisions were essentially turf wars and squabbles over tactics and leadership positions than any deep-seated ideological differences, their exposure in the Egyptian media meant that what had always been a highly secretive movement seemed to be losing its grip. There was, moreover, a growing feeling among the more conservative elements that the struggle to enter the formal political arena had not been worth the effort. These elements, who by 2010 had come to reassert their domination of the movement's leadership, believed it was time to refocus on the Brotherhood's traditional activities of preaching and education. By the eve of the protests, therefore, the movement appeared more inward-looking and disengaged from politics than ever before.

Given this history, it was little surprise that the Brotherhood was hesitant about joining the protests of 25 January 2011, timed to coincide with National Police Day. Moreover, it remained unclear at this point exactly who was behind the protests and, more importantly, whether they would endure. As in Tunisia, the protestors seemed to have come almost out of nowhere, in a spontaneous outpouring of anger at the status quo. Although groups of youth activists had put out calls on social media sites for a 'Day of Rage' on 25 January, there was still much confusion about what was unfolding. There was also a strong sense among Egyptians that their own regime would not be as easy to bring down as that of President Ben Ali in Tunisia. As one Nasserite Party member commented at the time, 'The security brigades won't give ordinary people and political activists the chance to demonstrate. Egyptians know how to talk more than they know how to act.'[10] After almost a century in existence, the Brotherhood was not going to rush to entangle itself with a protest that might fizzle into nothing. On 11 January the Brotherhood announced that it would not be taking part in the planned demonstrations, out of respect for the 'the national occasion that Egyptians ought to celebrate altogether'.[11]

Furthermore, the Brotherhood was not ready to engage in anything that would leave it vulnerable to retaliation by the security services. Regardless of who was behind the protests, the Brotherhood knew that it would be the first to be scapegoated if it joined in. Security forces had already threatened a number of Brotherhood leaders in the days leading up to 25 January, and the movement feared further reprisals. Ahmed Rami, a middle-ranking Brotherhood leader explained: 'The movement believed that 25 January wouldn't be a popular event and that if it took part with all its power and headed the scene that it would ... provoke the security [apparatus] and give it the pretext to repress its members.'[12] The Brotherhood had suffered enough persecution at the hands of these security forces over the decades to make self-preservation an overriding preoccupation.

Moreover, given its natural aversion to revolution, the Brotherhood felt decidedly uncomfortable about engaging in anything that might bring the regime down. At a secret meeting of opposition elements on 23 January 2011, Brotherhood veteran and member of its Guidance Office (most senior leadership body) Mohamed Beltagi refused to sign a statement calling for a peaceful end to rule by Mubarak and his family. Beltagi declared that the Brotherhood would never agree to add its signature to a statement in which Mubarak's name was mentioned or in which there was a call to get rid of him, asserting: 'We want the demands to be confined to dissolving the People's Assembly and the Shura Council.'[13]

But at the same time the Brotherhood did not want to be left entirely out of the picture. If the Tunisian scenario was going to be replicated in Egypt, the movement could not afford to sit on the side-lines if it wanted to play a part in the country's future. Furthermore many of its younger cadres, who were more in tune with what was happening in the street, were pushing hard to join the protests. Typically, therefore, the movement opted for a risk-averse approach that combined both positions. The Brotherhood refused to endorse the protests as an organisation, but permitted its members to take part in an individual capacity. Ahmed Rami explained how, on 24 January, his immediate leader in the movement had received instructions from the Brotherhood's leadership confirming that anyone who wanted to take part in the demonstrations was free to do so, but that there was no obligation from the movement as a whole.[14]

Even when it first became apparent that the unfolding events were bigger than anyone had anticipated, the Brotherhood persisted with this two-pronged approach. At 8 p.m. on the evening of 25 January, a group of Brotherhood students went to the movement's Guidance Office to try to persuade the leadership to support the protests. Some of the Brotherhood's biggest names were there, including Mahmoud Izzat, Mahmoud Ghozlan, Mohamed Morsi, Issam Al-Araian, Saad Al-Katatni, Mohamed Beltagi and Husham Issa. The students explained to these Brotherhood veterans the significance of what was happening in the streets, and impressed upon them that, if the movement put its weight behind the demonstrations and provided finance for the sit-ins, then the protests would succeed. But this was not sufficient to convince the leadership. Mahmoud Izzat held to the movement's restrained response, responding that the demonstrations had begun in a popular fashion and that they should continue in the same way: 'The movement's stance is well-known and it is clear. Go and be with the people in the street. If they stay in the square stay with them and if they leave, then leave too.'[15] However, Izzat agreed to send Beltagi to accompany the students so that, like other political forces, the Brotherhood would be represented in the protests by one of its well-known leaders.

By the next day, however, the Brotherhood's position had shifted. When the Brotherhood began to realise the scale and significance of what was unfolding as the protests gathered momentum and spread beyond Cairo, it issued a statement announcing that it would take part in the 'Friday of Rage' demonstrations that were planned for 28 January. It duly took part in these protests and joined those of the following days, including the March of the Millions on 1 February. The Brotherhood had come to understand that the protests represented a unique opportunity, and that it was time to grasp the moment. Thus, the revolution finally awakened what was a large, lumbering elephant of a movement.

However, the movement was politically astute enough to ensure that it did not push itself forward too overtly. Leading Brotherhood member Rashad Al-Bayoumi explained: 'We are keeping a low profile as an organisation. We are not marching with our slogans. We don't want this revolution to be portrayed as a revolution of the Muslim Brothers, as an Islamic revolution.'[16] Notably, when some Brotherhood members in Tahrir Square began chanting 'Allah u'Akhbar' ('God is great') and 'W'Allah Al-Hamd' ('thanks to Allah'), Brotherhood leaders including Beltagi told them that they should shout 'Long live Egypt', in order to 'reflect their awareness that the Brothers are participants in the revolution and not the ones who carried it out or led it'.[17] One Western journalist recounted, too, how a member of the Brotherhood's youth movement had told another member who was holding up a copy of the Qu'ran in front of a television camera: 'For God's sake, don't hold up your Qu'ran. Hold up an Egyptian flag ... That's not for the media.'[18] It was clear, therefore, that the Brotherhood was playing a clever game, providing the protests with critical mass while at the same time preventing them from being portrayed as an Islamist power grab.

On the ground, though, the Brotherhood was most definitely making its presence felt. It cannily employed the decades of experience it had built up in the social arena through its charity and welfare networks to take on the role of arch-organiser. Brotherhood members strung up plastic sheeting in Tahrir Square to serve as tents, brought food and hot tea for their fellow demonstrators, distributed blankets, and set up an emergency first aid clinic inside the square.[19] They also rigged up the first microphones, giving them control over the messages that were being pumped out to the demonstrators.[20] In conjunction with other opposition groups, Brotherhood members also took on the role of protector, regulating entry and exit points to Tahrir Square, searching those entering in order to prevent government thugs and intruders from infiltrating the demonstrations.[21] The Brotherhood was in its element.

But when the infamous Battle of the Camels erupted on

2 February, the Brotherhood suddenly wavered. The previous evening Mubarak had given a speech offering a series of concessions, including a promise to hold elections in which he would not stand. Although some protestors left the square in response to this speech, the majority refused to disperse, demanding nothing short of Mubarak's immediate departure. The regime responded by getting tough. Pro-regime thugs, or *beltagiya*, armed with clubs, bats and knives, and some of them on camels and horseback, charged into Tahrir Square and began attacking the protestors, killing eleven and injuring some two thousand people.

This last-ditch attempt at survival by Mubarak placed the Brotherhood in a quandary, and its immediate reaction was to withdraw from the protests. As one of the Brotherhood's youth recalled,

> During the clashes we were told by one of the brothers from downtown Cairo that the movement had issued a decision to pull out. We asked Brother Tariq Abdeljawad to go to the Guidance Office on his way to Tahrir Square on Wednesday evening [2 February] to clarify. He met with Dr Mahmoud Izzat who told him, 'I am telling you we took the decision to pull out and we informed [our people in] the square of that decision.'[22]

Abdelmonem Abul Futuh, despite being a senior Brotherhood member at that time, was critical of the Brotherhood's decision: 'The Battle of the Camels was a battle in which Muslim Brotherhood members strove hard. But the Guidance Office intervened to pull the Muslim Brotherhood youth out. I told them, "Shame on you to pull out of the battle and leave others there."'[23]

But the young Brotherhood members refused to follow the leadership's instructions. There were a series of heated telephone conversations between the leadership and the youth, the latter making clear that they were fully intent on defending the square 'until the last man standing'. When it became clear that these youth were staying put, the Brotherhood relented, retracting its decision to withdraw. According to some reports, its decision was hastened by the fact that, at the request of some Brotherhood youth, the Islamic scholar and spiritual reference for the Brotherhood, Sheikh Yousef Al-Qaradawi, appeared on Al-Jazeera to back the protests. Whether Qaradawi's intervention was decisive in the Brotherhood's calculations, it clearly concluded that its best option was to allow its cadres to continue protesting. As Abul Futuh recalled, 'The youth of the Muslim Brotherhood refused to implement the Guidance Office's demands to withdraw, and soon enough the Guidance Office retracted and agreed that the youth of the Muslim Brotherhood could continue in their battle.'[24]

This change of heart on the leadership's part resulted in the wholesale mobilisation of Brotherhood's members and supporters, who joined the battle that continued throughout 3 February. Their presence turned out to be pivotal. As Egyptian intellectual Dr Saad Eddine Ibrahim commented, 'The Muslim Brotherhood stopped all these *beltagiya* that were sent by the Mubarak regime. The Muslim Brotherhood youth were the first defenders of those in the square.'[25] In fact, had it not been for the Brotherhood cadres, the revolution may well have been quashed there and then. As Egyptian Islamist thinker Mohamed Salim Al-Awa has argued, 'If it wasn't for the Muslim Brotherhood's confronting the giant in the battle of the camels, the revolution wouldn't have been successful.'[26] Similarly, Ahmed Doma, a member of the Revolutionary Youth Alliance, commented: 'If it wasn't for the Brotherhood youth and their heroic stance, the balance of forces would have changed.'[27]

While the Brotherhood as an organisation may have started out as a reluctant revolutionary, the Battle of the Camels saw it throw its weight fully behind the struggle that would signal the beginning of the end for the Mubarak regime. More importantly, it was in this battle that the Brotherhood came to realise its own strength. From this moment, the movement developed a strong sense of its own power and importance, as well as the mobilising power of the street. From now on the Brotherhood was going to call the shots, directing the revolution as it saw fit.

Between Revolution and Negotiation

The Brotherhood's first act after realising its own might, however, was not to engage in further revolutionary action but rather to harness its power to try to cut a deal with the regime. Although the Brotherhood had proclaimed on a number of occasions at the start of February that it would not deal with what it described as an 'illegitimate regime', on 5 February it announced that it was accepting the offer made by Vice-President Omar Suleiman to all political forces to take part in a dialogue to try to calm the streets. The Brotherhood's acceptance of this offer did not go down well with protestors in the square who were horrified at the ease with which this new revolutionary actor was willing to compromise. The move did not sit well with the Brotherhood's own youth, either. When Mohamed Morsi, who was head of the Brotherhood's political office at the time, told the Brotherhood's youth to choose representatives to attend the dialogue, the youth baulked and refused point blank to take part.[28]

For the Brotherhood, however, here was an opportunity to bargain with the regime in a bid to win more space for itself. Indeed, the movement had no qualms about negotiating with the regime at the same time as calling for its downfall. Or, as the late Hossam Tammam observed, 'By virtue of their history, the Brotherhood were always with the regime, even when they confronted it and took part in a revolution against it.'[29] The Brotherhood pressed ahead, therefore, and on 6 February Mohamed Morsi and Guidance Office member Saad Al-Katatni sat around the table with Suleiman. They were not the only ones to have accepted Suleiman's offer. A handful of other opposition forces, including Tagammu and the National Association for Change, joined the meeting, in which Suleiman sat underneath a looming portrait of Mubarak, prompting one Egyptian writer to comment that when the participants looked at Suleiman, above him they could see Mubarak – under whose shadow the dialogue was being conducted.[30]

During the discussions, Suleiman reportedly offered to release prominent Brotherhood members Khairet Al-Shater and Hassan Malik from prison, in return for the movement's agreement to pull its supporters out of Tahrir Square.[31] Having realised the power that the street enabled it to wield, however, the Brotherhood refused the offer, focusing instead on discussions about establishing a committee to amend the most controversial articles in Egypt's constitution. It also demanded the dissolution of the People's Assembly, the release of all political prisoners, and an end to the state of emergency. Astonishingly, it also began to argue that Mubarak should stay in power in order for him to amend the constitution. As Al-Katatni explained, 'It's safer that the president stays until he makes these amendments to speed things up because of the constitutional power he holds.'[32]

The ease with which the Brotherhood seemed to sell out on the revolution drew the ire of those still protesting, for whom the negotiations were a betrayal. For these protestors the Brotherhood's stance was all the more difficult to digest given the violence that had just been meted out, during the Battle of the Camels. Slogans began to be chanted in Tahrir Square accusing the Brotherhood of selling out the revolution; protestors held up banners reading: 'No negotiation, no representation before [Mubarak] leaving! No wise men! No Brotherhood! The demands are in the Square.'[33]

The Brotherhood justified its stance by arguing that it was doing no more than putting the 'people's demands' to the vice-president. By this point the Brotherhood's sense of its own importance was such that it had no misgivings about speaking in the name of the masses. Such arrogance only fuelled the anger of those who were still protesting, who also began accusing the Brotherhood of having hijacked the revolution. But the Brotherhood was so preoccupied with its own agenda that it continued undeterred. In addition, the regime was making good on agreements it had reached to free political prisoners, many of them members of the Brotherhood. The Brotherhood was not going to stop now. On 10 February, therefore – the same day on which Mubarak stunned Egyptians by giving a speech refusing to stand down – Al-Katatni announced: 'We will participate in the second round of the dialogue with Egypt's vice-president Omar Suleiman ... We have decided to take part in the talks to find a way out of the current crisis.'[34]

The dialogue did not go ahead. The surge of anger prompted by Mubarak's refusal to step down prompted an escalation in the protests, and on 11 February demonstrators surged towards and surrounded the presidential palace, prompting the president to flee. That evening Omar Suleiman announced that the president had gone, and that the army in the form of the Supreme Council of Armed Forces (SCAF) would take over the running of the country.

Even at this early stage, therefore, the Brotherhood had chosen appeasement over real change, its desire to direct the transition trumping any impulse to struggle for genuine democracy.

The Brotherhood's preference for appeasement became even more evident following Mubarak's departure. With the president gone, the Brotherhood wanted to bring a halt to the protests and get down to the business of negotiating the transition – even if that meant negotiating with the military. According to Brotherhood leader Mohamed Soudan, 'After 11 February most leaders of the Brotherhood said, "Let's go and calm the country down and let's stop the protests and make a deal with the army."'[35] This reflected the fact that, for the Brotherhood, Mubarak's departure signified the end of the revolutionary phase, and it had no interest in bringing down the forces that had been the power behind the president through revolutionary action. Rather, it sought to work with these forces, entering into an informal tactical alliance with the SCAF. This alliance was favourable to the Brotherhood for several reasons. Firstly, the Brotherhood feared that the military might suddenly turn against the forces of change, and that if it did so, it would leave the movement crushed. Secondly, the Brotherhood was acutely aware that, if it was going to play a part in the country's political future, it would need to be legitimised as a socio-religious movement and as a political actor, and that it would need to rely on the SCAF's good will to bestow such legitimation. Thirdly, it knew that, were it eventually to take power, it would be reliant on a strong military apparatus capable of providing security, and of confronting what was left of Mubarak's notorious security apparatus.[36]

Most importantly, however, the Brotherhood had calculated that the best way to direct the transition and to determine its place in the post-revolutionary order would be to use its new revolutionary might in its manoeuvring with the SCAF to extract as many concessions as possible. To this end, it began to court the SCAF. At a conference in Alexandria in March 2011, Mohamed Beltagi jumped in quickly to contradict Salafist leader Saleh Hazem Abu Ismail, who had expressed his view that it was a mistake to trust the army, telling him: 'We have a good army and we should trust it.'[37] The Brotherhood was also strikingly silent about some of the abuses that were being meted out to the protestors who were still in Tahrir Square. These included forced virginity tests performed on a number of female protestors on 9 March, which General Abdulfatah Al-Sissi, who was then head of military intelligence, claimed had been carried out to 'protect' the army against possible allegations of rape.[38] The Brotherhood, it seemed, was willing to put such uncomfortable issues to one side in the interests of making itself the SCAF's partner of choice.

But the Brotherhood was careful not to go too far in this direction. Fearful of alienating its supporters and losing its claim to oversee the revolution, it continued to lambast the SCAF at the same time as praising it. More importantly, it put its supporters back onto the streets whenever it needed to pressurise the SCAF, or to bolster its own revolutionary legitimacy. In early April, for example, the Brotherhood called for a million-man march, to be named the 'Day of Prosecution and Purging', to pressurise the caretaker government into pursuing legal cases against members of the old regime, who remained in positions of influence. This call was the Brotherhood's way of flexing its revolutionary muscles, reminding the SCAF of the power it could wield. The Brotherhood thus continued to navigate a course between the two opposing camps, picking and choosing when to adopt the mantle of revolutionary actor, and using the revolution as an instrument with which to press for its demands.

As for the SCAF, it was willing to align itself with the Brotherhood in this way because it wanted to calm the streets. As one retired general reflected, 'The SCAF's goal at the time was to calm down the streets, and with the Brothers being the most organised and numerous group, they naturally felt it made sense to let them have a critical say.'[39] Furthermore, if the SCAF was going to direct the transition it needed some popular political cover, and reaching an understanding with the most powerful force on the street was the obvious way of acquiring it. As the retired general put it, 'When you enter a new block, you usually look to see who is the strongest thugs (NB original uses the word thugs) with whom you could have an understanding. The SCAF was the newcomer, and the thug was the Muslim Brothers.'[40] These two institutions – both reactionary, and both, in the words of former Deputy Murshid Mohamed Habib, 'subject to the same culture of listening and obedience'[41] – entered into an uneasy marriage of convenience. So it was that what had started out as a revolution driven by young people seeking a fresh start mutated into a compromise between the same two old, tired, reactionary forces that had been battling each other for decades.

This marriage of convenience, which cut off the revolution in its infancy, was to have far-reaching consequences for both Egypt and the Brotherhood. By joining hands with the SCAF, the Brotherhood had effectively breathed new life into the very power that would cut it down so brutally a little over two years later. Indeed, many Brotherhood members were to lament trusting the SCAF as perhaps its greatest mistake. 'There is a strong realisation among the leaders of the Muslim Brotherhood that we made a mistake, that we were not revolutionary enough', explained FJP MP Abdelmawgoud Dardery.[42] Mohamed Soudan reflected: 'It was our mistake, or the mistake of our leaders, to order the protestors to go home.'[43]

But at this point the Brotherhood was so sure of itself and its power that it was blinded to the potential consequences of its actions. In its rush to take control of the transition, it could not anticipate that, by employing its usual accommodationist approach, it would sow the seeds of its own downfall. Rather, in the euphoria of the revolution it seemed to believe that, with the street in its hands, along with the rallying force of Islam, it would be able to outmanoeuvre the forces that had held the country in their grip since the middle of the previous century. As far as the Brotherhood was concerned, this was its moment, and nothing was going to stand in its way.

Securing Electoral Legitimacy

With Mubarak gone and the SCAF open to negotiating, the Brotherhood turned its attentions to legitimising its newfound power. By virtue of being the most organised political force, whose years of underground activism had spawned extensive networks of supporters, as well as its reputation for being 'clean' and uncorrupted, the Brotherhood knew that it was better placed than other political players to succeed in parliamentary elections. Furthermore, unlike the more urban and elitist secular or nationalist parties that worked only through the lens of politics, it could capitalise on being a socio-religious movement as well as a political one, meaning that it could mobilise more adherents to support it in the polls.

The Brotherhood therefore poured all its energies into getting Egypt to the polls as early as possible. To this end, it gave its backing to the Constitutional Review Committee set up in the middle of February, which included among its members lawyer and Muslim Brotherhood member Soleh Sobhi, as well as Judge Tariq Al-Bishri, the former head of Egypt's administrative court. This committee was tasked with drafting a series of amendments to the constitution that would regulate parliamentary and presidential elections that the SCAF had announced would take place in June and later in the summer of 2011, respectively, and that would be put to the people in a referendum. These amendments included specifications that the presidential mandate be reduced from six to four years, and limited to two terms only; that the judiciary should return to supervise elections; and that a 100-member Constituent Assembly be elected by a majority of members of the People's Assembly and Shura Council, and that this assembly should draft a new constitution within six months and submit it to a popular referendum.[44]

While such proposals fell in line with the spirit of the revolution and tallied with some of the demands made by opposition groups over previous years, the amendments did not go far enough for many activists, who had wanted the constitution to be scrapped completely and replaced with an entirely new document. There was also a strong push by some groups for a new constitution to be written before parliamentary elections took place. But the Brotherhood was in a rush to get these amendments approved as quickly as possible. This had nothing to do with lofty ideals about the transition to democracy, but was because their approval would open the way for elections to be held. Moreover, these amendments had an added bonus. If approved, they would mean that the People's Assembly, which the Brotherhood expected to dominate, would write the constitution.

It was little surprise, therefore, that the Brotherhood brought all of its mobilising powers to bear in the run-up to the March 2011 referendum on the amendments. It was particularly significant that the movement began to conflate voting 'Yes' with a vote for Islam. Such tactics were nothing new. Despite the Brotherhood's repeated assertions over the years that it did not equate itself with Islam, it often portrayed its political preferences as a choice in favour of the faith and of morality. This campaign was no different. The movement made repeated references to Article 2 of the constitution ('Islam is the religion of the state and Arabic its official language. Principles of Islamic law [Sharia] are the principal source of legislation'), despite the fact that this was not one of the articles up for amendment. It warned voters that opposing the amendments would be tantamount to rejecting Article 2, and by extension Islam itself.[45] The Brotherhood also adopted slogans such as 'Voting yes with Allah' and 'We are bringing goodness to Egypt'. Already, therefore, the Brotherhood was dividing Egyptians between the faithful and the unfaithful, the pure and the impure, playing on morality as a means of forcing the political outcome it desired.

Whether as a result of the Brotherhood's campaign or not, the results went in its favour. The amendments were passed with 77.3 per cent of the vote, opening the door to parliamentary elections. In order to be able to contest the elections, however, the movement needed to establish a political party of its own. In April 2011, therefore, it set up the Freedom and Justice Party. This was a significant shift in direction for the movement. For all that the Brotherhood concerned itself with politics, it had always shied away from forming a political party. This was directly in line with the teachings of Al-Banna, who had always argued vehemently against political parties, viewing them as un-Islamic, divisive and contrary to the unifying spirit of the Ummah. The movement, and especially the conservatives in it, had stuck to this view, and had continued to oppose the idea of establishing a party. When a group of reform-minded brothers applied to form their own Al-Wasat party in 1996, they were mercilessly expelled from the movement. While some of the anger against the Al-Wasat group was because they had dared to bypass the Brotherhood's official hierarchy, there was nevertheless a strong ideological resistance to the idea of setting up a party, which was still considered as an imported and alien concept. As late as April 2011, Khairet Al-Shater gave a lecture in Alexandria following his release from prison, in which he declared,

> 'The [political] party, my brothers, as an instrument, means, or vessel, is not born of the Islamic idea, or of the Islamic experience, or of the Islamic model. Rather, it is one of the various products of Western civilization, the Western model, or the Western renaissance. It is an instrument or a vessel for the deliberation of power in the political space, an instrument for [engaging in] the conflict for the sake of obtaining power.'[46]

Al-Shater went on to stress that, while the movement could establish a party, this should only be for 'secondary tasks'.[47]

But when the opportunity to come to power presented itself, these longstanding objections were cast aside seemingly without a second thought. This change of heart was not the result of any altered conviction on the Brotherhood's part about the nature of the political party as an institution or instrument. Rather, the Brotherhood saw in the political party the quickest means to get into power. However, the setting up of the FJP unleashed much internal debate about what the relationship between the party and the movement should be. Predictably enough, the Brotherhood insisted publicly that the party and the movement were to be two separate entities. Rashid Al-Bayoumi told the *Asharq Al-Awsat* newspaper that, while the FJP would share the Brotherhood's ideological framework, it would be completely separate.[48] Similarly, Brotherhood spokesman Walid Shalabi insisted that the party and the movement might share the same Islamic ideals and would support each other when necessary, but that they would be completely separate in matters of management and finance.[49]

But the Brotherhood seemed to see no contradiction between such statements and the fact that three members of the Brotherhood's Guidance Office were appointed to lead the party – Mohamed Morsi as leader, Issam Al-Arian as party deputy leader, and Saad Al-Katatni as secretary-general. These were no ordinary Brotherhood members either, but some of the biggest names in the movement's leadership. In addition, the Brotherhood wrote the party's platform and approved its bylaws.[50] Even more tellingly, although membership of the FJP was not obligatory for the movement, Supreme Guide Mohamed Badie forbade all Brotherhood members from joining any other political party. It was no surprise, then, that when it applied for official recognition on 18 May 2011, it already boasted some 9,000 founding members.[51]

Furthermore, party members gave contradictory statements on the relationship between the two entities. Some were more circumspect about the closeness of the relationship. The

Brotherhood's secretary-general, Mahmoud Hussein, explained: 'The party is independent vis-à-vis all its members, finance and decisions. But there are certain issues that affect both and therefore they have to sit together ... the movement takes its decision and the party takes its decision and they meet to co-ordinate.'[52] Al-Arian, meanwhile, revealed that there was a joint committee between the two to co-ordinate on decisions related to the state.[53]

Others were more frank. FJP member and former planning and international co-operation minister, Amr Darrag, explained:

> We wanted [the FJP] to be independent, but we couldn't do it in the beginning. We would be foolish if we formed a party and forgot about the support of the movement. Because where were we getting our support from? ... It would be a ridiculous thing to get rid of all this [support], I mean to start like any other party.[54]

In April 2011, meanwhile, Mahmoud Izzat told a mass rally in the Imbaba neighbourhood of Cairo, a well-known Islamist stronghold, 'The movement will never run the FJP but it will share achieving the same strategic and political goals. The party is a tool with which to rule.'[55]

The Brotherhood failed, therefore, to distinguish between its role as a political party and its role as a socio-religious movement. It also failed to comprehend that, by its continued insistence that the party and the movement were two completely separate entities – something that was blatantly untrue – it further undermined its credibility in the eyes of the populace. For a movement whose history had been dogged by accusations of doublespeak, its inability to separate the two or to articulate a convincing narrative about the nature of the relationship was a serious political misjudgement.

At this point, however, such issues seemed almost trivial. The Brotherhood was focusing all of its energies on ensuring that its popular support was going to be translated into tangible political gains in the elections that were now scheduled for November.

But the situation was proving trickier than the Brotherhood had anticipated. While the SCAF had been willing to negotiate with the Brotherhood over the transition, it did not want to see a Brotherhood-dominated parliament, and certainly did not want the Brotherhood to dictate the process of writing the constitution.

It therefore set about moving the goalposts, taking a series of steps to try to ring-fence the Brotherhood. In July 2011 the SCAF issued a new parliament law stipulating that 50 per cent of seats in the lower house of parliament be reserved for individual candidates, with the remaining 50 per cent to be elected under a party-list system. The law also stated that in the Shura Council, or upper house, sixty-five electoral constituencies would be reserved for individual candidates, while twenty-eight would follow closed party lists. This was disastrous for the FJP, as well as for other political forces. Although, under intense public pressure, the SCAF decided in September to increase the share of party lists from 50 per cent to two-thirds of seats, this was still a blow to the Brotherhood's ambitions.

The movement responded by announcing that it had decided to nominate candidates for all available seats in the parliament. In line with its cautious approach and its desire not to be seen to be grasping for power, the Brotherhood had initially declared that it would nominate candidates for thirty-five seats only. In April 2011 it increased this number to fifty seats. However, faced with the limitations imposed by the SCAF, it went all-out to contest all available seats through the alliance it had teamed up with, the Democratic Alliance for Egypt, in which it was by far the dominant player.

But as the elections approached the SCAF raised the stakes again, announcing a series of supra-constitutional principles that included awarding itself the authority to hand-pick eighty of the 100 members of the Constituent Assembly; to force the Constituent Assembly to reconsider any provisions in the draft that it objected to and to refer these provisions to the Supreme Constitutional Court (whose decisions on the matter were to be binding); and to have the right to convene a new Constituent Assembly if the body failed to draw up a constitution within six months. This was too much for the Brotherhood, and it returned to the streets. The movement assumed a revolutionary role once more, joining with the other political forces in Tahrir Square to demand the principles be retracted. This was no half-hearted move. The Brotherhood mobilised its members to come out in full force, as if to demonstrate to the SCAF that if it did not retract it would be at the mercy of the masses once again. Indeed, throughout this period the Brotherhood engaged in wholly reactive policymaking, responding to each situation as it arose and taking desperate measures such as appealing to the street when it appeared to have no alternative. While such an approach was hardly surprising given the unstable environment in which it was operating, it exposed the fact that the Brotherhood had no real vision of how to deal with the transition, and that its only real preoccupation was to achieve power, regardless of how it did so.

In the face of such pressure, the SCAF duly backtracked, announcing that its supra-constitutional principles would be advisory rather than binding. The way was open at last for the Brotherhood to launch itself with full force into the elections. The result of the polling, which lasted from 28 November 2011 to 11 January 2012, was hardly a surprise. The FJP powered to victory, its coalition taking 235 seats, representing 47.2 per cent of the total vote and making it the largest bloc by far. The Brotherhood's confidence in the polls and in its ability to mobilise its supporters had not been misplaced. As well as its core support base, it had also attracted significant popular support from those Egyptians prepared to give it the benefit of the doubt on the grounds that it appeared to be a pure and untested alternative to what had come before. In addition, for some Egyptians the Brotherhood represented Islam itself, and was therefore worthy of support.

Although the Brotherhood was the clear frontrunner, the Salafists, led by the Al-Nour party, also made a good showing, taking 120 seats. The Islamists in their different hues thus ended up taking 355 of the 508 seats in the People's Assembly. Although the revolution had been launched by young people who had no specific ideological agenda, it was the Islamists who succeeded in capitalising on the situation, and were therefore set to run the show. The future looked bright for the Brotherhood, which could claim not only revolutionary but also electoral legitimacy.

But it soon became apparent that the SCAF was not going to allow it free rein to rule. Concerned by the Islamists' dominance in the new parliament, the SCAF took further steps to limit the Brotherhood's room for manoeuvre. It refused to dissolve the government of Prime Minister Kamel Ganzouri, which it had appointed just prior to the elections. The head of the SCAF, Field Marshal Tantawi, meanwhile began issuing threats to dissolve the parliament if it discussed withdrawing confidence from the Ganzouri government.[56] According to the Brotherhood, the SCAF also threatened to dissolve the parliament if it followed up on a proposal put forward by the FJP to monitor the military budget. The Brotherhood's attempt to address such a sensitive issue was clearly a step too far for the SCAF. Mohamed Soudan explained: 'After the FJP suggested monitoring the military budget in the parliament, Saad Al-Katatni was summoned by the army and was told, "Listen, I have a piece of paper in my drawer to dissolve the parliament. If you talk again about monitoring the army's budget the parliament will be dissolved."'[57]

Fearing that its achievements were about to be snatched from under its nose, the Brotherhood moved the goalposts again, announcing that it had decided to field a candidate for the upcoming presidential elections. This announcement came as a bombshell. As part of its desire to reassure both domestic and international audiences, the Brotherhood had repeated time and time again since the early days of the revolution that it had no intention of contesting the presidency. As early as 4 February 2011, Beltagi told Al-Jazeera, 'We have said clearly we have no ambitions to run for the presidency, or posts in a coalition government'.[58] Furthermore, there was a strong reluctance among the movement's leadership for the Brotherhood to take on the responsibility of the presidency. Former Murshid Mehdi Akef, for example, warned against it, saying, "It is dangerous for us to nominate a presidential candidate."[59] At its first formal meeting in sixteen years, the Brotherhood's Shura Council voted in February 2011 not to nominate anyone for the presidency, ruling that anyone who did so would be contravening the Shura Council's decision.[60]

The Brotherhood upheld this stance in April 2011, when Abdelmonem Abul Futuh challenged this decision and announced his intention to stand for the presidency. Known as one of the more liberal and reform-minded leaders in the movement, Abul Futuh had always been something of a maverick, who often transgressed the official Brotherhood line. His announcement still came as a shock to the movement, which dispatched a number of its leaders to convince him to change his mind. When he refused and insisted on contesting the elections as an independent candidate, the Shura Council duly expelled him from the movement.[61] Typical of the Brotherhood's response to those who contravene its members' trademark obedience, Abul Futuh was shown little mercy. Al-Arian proclaimed: 'He has nothing to do with us now ... We cannot support anyone violating our decisions.'[62] Abul Futuh therefore left the movement, and contested the presidential elections independently of the Brotherhood.

Yet for all its indignation at Abul Futuh's decision, once the Brotherhood felt it was being cornered by the SCAF and was at risk of losing the endgame, it raised the stakes by announcing its intention to put forward a candidate for the presidency. In March 2012, therefore, it made what was arguably its second catastrophic decision since the outbreak of the revolution, declaring that it was nominating Brotherhood powerhouse Khairet Al-Shater, as a candidate. It justified this volte-face by explaining: 'We have chosen the path of the presidency not because we are greedy for power but because we have a majority in parliament which is unable to fulfil its duties.'[63]

It had not been an easy decision. There were plenty of senior Brotherhood figures who remained firmly opposed to the idea. These included Beltagi, who wrote on his Facebook page after the announcement had been made: 'I oppose the Brotherhood's nomination of one of its own for the presidency ... It harms the Brotherhood and the nation, to have one faction assume all the responsibility under these conditions.'[64] Many Shura Council members were also difficult to convince. When the Council met to vote on the issue, the disagreements were so intense that the session had to be postponed. But certain figures in the Brotherhood's leadership were determined to get their own way. Having come this far, they were not going to let power slip through their hands now.

According to Mohamed Habib, the Guidance Office began putting pressure on those Shura Council members who were objecting to the presidential nomination to change their stance.[65] Likewise, Abul Futuh explained how Shura Council members were pressurised into voting in favour of the nomination, claiming that much of this pressure came directly from Al-Shater himself, who he claimed had a strong desire 'to take control'.[66] He commented: 'Al-Shater put huge pressure on members of the Shura Council until they gave way and agreed to nominate him.'[67] When the Shura Council reconvened, fifty-six members voted in favour of nominating a presidential candidate, while fifty-two voted against. Although the final count was a close call, the Brotherhood's leadership had got its way.

Al-Shater's nomination infuriated the SCAF which, in the cat-and-mouse game that had developed between these two large forces, retaliated on 14 April by disqualifying Al-Shater over a disputed criminal conviction related to alleged money-laundering and funding of a banned group. It also barred nine other presidential candidates, including Salafist leader Hazem Salah Abu Ismail, and, in what was perceived as a bid to appear even-handed, Ahmed Shafik, who was viewed as the SCAF's own candidate.

Despite this blow, the Brotherhood was not going to back down. It proposed an alternative nomination, choosing Mohamed Morsi instead. Morsi was a curious choice, and could not have been more different in terms of personality from the powerful and charismatic leader and businessman Al-Shater. The son of a rice and cotton farmer from the Nile Delta, Morsi was an engineer by profession. He had studied for a PhD in materials science at the University of California before going to work as an assistant professor at California State University in Northridge. However, he seems to have struggled to master the English language. As the grandson of one former pupil explained, 'My grandfather said that his professor [Morsi] seemed to have good teaching skills, however his English destroyed many students'. Morsi had been forced to write out his answers to questions on the blackboard in order to make himself understood.[68]

Morsi joined the Brotherhood in the late 1970s, rising up through the ranks to serve as a Brotherhood MP (as an independent candidate) from 2000 to 2005, when he led the movement's parliamentary bloc. But, as Mohamed Habib recalls, Morsi's appointment to lead this bloc was decided more by chance than by any resounding endorsement of his political abilities. Habib recounts how, in 2000, when he was an MP, he was telephoned by Guidance Office member Mohamed Ali Bishr, who suggested that Morsi be chosen to head up the bloc because he knew him from the time when they had both been in the United States. Habib discussed Bishr's suggestion with the seventeen Brotherhood MPs in the bloc. 'When I mentioned his name', he recalls, 'they were surprised, especially because it was the first time that Morsi had entered the parliament and he had no experience, while others had already been in parliament before.'[69] However, these MPs accepted Morsi's appointment because they believed that Habib's suggestion was 'an expression of the Guidance Office's wishes', and that they should therefore accept it.[70]

Morsi's time in the parliament was hardly remarkable. He became known for weaving Qu'ranic verses and the sayings of the Prophet into his political discourse, and had a particular preoccupation with public morality, questioning the former information minister about publications in the state-run media that were running 'naked pictures' on their covers, and about video clips showing 'naked people'.[71] He spoke out, too, against the Miss Egypt beauty contest, issuing an urgent statement on the matter. But Morsi did sufficiently well to be appointed as leader of the Brotherhood's Political Office, as well as a member of its Guidance Office – though he was hardly natural leadership material. Abul Futuh commented: 'He is an excellent person and he is kind. But he isn't fit to run a ministry. The Brotherhood has many people who have charisma and expertise. Morsi has neither. The fact is that, unlike Al-Arian, he had no relationship with other political parties. He was an isolated man.'[72] Morsi also seems to have been reluctant to be put forward for the post. According to Isama Yassine, a senior Brotherhood spokesman and youth minister in the government of Hisham Qandil, when the party nominated him Morsi put his head in his hands and declared, 'May Allah forgive you!'[73]

Despite Morsi's obvious weaknesses, the Brotherhood appears to have had no qualms about putting him forward as its candidate of choice. This reflects the fact that personality has generally been of little consequence to the Brotherhood. The machinery of the movement has always been the Brotherhood's driving force, organisation and obedience being the overriding preoccupations. The Brotherhood therefore seems to have believed that the power of the movement, rather than the man, would be sufficient to carry it through the polls.

This turned out to be correct – though the presidential elections were not as easy a victory for the Brotherhood as the parliamentary polls had been. In results that should have served as a warning to the Brotherhood, Morsi won just 24.7 per cent of the vote in the first round, securing him a place in a runoff against Ahmed Shafiq, who had been reinstated since his disqualification. This meant that the second round became a choice between the old regime and the unknown – but an unknown that at least offered the prospect of a new and better Egypt. Many Egyptians therefore voted for Morsi because they wanted to see an end to the old regime, rather than because they necessarily believed in him or what he stood for. Furthermore, during his campaign Morsi had emphasised that he wished to be president for all Egyptians, not just for the Brotherhood. Even so, it was a close-run thing, Morsi winning the second round with just 51.7 per cent of the vote. On 24 June 2012, Morsi was declared Egypt's first civilian president.

Through this victory, the Brotherhood secured the ultimate triumph. Although it had never claimed to want to rule, it now held both the legislative and executive branches of power in its hands, as well as enjoying the added legitimacy conferred by Morsi's status as Egypt's first democratically elected president. Although its constant political manoeuvring and reneging on its promises had alienated some of those who had taken part in the revolution, it was precisely this kind of manoeuvring that had enabled it to reach its end goal.

In addition, while the Brotherhood may have been a reluctant revolutionary force, it could claim revolutionary legitimacy too. Although many still accused it of having sold the revolution out in order to muscle its way to power, as far as the Brotherhood was concerned it had shouldered the revolution, driving it forward when it was most at risk. It also believed that, through its negotiations with the SCAF, it had not only delivered a successful transition, but had avoided bloodshed in the process. In the Brotherhood's eyes, therefore, the long years of struggle and endurance had finally born fruit, and it had at last attained its just reward.

The future seemed to belong to the Brotherhood, and the way was finally open for it to put its ideology into practice, thereby demonstrating to Egyptians and the rest of the world that Islam really was the solution. But the Egyptian Brotherhood bore a special responsibility on its shoulders. Given that Egypt was the birthplace of reformist political Islam, and that the Egyptian Brotherhood was the 'mother branch' of a whole transnational movement, it knew that its experience in power would serve as a test case for the entire Islamist project that had been waiting in the wings for so long. With Islamist parties coming to power in Tunisia and looking set to play a key role in Libya, the burden of responsibility was all the heavier. It was essential, therefore, that the Brotherhood's time in power be a success.

TWO

BROTHERHOOD IN POWER: A HOLLOW VISION

Mohamed Morsi's assumption of power on 30 June 2012 marked a momentous occasion for the Brotherhood. Within a matter of months, it had gone from a semi-clandestine opposition movement crouching in the shadows and looking over its shoulder at every turn, to a democratically elected power mandated to lead Egypt through this critical moment in its contemporary history. With two elections under its belt and significant popular support, the Brotherhood had seemingly turned itself into a credible political force that was ready to govern.

But for the Brotherhood this moment was about more than just worldly politics; it had a divine dimension, too. The movement's triumph heralded the coming to power of a project that would bring Islam to the fore and mark a new dawn for the whole of the Ummah (Islamic nation). The Brotherhood, it seemed, was finally meeting its own destiny. Prior to taking up the presidency, Morsi had proclaimed that the Brotherhood would reconquer Egypt Islamically, and would build 'the Islamic State in Egypt on the same principle of the first Islamic state that was established in Al-Medina'.[1] Morsi presumably was not equating himself directly with the Prophet here. He doubtless did not mean to castigate pre-revolutionary Egypt as a *jahili* society either, as his comments would seem to imply. Instead, Morsi seems to have been carried away by the euphoria of the moment. But it was clear that, amid the heady elation, the Brotherhood believed in its own rhetoric, and thought itself to be unstoppable.

In reality, the picture was less rosy. Although the Brotherhood had successfully manoeuvred its way around the SCAF to craft the post-revolutionary order to its advantage, the latter was still a force to be reckoned with. And while the Brotherhood might have won the trust of a significant body of the electorate, there were whole swathes of Egyptian society that, if not openly hostile, were deeply suspicious of it before it had even started. This included large sections of the state, for whom the Brotherhood represented the very antithesis of what was required to lead a power such as Egypt. Furthermore, while the Brotherhood might have achieved electoral legitimacy, it was subsisting on a borrowed mandate. Although the Brotherhood could be sure of its own core support base, many Egyptians had voted for it because it was an untested power that represented an untainted moral force – and, more importantly, because they saw in it a break from the past. Many gave their votes to Morsi in the second round of the presidential elections to prevent the SCAF's candidate, Ahmed Shafiq, from coming to power. In addition, those opposition figures who had thrown their weight behind Morsi in this second round had done so on a promise that he would move beyond the Brotherhood and be a president for all Egyptians. The Brotherhood thus came to rule with one hand already tied behind its back.

Yet, despite these challenges, few could have predicted quite how short-lived Morsi's time in office would turn out to be. Few would have guessed either that, after just one year, the Brotherhood would be not only forced out of the political arena, but brought completely to its knees.

The roots of this cataclysmic fall from grace, which at a single blow reversed all the painstaking gains the Brotherhood had made over the decades, lie partly in objective factors, not least of which was the mountain of challenges facing the country at that time. However, the Brotherhood's failings were also due to subjective factors. Indeed, right from the start, the Brotherhood was out of its depth, flailing desperately like a drowning man, as it struggled to meet the challenges of governing in a modern age. In spite of the various reformist platforms it had drawn up during the 2000s, as well as its own electoral programme based on its An-Nahda ('Renaissance') project, the Brotherhood came to power with no vision and no real awareness of the world it was operating in. It is true that the Brotherhood had never claimed to want to rule, but it arrived on the scene looking like a movement that had barely even considered what it would do when it achieved power, and was walking blindly into the unknown. As former foreign minister and Arab League chief Amr Moussa noted, 'They weren't ready to rule Egypt and they hadn't prepared themselves to do so. Even coming to power was a surprise for them.'[2]

Once the Brotherhood began ruling, things did not improve. Its lack of any real vision meant that it very quickly turned to reactive policymaking as it stumbled its way through the challenges thrown at it from every side. It also fell back on its old friend, informal politics, manoeuvring its way through problems by striking deals, in an increasingly frantic bid to appease all sides. Despite being considered as the standard-bearer of political Islam, therefore, when it came to putting its project into practice the Brotherhood proved incapable. Both its political and Islamic aspirations turned out to be empty, comprising mainly slogans and generalities that could not be translated into concrete outcomes. Instead, the Brotherhood relied on a faith in its own cadres and a belief that, if these pious individuals came to power, everything would fall into place. Al-Banna himself had once said, 'My job is to write men rather than to write books',[3] and, 'In the time that I would waste in writing a book, I could write 100 young Muslims. Every one of them would be a living, speaking, influential book.'[4] The Brotherhood seems to have believed that this would be sufficient to steer Egypt through such tumultuous times. For all its talk of being a modern, progressive party, the Brotherhood fell back on its belief that the 'reformed' individual who had Islam at his core could carry the day. Beyond that, there seemed to be only a big black hole.

A Lack of Vision

That the Brotherhood should have come to power with no tangible vision or political programme to match its grandiose ambitions was in many ways unsurprising. Although the movement had been engaged in political activism for decades, some of its members serving as MPs, the Brotherhood had always struggled to articulate its ideas and concepts. It had also always been far better at expressing what it was against than forging any coherent vision of what it stood for, taking refuge in the realm of the general whenever called upon to do so. The series of reform platforms published in the mid to late 2000s, aimed at demonstrating that the Brotherhood had moved on and was now a modern, progressive movement, were a case in point. These platforms, which laid out the Brotherhood's vision across the political, economic and social spheres, were vague, often contradictory, and preoccupied with ill-defined concepts. They were also notably lacking in concrete policy proposals or solutions.[5] Although it circulated plenty of buzzwords about democracy, social justice and the rule of law, the Brotherhood struggled at the most basic level to articulate even some of its defining concepts, such as what exactly it meant by a 'civil state run along Islamic principles'.

When it was an opposition movement, this lack of a coherent vision did not seem to matter too much. Many of the Brotherhood's adherents supported it not because of its politics, but because it was a socio-religious movement and moral force whose association with Islam was such that, for them, it represented Islam itself. Even after the revolution, there was no need to dazzle these supporters with any grand plan or political programme, let alone fancy talk of social justice and Islamic democracy. This support base was guaranteed.

But once the revolution brought it out into the open, and as the elections approached, the Brotherhood had to convince others, namely the secular opposition and the West, which were both suspicious of the movement's intentions and capabilities, that it was up to the job of ruling. It therefore needed some sort of grand plan or programme equal to the momentous changes unfolding in Egypt and throughout the region. The Brotherhood turned, therefore, to its An-Nahda project. It was with this project, which served as the peg upon which Morsi hung his election campaign, that the Brotherhood promised to transform Egypt and save the country from itself.

This Renaissance project was not a new initiative. The brainchild of Brotherhood powerhouse Khairet Al-Shater, it had been many years in the making. As the Brotherhood stated in 2012, 'This project and programme is the result of a tremendous effort and hard work that lasted well over fifteen years.'[6] Yet despite all the time invested in it, when the revolution erupted it was clear that this project was far from developed. As Al-Shater himself acknowledged in April 2011, 'The issue of the Nahda ... my brothers, is not as easy a subject as its title suggests, because this project of the Ummah's Nahda does not exist on the level of planning or formulation.'[7] As late as July 2012, after Morsi had campaigned and been elected on the basis of the programme, Secretary-General Mahmoud Hussein, stated that the movement had only 'put down the seeds and roots' of the An-Nahda project, and that it still required 'experts and specialised people' to come together in forums to 'mend it so that it becomes a project for Egypt'.[8]

Despite being undeveloped, the An-Nahda project still promised the earth. It was an almost utopian document, painting an ideal picture of a happy and prosperous Egypt regaining its rightful place in the world: 'The Project is based upon empowering the people and placing their destinies in their own hands', it stated, promising to build 'a society endowed with lofty values, science and thought' and a state that 'provides people access to education, healthcare, jobs, investment, and business building opportunities; and protects their rights and dignity within and outside the country.'[9] A leaflet explaining the programme that was distributed during Morsi's election campaign promised even more dizzying achievements: 'The project's origin is based on the project of the Prophet (pbuh) which is about transforming shepherds and idol worshipers into the patrons of nations and the makers of the greatest civilisation known to mankind.'[10]

The An-Nahda project was also a programme of salvation. In line with the Brotherhood's preoccupation with improving the individual, there was a strong focus on saving the Egyptian people, as though they were somehow corrupted and in need of redemption from the moral quagmire into which they had sunk. The project stated its intention to 'rebuild the Egyptian person' and to employ 'quick and intensive efforts to save the Egyptian family.' It had the feel of a religious mission, with a strong focus on individual morality and piety rather than that of a modern political programme designed to deal with the complex set of challenges facing a country about to embark upon the most profound transformation of its contemporary history.

Furthermore, although the Brotherhood explained that the An-Nahda project represented the 'practical application' of its age-old slogan, 'Islam is the Solution',[11] there were few practical details of how it intended to implement its vision. While parts of the document read rather like a Western management manual, with its talk of 'empowered institutions' and a 'productive value-added economy', there were no concrete plans about how it would go about achieving these high-minded ideals. In fact, while the programme was explicit in its commitment to democracy, a broad-based coalition government and free-market economics, there was nothing explaining what it actually intended to do other than some vague notions such as a plan to launch 100 national projects each exceeding $1 billion, and guaranteeing an annual growth rate of 6.5–7 per cent every year for five years, and some promises to improve traffic and security. There was a sense, therefore, that the programme had been drawn up in a vacuum, in isolation not only from the realities of Egypt itself but from the wider world around it. Neither was there any sense in it that Egypt was going through exceptional circumstances, and required a tailored set of responses and solutions.

Many Egyptians found the programme both perplexing and insulting. Well-known Islamic thinker Mohamed Salim Al-Awa complained: 'This project doesn't respect our minds. They are selling us air ... The candidate who tells us he will implement a renaissance project within four years doesn't respect our minds. We can't change the country in four years.'[12] Former deputy Murshid, Mohamed Habib, issued an equally damning criticism asserting that, once Morsi had come to power, 'we discovered that the Renaissance Project was just ideas and headlines'.[13] The project also drew ridicule. A Twitter feed emerged including parodies of film titles with offerings such as 'The Devil Wears Nahda', 'Around the Nahda in Morsi Days', 'Nahda Impossible' and 'Nahda in Wonderland'.[14]

For all its grandiosity, therefore, the project turned out to be hopelessly ambitious and out of touch with realities on the ground. Phase 1, in which Morsi promised to solve more than sixty specific issues ranging from security to sanitation and transport within his first three months in office, was a case in point. Given the extent of upheaval the country was undergoing, remedying such problems within such a short time was impossible. It was little surprise, then, that once the pressing challenges of rule became a reality, the An-Nahda Project was put quietly on the backburner. At one point Al-Shater even denied that the project had ever existed: 'This project doesn't exist and it is the creation of the media.'[15]

Yet this renaissance project somehow summarised the Brotherhood. Full of vague ideals but lacking in substance, it reflected the movement's general lack of experience and self-awareness, as well as its failure to understand the new reality within which it operated. While such a project may have sat well with its core supporters, as well as with parts of a wider constituency, it was not sufficient to convince others, particularly those in the elite, that the Brotherhood was qualified to take on the job it had been tasked with.

This lack of awareness was also reflected in the Brotherhood's choice of presidential candidate. The Brotherhood seems to have been insufficiently aware, or even concerned, about how Morsi would be perceived by the wider public. As noted in Chapter One, the Brotherhood had always prioritised the machinery of the movement over individual personalities, meaning that the charisma and personality of the president was almost immaterial. Even Al-Shater, who was the Brotherhood's first choice of candidate, though he may have been more charismatic than Morsi, was hardly a natural leader, having always preferred to operate behind the scenes. Thus the Brotherhood saw nothing wrong in propelling Morsi to the fore. In fact, Morsi was the typical Brotherhood man: drawn from the professional classes, but of humble origin, he displayed sincerity and piousness, but was hardly going to set the world alight.

While many ordinary Egyptians saw in Morsi a simple, unaffected man who was sincere and who was one of them, to many others he was nothing short of an embarrassment. With his bumbling, awkward manner, for many he was simply not up to the job – especially given that the presidential post carries a special symbolic resonance in Egypt, imbued with the values of patriotism and heroism, with the incumbent expected to serve as father to the nation. The indignation of the Egyptian elite was encapsulated by Mona Makram Ebeid, a professor at the American University in Cairo, who exclaimed: 'Egyptians felt humiliated when they saw him. Can this be the president of Egypt? It is not Timbuktu we're talking about. It's Egypt with 90 million people and 7,000 years of civilisation.'[16] Indeed, for the Egyptian elite, Morsi represented all that was backward and unsophisticated about the Brotherhood and the Islamists more widely.

Such views were evident in some of the stories that did the rounds, such as that related by a former senior state security official who claimed that, upon seeing the priceless antique carpets and furniture in the presidential palace for the first time, Morsi and his team demanded to know, 'Why have you given us such old stuff? Is it because we are from the Brotherhood? We don't want this old stuff, we want new things!'[17] The same official also complained that the smell of food 'wafted constantly from the palace, even at ten in the morning'.[18] Meanwhile, the new president was held up as a figure of ridicule in the media, mocked mercilessly for his lack of sophistication and statesmanship. In the words of Alaa Abu Al-

Nasser, the general secretary of the Construction and Development Party (the political arm of Al-Gama'a Al-Islamiya), 'the media made mincemeat out of him'.[19]

Even some former members of the Brotherhood struggled with the anomaly of Morsi's assumption of the presidential post. Former deputy Murshid Mohamed Habib complained that Morsi ran the state as if it had no 'history or status or tradition'.[20] Habib complained, too, about Morsi's habit of delivering long and rambling speeches: 'When Morsi took over he talked on every important and unimportant occasion. To be fair, some of those speeches were close to the layman, but in many others he was so unsuccessful to the extent that I was fearful anytime I heard he was going to speak.'[21] Abdulmonem Abul Futuh meanwhile accused Morsi of lacking political imagination: 'He talks in generalities and slogans, and he talks in a way that is closer to a preacher than a president. His speeches are not clear.'[22] Abul Futuh touches on an important point. Many complained that Morsi was more like an imam than a political leader. The fact that he chose to give some of his speeches inside mosques, seemingly not distinguishing between the roles of president and preacher, certainly contributed to this impression.

Thus the Brotherhood came to power lacking not only any clear vision of what it wanted to achieve, but also a strong or charismatic president. It also arrived in office already emasculated. The Brotherhood's decision to cut short the revolution and negotiate with the SCAF may have helped secure its place in the transition, but it also left it facing a formidable force that was intent on undermining it at every turn. Just two days before the second round of presidential elections, the Supreme Constitutional Court – still the domain of Mubarak-era judges – had ruled that the House of Representatives, the lower house of parliament, was unconstitutional because one-third of its members had been elected illegally.[23] The SCAF duly dissolved the house. It also took further steps to restrict the Brotherhood, issuing a Supplementary Constitutional Decree on 17 June 2012 limiting the president's powers and handing legislative authority over to the SCAF. This was disastrous for the Brotherhood, and left Morsi as a president who had promised the earth and more, but who had no real capacity to deliver.

Politics 'on the Hoof'

With no real vision to draw upon, the Brotherhood inevitably fell back on reactive policymaking, responding to each crisis as and when it arose. In this vein, it also continued to rely on the dualistic approach it had adopted during the revolution, mixing appeasement on one hand with appeals to the street on the other. Indeed, whenever things got tough, it re-assumed the mantle of a revolutionary actor, as if it was mobilising the street against the very state it purported to lead.

Such traits were evident from the start, with Morsi's swearing of the presidential oath. The constitutional amendments passed by referendum in March 2011 had stipulated that the new president was to be sworn in in front of the parliament. But the lower house of the parliament was now dissolved, and Article 30 of the Supplementary Constitutional Decree, issued by the SCAF on 17 June 2012, specified that the president elect should be sworn into office before the General Assembly of the Constitutional Court.

This demand outraged the revolutionaries who had poured back into Tahrir Square and were calling on Morsi to refuse to take the oath in front of the Constitutional Court. Morsi was thus thrown immediately into a serious dilemma. On one hand, he felt the need to bolster his revolutionary credentials by standing up to the SCAF and proving that he meant business. At the same time, however, he knew he could not afford to push the SCAF too far, and feared entering into any kind of confrontation with it. He therefore tried to steer a middle course that played to both camps simultaneously. On 29 June, after performing noon prayers at Cairo's Al-Azhar mosque, Morsi headed to Tahrir Square, where he proceeded to swear the oath of office in front of cheering supporters. 'This is an oath to you', he told the crowd, before going on to recite the presidential oath of office.[24] Morsi told his audience on more than one occasion, 'I love you', and, in what appeared rather like a clumsy piece of theatre, lifted his jacket to show the crowds that he was not wearing a bullet-proof vest.

What was especially notable about this rabble-rousing speech, however, was Morsi's proclamation that 'No power is above this power. No power is above you. No power is above your will. You are the rulers. You are the owners of the will. You are the source of this power and authority.'[25] Morsi's speech, with its appeal to 'people power', therefore appeared more like a mass rally to mobilise support against the SCAF and the state than the speech of a president taking office. Moreover, here was Morsi, who had never had a revolutionary bone in his body, taking on the mantle of revolutionary leader as if he had personally led and delivered the revolution. This was a guise that Morsi was to adopt repeatedly throughout his presidency.

Following this grand display of revolutionary defiance, however, Morsi proceeded to comply with the SCAF's wishes, and the next day duly swore the oath of office before the Constitutional Court. Morsi, who turned up at the ceremony forty-five minutes late, purportedly because of the notorious Cairo traffic, was clearly resentful, especially given that the whole ceremony was to be broadcast live on television. Morsi had objected to its being broadcast live, but after the court insisted and three judges threatened to pull out, he submitted.[26] Indeed, while the Brotherhood may have begrudged being forced to comply with such demands, it feared entering into any serious confrontation with the SCAF. As the Brotherhood's secretary-general, Mahmoud Hussein, explained,

> SCAF's insistence on having the oath delivered before the Supreme Constitutional Court disregarded the people's opinion and the political forces that want the president to take the oath in the people's assembly, which was elected by the people. But the current

> crisis has given Morsi no choice but to accept ... in order to avoid entering into early differences with the SCAF.[27]

In the event the ceremony was a sombre affair. In seeming contradiction to the stirring speech he had given the day before, a grim-faced Morsi declared solemnly, 'I respect the constitutional court and I respect its rulings. I respect the judiciary, its rulings and its institutions.'[28] Yet Morsi went further, and began to lavish praise on the judiciary: 'I thank Allah that we have these institutions with men who are loyal to their country and keen to achieve its interests and who know and understand the meaning of respecting the constitution, the law and the rulings.'[29]

Two hours later Morsi made his inaugural speech at Cairo University in front of an audience of intellectuals, politicians and public figures. A million miles away from the revolutionary stance he had taken in Tahrir Square, it was now the turn of the SCAF to be the recipient of the president's lavish praise. Morsi lauded the SCAF as 'the shield and sword of the nation', and pledged to preserve it and 'safeguard its members, recruits and commanders, and to enhance and elevate its status, and to boost it by all means possible to make it stronger than ever before and continue to be steadfast, with the people's support in all it does'.[30] As with the judiciary, this excessive tribute to the SCAF was Morsi's way of trying to bring it on-side and avoid any direct confrontation. However, to many, including the revolutionaries, it looked like an odd sort of capitulation to the very forces that were denying the Brotherhood real power, and that the revolution had sought to overturn.

Not all Brotherhood members shared Morsi's enthusiasm for appeasing the military in this way. Despite Morsi's having given Field Marshal Tantawi his personal assurances that the Brotherhood would not insult the military during the gathering, FJP secretary-general Mohamed Beltagi began leading chants of 'Down with military rule!' This drove the SCAF to threaten to withdraw from the event, which in turn caused the Brotherhood's supreme guide, Mohamed Al-Badie, to step in and ban such slogans from being chanted.[31]

Although the difficulty of the Brotherhood's position at this time was unquestionable, its vacillation between populism and appeasement gave the impression that its politics were muddled and made up on the hoof. This was hardly helpful for a movement that, throughout its history, had been accused of deception and double-speak. Although the Brotherhood's dualistic approach was simply its way of trying to keep the different constituencies on board at the same time, rather than any kind of deliberate deception, the movement should have had a greater understanding of how its actions would be perceived. Yet the Brotherhood seemed to be so wrapped up in the feverish cheers of its supporters that it was unaware, or insufficiently concerned, about how its actions appeared to others as it blundered from one stance to another, responding to each situation as it arose.

As well as this twin-track approach, the Brotherhood also turned to informal policymaking as a means of manoeuvre. While this was partly because of the constraints it was working under, it was also symptomatic of the movement's wider approach to politics. The Brotherhood had always been most comfortable when working through personal connections and informal agreements in order to achieve its objectives. It had always been happy to strike informal deals with successive regimes or forces, however repressive they may have been, this being a manifestation of its status as a semi-underground opposition movement. Yet it continued to operate in this informal manner even after it came to power, as if it was still not part of the state it had been elected to lead.

Within this context, the Brotherhood struggled to move away from a decades-old habit of trusting only its own. Despite all its talk of consensus politics, when it came to ruling, the movement proved reluctant to rely on those outside its own circle. And when it did bring in others it ensured that it chose individuals who were completely on-side, and would follow its lead. As Abul Futuh observed, 'The nature of the Brotherhood's leadership is closed. They don't trust anybody but themselves. Even when they brought in people outside of the Muslim Brotherhood they chose them on the basis that they would be followers.'[32]

This was certainly true when it came to Morsi's appointment of his first cabinet, in August 2012. There was a strong expectation that Egypt's first proper post-revolutionary government would mirror the different forces that had come together to oust the Mubarak regime, and that it would mark the launch of a new phase in Egypt's political history. But what emerged could not have been further from these expectations. As liberal activist Shahir George complained, 'It is not a revolutionary government at all, merely another caretaker government.'[33]

This new government was headed by Prime Minister Hisham Qandil, who had been minister of irrigation and water in the outgoing government. Although he was not a member of the Brotherhood, Qandil had Islamist sympathies; in the words of Abul Futuh, 'He may not have been from the Brotherhood but his character indicated he would follow them.'[34] Somewhat judiciously, the FJP took only five portfolios for itself – information, housing, higher education, youth and manpower – none of them sovereign, and most related to services, an arena in which the Brotherhood felt it could excel. Indeed, the movement was well aware at this point that it did not have enough qualified or experienced people to take up ministerial posts. As Amr Darrag explained, because ministers were traditionally drawn from the sectors they represented, the FJP 'did not have that many politicians who could really function as different ministers'.[35] Moreover, the Brotherhood was aware of the need to be seen to be consensual.

The remainder of the posts were divided between technocrats and independents, some of whom had served in the outgoing government, as well as a number of rather formidable figures from the former regime. These included Hussain Tantawi, who stayed on as defence minister, and Ahmed Gamal Al-Din, a retired general and police officer who was appointed as interior minister. Members of the Brotherhood explained Tantawi's appointment in terms of the need to 'uphold tradition' by appointing a serving officer in the military to the post.[36] But the reality was that this was a cabinet of appeasement – a result of cautious choices aimed at maintaining the delicate balance of power between the SCAF and the Brotherhood, rather than the heralding of a new Egypt. The one exception was Ahmed Mekky, a former deputy of the court of cassation, who was made justice minister. His appointment was viewed as a challenge to the judiciary, although notably he was also sympathetic to the Brotherhood.

What was particularly striking about this cabinet, however, was that the Brotherhood had given no space to other political parties. These included the Salafist Al-Nour party, which on the basis of its election results had expected to get a share of the posts, and which issued a statement on 2 August criticising Morsi for having failed to establish a broad-based government.[37] The anger of many parties was all the more bitter because, prior to his election, Morsi had given them his word that he would include all political forces in a national unity government. At a meeting at Cairo's upmarket Fairmont Hotel on 21 June, tens of leading opposition figures came together with the Brotherhood to show a united front against the former regime, which they believed was manoeuvring to rig the presidential election results to ensure that its candidate Ahmed Shafiq was triumphant. In return for these parties pledging him their support, Morsi promised to launch a comprehensive national project and to form a national salvation government that would be headed by an independent political figure and include representatives from all political factions. Morsi also agreed to establish a presidential team that would reflect Egypt's diverse political makeup.

Morsi's willingness to agree to these conditions was driven by what one opposition leader present at the Fairmont meeting described as his need to 'create a front of support'.[38] But once his presidency was confirmed, Morsi dropped these opposition figures apparently without a second thought, while his promise to create a national unity government evaporated into thin air. The Brotherhood has claimed that it had in fact approached some of these political factions about taking on ministerial posts. Brotherhood spokesman Mourad Ali insisted: 'We offered cabinet positions to figures from other groups, but they refused.'[39] Mahmoud Hussein was more specific: 'We talked to Abul Futuh and Hamdeen Sabahi about being assistants to Morsi prior to the [presidential] election and after it. But they imposed conditions that no one else apart from them would be appointed as assistants and that Morsi couldn't take any decision without their consent.'[40] But Abul Futuh has insisted on more than one occasion that he was never contacted about any post. He told Al-Jazeera, 'I know very well that no contacts were made with any of the previous [presidential] candidates in that respect, including me. No contact was made with Dr Baradei or with Hamdeen, and I am in contact with them all. There were no contacts made to that effect. What is being suggested is just talk in the media, and doesn't reflect reality.'[41] In fact, Abul Futuh claims that he had already been cut off by the movement following his bid to stand for the presidency, complaining, 'That's their way of dealing with things. They drop you.'[42]

It appears, therefore, that the Brotherhood had such an inflated sense of its own power that it believed it did not need to bring in other forces, regardless of the promises it may or may not have made – especially those forces that might pose a challenge to its own hegemony. Indeed, because it believed these opposition forces to be weak and itself to be strong, the Brotherhood assumed they did not matter.[43] Furthermore, the Brotherhood clearly hadn't yet realised the true danger posed by the SCAF, and saw no value in creating a broad-based platform with which to chip away at the SCAF's power. Instead it seemed to feel far more comfortable working alongside the familiar enemy of the SCAF than it did with reaching out to other forces. As Islam Al-Katatni, the brother of senior Brotherhood figure Saad Al-Katatni, commented, 'The Muslim Brotherhood doubt everyone other than themselves. They don't trust anyone.'[44]

Morsi's Consultants' Committee, or advisory team, appointed at the end of August, was equally short on members of other political parties. Just like the cabinet, this seventeen-member team was meant to give the impression of inclusiveness. Although one of his deputies, Essam Al-Haddad, was a Brotherhood Guidance Office member, the remaining three deputies comprised a Copt, Samir Morcos; a female academic, Pakinam Al-Sharkawy; and a Salafist, Emad Abdelgafour, who was head of the Al-Nour party. There were also a number of liberal faces in the team, such as writer Sekina Fouad, poet Farouq Gouieda and TV host Amr Al-Leithi.

But the team was strongly dominated by Islamists from the Brotherhood and the FJP, such as Issam Al-Arian, Mohei Hamed Mohamed, Omamia Kamel, and Hussein Mohamed Al-Kazzazz. There were also some members from the Salafist current. Furthermore, as well as this advisory council Morsi appointed a raft of Brotherhood members to positions of power. These included Ahmed Abdel-Ati, who became the head of Morsi's office; Assad Al-Shaikha, Morsi's nephew, who became deputy chief of staff and who was sometimes referred to as the 'president's shadow'; and Muslim Brotherhood member Yasser Ali, who was appointed as Morsi's spokesman, among others.[45] Thus, while the cabinet and main advisory team were meant to appear inclusive, in reality Morsi surrounded himself with a tightknit team of faithful allies in whom he could place his trust. In fact, loyalty often trumped suitability for the job in question. Former Brotherhood member Kamal Helbawy complained that the Brotherhood had 'appointed certain advisors who had no experience whatsoever'. He cited Essam Al-Haddad, for example, who had been a student of his in the late 1970s: 'He became Morsi's assistant for foreign affairs, but he has no relation to foreign affairs. He was working in relief agencies.'[46] Ahmed Abdel-Ati, meanwhile, was a pharmacist by trade who was virtually unknown outside Brotherhood circles until he became Morsi's presidential campaign co-ordinator.[47]

The Brotherhood was also accused of allowing these figures to overshadow government ministers in what was a further demonstration of its preference for informal politics. As one Egyptian journalist complained, 'Essam al-Haddad was a medical doctor who suddenly became advisor to Morsi in foreign affairs. The foreign affairs minister was rendered useless because of him.

Suddenly Al-Haddad started touring different countries as if he was higher than the minister. Everyone in Egypt started wondering where the foreign ministry was.'[48] Although the foreign minister, Mohamed Kamel Amr, denied these allegations, Helbawy made similar observations: 'Al-Haddad became higher than the minister of foreign affairs and the intelligence chief ... He was always just behind Morsi.'[49] The Brotherhood appeared to have no compunction, either, about pursuing politics through the party rather than the relevant government bodies. In December 2011, for example, the FJP agreed directly with the Turkish ambassador to Egypt that Ankara would run a large campaign on Turkish television promoting tourism in Egypt, free of charge. According to Mohamed Soudan, who was the FJP's secretary-general in Alexandria, the FJP entrusted a development committee to contact officials in the Tourism Ministry to see whether they had any readymade advertisements that could be shown on Turkish television as part of this campaign – or, failing that, whether they could produce some in the Turkish language.[50]

This kind of informal policymaking made the decision-making process seem particularly opaque, including for some members of the presidential team who, being outside Morsi's inner circle, were themselves perplexed about how matters were decided. Nationalist member of the presidential advisory team Mohamed Seif El-Dawla complained: 'The decision-making process is like walking in a minefield without a map.'[51] Ayman Al-Said, another of Morsi's advisors, commented that Morsi 'listens to a very wide circle of advisers and experts. But decision-taking is different. I don't know who makes final decisions.'[52]

Thus, despite all the formal mechanisms associated with the presidency, Morsi continued to operate through informal channels, undermining the very state he was supposed to be leading. Furthermore, he could not dispel the belief that he was just a front man, and that the Brotherhood was pulling his strings. Judge Mohamed Fuad Jadallah, Morsi's legal advisor, reflected that presidential decisions often came 'readymade from outside the palace'.[53] Likewise, Mohamed Habib explained: 'I warned many times that there was someone intervening in presidential affairs and in the job of the president. I said that this was one of the reasons for the shaky nature of the president's decisions. This way of ruling doesn't fit running a state the size and weight of Egypt.'[54] Abul Futuh complained that, despite Morsi's having given him a written promise before the presidential elections that he would be independent

> Right from the first day he wouldn't do anything without consulting the leaders of the Muslim Brotherhood ... He ran the state like he was running the Brotherhood, as if the presidency was just another branch of the movement. He ran meetings in the presidency exactly as he used to run the meetings of the politburo of his party, the FJP. When he was holding a meeting with the party and they took a decision, he always used to say, 'We have to wait until we put the decision to the leadership of the Muslim Brotherhood.' And whatever the leadership decided would be the decision that was taken.[55]

Abul Futuh also claimed that it was Al-Shater who was really in control: 'He [Al-Shater] was running everything like a puppet show from behind ... Egypt had two presidents, a real one – Khairet Al-Shater – and an official one – Mohamed Morsi.'[56] While such comments may be somewhat exaggerated, even members of the Brotherhood acknowledged that the Guidance Office was in contact with him over policy decisions. As Mohamed Soudan explained, 'The Guidance Office used to send Morsi messages. We sent him a message warning him about Interior Minister Ibrahim. He said, "No, he is good. Let me do what is right." He accepted a few of these messages and ignored many others.'[57] Although the Brotherhood had made a point of telling Egyptians that, once he came to power, Morsi's allegiance would be to 'Allah and Egypt', and no longer to the Murshid, the president struggled to dispel the impression that he was merely the puppet of the Brotherhood – an impression that would haunt the movement throughout its time in power.

Morsi failed, too, to convince Egyptians that he was working in the interests of the movement, and that he could be a national figure. All this fed into a narrative that emerged soon after the Brotherhood came to power, holding that it was engaged in a wholesale process of Ikwhanisation, or Brotherhoodisation, of the state. Such accusations, trumpeted by Brotherhood opponents and parts of the media, were wildly exaggerated. While Morsi may have surrounded himself with a close-knit group of Brotherhood loyalists who operated like a private club, he was unable even to scratch the surface of the Egyptian state, let alone Ikwhanise it. As Abul Futuh commented, 'Although people accused them of Ikwhanisation, the reality is that the state was bigger than them.'[58]

The Brotherhood and the Deep State

The state certainly represented an ominous body for the Brotherhood. This was hardly surprising. Upon coming to power, the movement was parachuted into the middle of a bureaucracy that was at best ambivalent towards it. Many state institutions had a mind-set that was antithetical to the Brotherhood, having been brought up on a diet replete with anti-Islamist propaganda. Not that the whole of the administration was entirely hostile. As Amr Mousa has argued, 'Some people [in the state] were willing to give them a chance. It was only fair to give them a chance.'[59] But as the Brotherhood saw it, it was surrounded by a large and immovable body that was determined to prevent it from succeeding. This was true most of all of the security apparatus, whose main task over the past decades had been to repress the Islamist current. As former FJP MP Gamal Heshmat commented, 'The security apparatus was brought up to be hostile to the Islamists, and when Islamists took over they couldn't handle it.'[60] One high-ranking former member of state security services was more explicit, exclaiming: 'Inside the police they wanted to choke them [the Brotherhood] to death.'[61]

Furthermore, despite the fact that the upper echelons of state institutions were stuffed full of retired military and police personnel who were milking the system for all it was worth, the Egyptian state still had an image of itself as a modernist and progressive body that was distinctly at odds with Islamist rule.[62] It therefore feared that the Brotherhood was intent on Islamicising the state, bringing in its own cadres and clearing out those who did not adhere to its ideology. There was also a real anxiety inside the administration that the Brotherhood would try to dismantle the myriad layers of privilege and patronage that had been built up over generations. Yazid Sayegh has expertly described what the Brotherhood was up against:

> Senior officers have access to a wide array of government posts after retirement, subsidized services and goods, the command of significant resources and opportunities within the civilian economy, and elevated social status. The officers' republic additionally exercises exclusive control over the defence budget, US military assistance, and military-owned businesses. Moreover, it is underpinned by a deep sense of institutional and personal entitlement.[63]

Those within these institutions feared that the Brotherhood was going to embark upon a mass purge that would put an end to their privileges. Early moves to retire hundreds of police officers did little to assuage these fears. These bodies were thus, in many ways, steeled against Morsi before his administration had even begun.

The extent of hostility certainly seems to have come as a surprise to the Brotherhood. As senior Brotherhood member Ashraf Abdel Gaffar explained, 'We were aware of it but the question was: To what extent? We didn't expect it to be that deep.'[64] The experience of Gamal Abdelsattar, the deputy awqaf (religious affairs and endowments) minister, was typical. He recounted how, when he began work at the ministry, he was surprised to find that it was being run by five retired military personnel who had been appointed as deputy ministers.[65] He was surprised, too, at the levels of corruption inside the ministry, and how, when they had tried to refer corrupt individuals to investigative committees, they discovered that these committees were also corrupt. The situation was so dire that it prompted him to exclaim: 'The devil is having private lessons here!'[66]

Of course, one should not overplay the idea of the deep state. These were not monolithic institutions, and many contained currents that had been pushing for change and reform for some time. Pro-reform groups such as Officers But Honourable, in the police, along with similar bodies in the judiciary, were hungry for change, and were keen proponents of the revolution against the former regime. There were also plenty of individuals within the state bureaucracy who had supported the revolution, and who wanted to be rid of Mubarak and his cronies. However, this did not mean they were ready for real reform inside their own institutions.

They need not have worried, however. For all that the Brotherhood lacked the stomach for revolution, it had little appetite for reform either. Despite the fact that it had a broad popular mandate to bring about change, and had always identified itself as a reformist movement, it did very little to try to reform these institutions in any meaningful or systematic way. This was certainly true where the Interior Ministry was concerned. Although Amr Darrag had identified security sector reform as the most important issue the Brotherhood would like to tackle, it did almost nothing to reform either the Interior Ministry or the police.[67] Before its dissolution, the Islamist-dominated lower house of parliament had amended the police authority law – but these amendments were minimal, and included introducing improved pay and pensions for police officers. Morsi did even less. Although the Interior Ministry forced 454 senior officers into retirement, there was no substantive talk of reform from the presidency, let alone any action on the matter. This is not to suggest that reforming these creaking institutions would have been easy, or even practicable; but the Brotherhood appeared to have no roadmap for how it intended to change these bodies.

Instead, the Brotherhood opted for a policy of persuasion,

seemingly believing that these institutions could be brought round by good-will alone. This was predicated on the movement's belief that these state institutions and those who worked in them were largely sound, but were being corrupted by rogue elements at the top. As Gamal Heshmat explained, 'We believed that there was good-will in many of the state institutions.'[68] Mahmoud Hussein noted that 'Dr Morsi and his presidential team thought that large numbers of the institutions of the deep state were nationalist and that we could rely on that.'[69] Morsi seemed to believe that if these institutions could only be made to understand that he was well-intentioned and sincere, then they could be persuaded to stand behind him. Tellingly, Mahmoud Hussein commented that 'Morsi looked at problems in a sincere way, and if there had been enough sincere people he would have solved them.'[70]

The Brotherhood also believed in the power of redemption. As Gamal Heshmat revealed, 'We wanted the police to be better, and to give them the chance to repent and change for the better, but none of them took up that opportunity.'[71] Ashraf Abdel Gaffar commented that the party 'offered a very decent civilised and human alternative for corrupt bureaucrats by asking them to stop what they were doing or else be taken to court. Or they had to show us their willingness to fix their mistakes, and we would let them go after that ... That was naive thinking. They needed harsh treatment.'[72] FJP member Abdelmawgud Dardery reiterated the same idea almost word for word:

> What the FJP did was they offered a very decent, very humane, very civilised alternative. These corrupt bureaucrats, we asked them to stop it or we would take them to court, or if they were willing to fix some of the problems they created we would let them go ... that was the theory, but now I think it was naive thinking because it seems that the deep state needed a harsh hand.[73]

This informal approach was directly in line with the movement's overall ethos of focusing on the individual as a means of building a better society. But it was also the thinking of a socio-religious proselyting movement rather than a contemporary political party armed with the necessary tools to reform and run a functioning state. Indeed, the Brotherhood appeared to have no real policy or long-term reform plan to deal with these very state institutions, relying instead on opportunistic policymaking, and on postures over substance.

One of the consequences of this lack of any long-term vision was that the Brotherhood was forced to rely increasingly on reactive gestures, responding to events as they arose and snatching opportunities where it could. Even what was considered to be Morsi's most serious attempt at dismantling the apparatus of the former regime – his expulsion of a raft of senior military figures in the SCAF in August 2012 – turned out to be little more than an opportunistic reaction to events. Indeed, their removal was not part of any considered plan to purge or reform the security apparatus in line with the spirit of the revolution. Instead, fate offered Morsi a chance, and he seized it with both hands. This chance came on 5 August 2012, when sixteen soldiers were killed and a further seven injured after militants attacked a military camp in Rafah, in the Sinai. Although the Sinai had long been a problematic region where militancy was not unknown, the fact that this incident had come so soon after Morsi's assumption of power sent shockwaves through the country. It also shook the presidency, not least because there was immediate speculation that the attack had been carried out by Islamist extremists linked to Palestinian elements from Gaza, which was under the control of Brotherhood offshoot Hamas.[74] There was also talk that some of the attackers were former Islamist prisoners who had been released from Egyptian prisons just forty-five days earlier. Although it had been the SCAF that, after the revolution, had started releasing Islamist prisoners, freeing over 800 of them while Morsi released just twenty-seven (admittedly most of them jihadists), there was a widespread belief that those who were freed had gone straight to the Sinai, and that Morsi was responsible.

The Rafah attack threatened, therefore, to be hugely embarrassing to the new president. On 6 August the situation deteriorated, when intelligence chief Mourad Mowafi revealed to the media that he had relayed intelligence information about an imminent attack against military units in the Sinai to the 'concerned authorities' before the attack.[75] He also indicated some of this intelligence had come from Israeli sources, suggesting that Palestinian elements may have been involved. Although the presidency issued a vehement denial that it had ever been passed this information, Mowafi's assertion fuelled the belief that Morsi, who had not provided information about the attackers, was somehow complicit in the incident, or at the very least was protecting his fellow Islamists.

By the day of the soldiers' funerals, anger against the Brotherhood and its government was mounting. Prime Minister Hisham Qandil was attacked by an angry mob as he left the Al-Rashad Mosque, where he had been attending funeral prayers. Protestors held their shoes in the air, chanting anti-Brotherhood and anti-Morsi slogans, including: 'You killed them, you dogs!'[76] When he heard about this incident, Morsi, who had been planning to attend the funerals, changed his mind and went to visit injured soldiers at the military hospital at Quba instead. But this last-minute no-show prompted further resentment and hostility.

For the Brotherhood, however, the whole episode raised fears that there was something afoot inside the security services. The woeful lack of security provision at the soldiers' funeral certainly left many inside the Brotherhood believing that there had been a deliberate ploy by the security services to leave the president exposed to the angry mob. As Mohamed Soudan recalled, 'Morsi wanted to attend the funeral. Our brothers phoned him to tell him that there was a trap set up for him. Morsi called the Cairo police, the head of Intelligence, the defence head, and they didn't answer him. There was a conspiracy, and the police didn't protect the prime minister.'[77] There was also a feeling among some Brotherhood members that this was part of a wider plot being hatched to assassinate Morsi, and that some sort of coup was brewing. While the security forces were certainly hostile to the Brotherhood, talk of a coup or assassination plot certainly appears overplayed. Yet it reflected the Brotherhood's inability to shake off the habit of viewing itself as the victim of a conspiracy. Indeed, the Brotherhood could only see the expression of public anger and grief that had erupted at the funeral through the lens of a wider plot against it.

Morsi retaliated harshly. On 8 August he seized upon the opportunity to expel Mowafi and a host of other senior security figures for their failings over the Rafah incident. Among those whose heads rolled were the chief of military police, several senior Interior Ministry officials, and the governor of North Sinai, Said Abdul Wahab Mabrouk. He also fired the head of the Presidential Guard for having failed to provide adequate security at the soldiers' funerals. It looked therefore as though Morsi was declaring war on the security sector and finally embarking upon the cull that the revolutionaries had been demanding.

For all the decisiveness of this moment, however, Mowafi's expulsion was executed in a typically shambolic and cack-handed fashion. On 8 August the Presidency called Mowafi's deputy, Rifat Shehata, to attend that day's meeting of the National Defence Council, instead of his boss.[78] A surprised Mowafi contacted Morsi only to be told, 'You are expelled from your job. I decided to give it to Shehata. He is now the head of the intelligence service.'[79] Shehata, meanwhile, turned up at the meeting to hear Morsi announce that he had been appointed in Mowafi's place – an announcement that prompted 'shock and silence' in the room, not to mention embarrassment on Shehata's part.[80]

Regardless of how it was done, however, this move against the security sector brought Morsi some welcome popular support. Egyptian journalist Hamid Qandil declared: 'Today is the day that the president took over the presidency.'[81] More notably, the revolutionary activist group known as the 6 April Movement gathered in front of presidential palace at Al-Ittihadiya, as well as in front of Morsi's house in Cairo and his family home in the Al-Sharqiya governorate, to demonstrate their support for the president's actions. But, while they praised him, they also made clear that they were waiting for 'more radical and hard-hitting' decisions against the deep state.

Morsi duly responded. Sensing he was on a roll, the president capitalised on the Rafah incident even further, staging what looked like an even more impressive coup against the forces of the old regime. On 12 August the president summoned Tantawi and chief of staff of the armed forces, Sami Anan, to the palace and informed them that he was referring them for retirement. The news reportedly came as a bolt from the blue. Fuad Jadallah described how Tantawi and Anan

> were sitting in the corridor [of the presidential palace] waiting to meet the president and they had no idea about the decision or its nature ... Tantawi and Anan were led to the president's office and ... Morsi informed them, and their surprise was massive, and they were sad. I learned later that they left Morsi and didn't know what to do.[82]

Tantawi, who Morsi had appointed as defence minister just ten days before, was replaced by the head of military intelligence, General Abdelfattah Al-Sissi, while Anan's post went to SCAF member General Mohamed Al-Asser. Morsi also took the chance to get rid of other senior military figures, including Navy Commander Mohab Memish and Air Force Commander Reda Hafez. He took the opportunity, too, to appoint Judge Mahmoud Mekki, who had been a tireless advocate for the independence of the judiciary, as his vice-president, suggesting that the president was intending to take the fight to the judiciary next.

Predictably enough, the expulsions elicited rapturous applause from the revolutionaries. Here at last was the decisive move that they had been waiting for, and here was Morsi acting in accordance with the revolutionary spirit that had infused his speech when he swore the oath of allegiance in front of the crowds at Tahrir Square. Liberal activist Shady Al-Ghazaly Harb proclaimed jubilantly: 'We had been chanting, "Down, down with military rule" ... Today it came true.'[83]

But it was not long before things began to sour. Soon enough, there was speculation that, rather than representing a definitive break between Morsi and the SCAF, these expulsions were actually part of a pre-arranged informal deal struck between the two sides. The fact that the SCAF did not try to resist this purge or make any public objection to it would seem to indicate that this may well have been the case, despite the Brotherhood's denials. Furthermore, Tantawi and Anan were not exactly sent away in disgrace. Both men were awarded medals, Tantawi receiving the Order of the Nile – the highest medal in the country. Both were also made military advisors to the president, who lavished them with praise. Such treatment was a far cry from the demands of the revolutionaries, who had wanted these figures to be held to account for the violence that had been meted out against protestors during the revolution. Some revolutionaries determined that Tantawi and Anan's expulsion was all part of a deal to provide these leading figures with a safe exit, guaranteeing them immunity from prosecution.[84]

The boldness of Morsi's action was also weakened by the fact that Tantawi was already planning to retire, allegedly telling Morsi on the day that he had taken his oath of office that he was intending to leave his post possibly as early as October 2012.[85] Tantawi was also already paving the way for Al-Sissi to take over his job, making it clear that he wanted no one else to succeed him. On the day after his expulsion, Tantawi went to Al-Sissi's office and told him, 'You are my son.'[86] Moreover, there were many inside the SCAF who were more than ready for Tantawi and Anan to go. There was a feeling inside the council that both men had committed mistakes, including over the Rafah incident, and that the army's reputation was being tarnished as a result. As Egyptian historian Zeinab Abul-Magd explained, 'There was a lot of discontent against them [in the ranks] ... Tantawi and Anan left quietly because they made huge mistakes.'[87] This coincided with a desire among younger elements inside the military to take their turn at the top. Journalist Abdullah Sanawi has explained that, although there was some consternation about the undignified way in which Tantawi was forced out, there was a feeling inside the SCAF that it was Al-Sissi's time to take over because it would 'renew the youth of the armed forces and their role'.[88]

Most tellingly, however, while Morsi made a big play of kicking out Tantawi, Anan and others, he replaced them with men who may have been younger but who were of much the same stripe. Al-Sissi was certainly of the same mettle as Tantawi – an establishment man through and through. The same was true of the other replacements. As analyst Issander El-Amrani has commented, there were no left-field appointees, and Morsi opted for continuity in a 'reconfigured SCAF'.[89] On closer inspection, therefore, this was not such a daring, revolutionary move on Morsi's part. It was not really a Brotherhood victory over the SCAF, either, but did represent a change in the balance of the relationship between the two forces that had been battling one another for decades. Morsi's move was therefore more a combination of coup and compromise than a full-blown revolutionary act.

Morsi's reticence about striking decisively against the SCAF was understandable. While he may have wanted to put the military firmly back in its barracks, he was well aware that he was wholly reliant on a strong security sector. As Mahmoud Hussein noted, 'Morsi was very keen to maintain the strength of the army and not to tamper with it. He didn't want to intervene with their privileges. He just wanted to downsize some of them, and even that he wasn't allowed to do.'[90] Furthermore, with the country in such an unstable state, and with the threat of economic crisis looming, the Brotherhood knew that placing itself in open confrontation with the SCAF would be suicidal. As Yahyia Hamid explained, 'We didn't want to be in conflict with state institutions ... we wanted to start changing it, but over a longer period of time ... We followed the reformist way while we should have followed the revolutionary way. But if we had followed the revolutionary way the state would have collapsed.'[91] Yet here again Morsi's approach could no more be described as reformist than as revolutionary. Rather, this was another half-hearted gesture of appeasement, meant to satisfy the revolutionaries on one side and the SCAF on the other. It was also a further example of the Brotherhood's reliance on the politics of good-will, accompanied by the hope that, by clearing out some of the 'corrupted' figures at the top, it could rely on figures such as Al-Sissi to work with it rather than against it.

But at the moment he struck, the expulsion of these figures gave the impression that Morsi had finally put himself in the driving seat and brought the revolution back on track, garnering much-needed popular support. It was little surprise, therefore, that Morsi tried to replicate the success he had scored with the SCAF by applying the same approach to the judiciary. The president already had a fractious relationship with the judiciary, not least because of the way in which he had gone about his swearing-in ceremony, but also because one of his first acts after coming to power was to issue a decree reinstating the People's Assembly that had been dissolved on the ruling of the Constitutional Court. Although Morsi was later forced to backtrack on this decree, the way in which he had challenged the court set him on course for a clash with the judiciary from the outset.

However, the Brotherhood still believed that, as with the security bodies, the problem with the judiciary lay with a few 'rotten apples' at the top. As Gamal Heshmat remarked, 'The body of the judiciary is good, but a few who were brought in by Mubarak and whose employment was extended time and time again, even after they reached retirement age, are the ones who are corrupt … Morsi had no problem with the judiciary. The judiciary had a problem with Morsi.'[92] Rather than any measured plan to reform or restructure the judiciary, therefore, Morsi focused his attentions on pursuing a hatchet-job against those at the top, in the hope of imposing his authority.

The opportunity arose with the ruling that was issued on 10 October by the Cairo Criminal Court acquitting all twenty-four defendants who were accused of killing protestors in the Battle of the Camels on 2 February 2011. The court ruled that there was insufficient evidence to convict the defendants, who included former ministers, businessmen, senior National Democratic Party (NDP) members, and the Mubarak-era parliamentary speaker. The acquittals sparked uproar, with revolutionaries and the families of the victims threatening to take to the streets in protest. Critically for Morsi, some activists began blaming the Brotherhood, claiming that it had been a party to the verdict that was a reflection of the new spirit of accommodation between the Brotherhood and the former regime. Activists such as Mohamed Abdel Aziz of the opposition Kifaya movement claimed that the acquittals were part of a 'reconciliation between the Muslim Brotherhood and the former regime'.[93] Others accused Brotherhood elements of being involved in the Battle of the Camels, claiming that this explained the acquittals.[94]

With the threat of demonstrations growing, Morsi knew he had to act – all the more so because there was a rising general dissatisfaction with the Brotherhood's performance, made worse by the fact that his first 100 days in office had come to an end and he had failed to meet the vast majority of the promises contained in his electoral programme. Calls for his resignation began to come thick and fast, and the mood was turning against him. In a bid to salvage the situation, Morsi used the acquittals to strike against the judiciary. As with the military, Morsi opted for a surgical approach, turning his attentions to the general prosecutor, Abdel Megid Mahmoud. Mahmoud was another potent symbol of the Mubarak regime, and the revolutionaries had long been demanding his removal. Protestors had regularly held up pictures of Mahmoud, indicating their desire to have him removed, and when mock people's courts had been set up in Tahrir Square in February 2011 to 'try' former regime officials, Mahmoud was found guilty of corrupting public life, and sentenced to death.[95] Thus Morsi believed that getting rid of Mahmoud would be a popular move that would bring him the renewed support of the revolutionaries.

Morsi therefore announced on 11 October that Mahmoud had been dismissed, and would be taking up a new post as Egypt's ambassador to the Holy See in the Vatican. Yet, in a move typical of the Brotherhood's informal way of operating, Morsi had first tried to strike a deal with Mahmoud over his demotion. This was partly because the president did not have the authority to remove the general prosecutor – a right reserved for the Supreme Judicial Council. Morsi therefore approached Mahmoud through a mediator, and tried to convince him to accept the ambassadorial post. But it was not all gentle persuasion. Issam Al-Arian tweeted: 'I whispered to Abdel Megid Mahmoud: The best choice for you is to accept the [ambassadorial] post with dignity. Think well. Other options are difficult.'[96] Mahmoud himself claimed he had been subjected to pressure and threats from Morsi's advisors.[97]

According to the Brotherhood, Mahmoud initially accepted the offer and allegedly 'did not protest', although according to some he asked to be appointed to an Arab-speaking country like Saudi Arabia, since he did not know any foreign languages.[98] But after thinking it had got Mahmoud out of the way, the Brotherhood was surprised when members of the judiciary, revolutionaries, and opposition and media figures suddenly rallied to Mahmoud's defence, attacking Morsi for making an attack against the independence of the judiciary. Judge Ahmed Zend, the head of the Judges' Club, called on all judges to stand behind Mahmoud, declaring: 'We are not like Tantawi and Anan.'[99] Opposition leader Hamdeen Sabahi went to visit Mahmoud, and accused Morsi of having 'violated the judiciary'.[100] Some have accused these opposition elements of seizing opportunistically on the general prosecutor's case as a means of denigrating the Brotherhood. There may well be some truth in these allegations, given that the opposition had been so keen for Mahmoud, as a symbol of the former regime, to go. But there was also a genuine concern among liberal elements at the way in which Morsi was behaving. This included his insistence on making arbitrary decisions that were seemingly plucked out of thin air, and taken unilaterally. Such decisions also contributed to the sense, whipped up by the media, that the Brotherhood was intent on dominating and controlling state institutions. There was thus a kind of closing of ranks against Morsi and the Brotherhood among the opposition, the revolutionaries and the judiciary that would become more pronounced.

Figures close to the Brotherhood were also troubled by the turn that events were taking. Islamist thinker and judge Tariq Al-Bishri commented in relation to Mahmoud's expulsion that it was 'an attack on judicial power, something I don't think has ever happened in Egypt's history ... The general prosecutor had nothing to do with the Battle of the Camels.'[101]

Meanwhile, the mood on the streets was becoming more turbulent, and revolutionary activists were calling for mass protests against the Brotherhood. Indeed, Morsi, who had been expecting his strike against the general prosecutor to be met with the same jubilation that had greeted his attack against Tantawi and Anan, had misjudged the public mood spectacularly. In response, the Brotherhood turned once again to the street. Seemingly not knowing what else to do, the movement issued a statement on 11 October calling on its supporters to mobilise against the judiciary and to stage protests to express the 'people's anger at the acquittals'.[102] Al-Arian issued another tweet calling on the Brotherhood's youth to gather in front of the Egyptian museum in Cairo, from where they could march on the Supreme Justice Courthouse.[103] As if to stoke further revolutionary sentiment, Mukhtar Ashri, the chairman of the FJP's Legal Committee, warned during a telephone interview with Al-Jazeera that 'defunct National Party leadership figures are already being released onto the street, and will no doubt lead the counter-revolution relentlessly'.[104]

Once again, therefore, the Brotherhood played the part of revolutionary actor opting for counter-mobilisation against the very state it was leading. It had no compunction either about the way it was operating, stating that it sought to use the demonstrations to 'pressure investigation bodies to submit whatever evidence they have to judges so they can indeed apply justice and achieve retribution' and to 'urge the public prosecutor ... to do his duty to protect society, to be truly loyal to the people and the goals of the revolution, not to the corrupt former regime and its cronies'.[105] Appealing to the masses in this way was hardly the approach one would expect of a movement in power, regardless of how constrained that power may have been.

Predictably enough, the demonstrations turned ugly as Brotherhood supporters clashed with their opponents. More than 110 people were injured in the violence, which saw hand-to-hand fighting in the streets. Meanwhile, Morsi was having trouble with the general prosecutor. Seeing the unexpected surge of support, Mahmoud refused to leave his post, duly turning up at work as normal. Morsi was thrown into a quandary. But seeing the intransigence of the judiciary, and aware that he had no legal mandate to force Mahmoud out, Morsi went back on his initial decision, meeting with Mahmoud on 13 October to thrash out a deal that would enable him to stay in office until he reached retirement age.

The Presidency tried desperately to sell this backtracking as a 'misunderstanding'. Deputy President Mahmoud Mekki told the media that Morsi had never intended to dismiss the general prosecutor: 'If the presidential office had intended to remove the public prosecutor it would have done so from day one of the presidency.'[106] Mekki also claimed that Morsi had simply 'suggested' to Mahmoud to leave his post, out of concern for his safety given the high levels of public anger against him.[107] But despite the backpedalling, the damage had already been done. Morsi's willingness to yield, and his doing so without any sign of a real fight, was to open the floodgates to further attacks and criticisms. As Minister of Parliamentary Affairs Mohamed Masoub was to comment, 'When Morsi retracted I thought it was the most disastrous decision. All failures started from there. Everyone realised that if you put pressure on the president he will back down.'[108]

Morsi's bid to strike at the judiciary was thus an abject failure, weakening his image and position even further. Indeed, by this point the Brotherhood was trailing behind. It had proved that it was politically incompetent, and could not break out of the mould that had shaped it over decades. In fact, it had become apparent that the Brotherhood had no politics of any real substance.

The movement had also delivered very little Islamically. Despite all the fears that the Brotherhood would Islamicise Egypt, it hardly moved on this front. Although the elite cultivated the impression that the Brotherhood was creating its very own Kandahar in Egypt, with stories of unveiled girls having their hair chopped off by scissor-wielding Islamists on public transport, this was a far cry from reality. In fact the movement did little to distinguish itself as a specifically Islamist party. Although the FJP had tried to introduce a bill to bolster Islamic finance that was disrupted when the parliament was dissolved, it did little to introduce Islamic laws. Even in matters of public morality, the one area where the Brotherhood has traditionally been better equipped to articulate its ideas, its efforts were limited. Saad Katatni told the *Al-Ahram* newspaper in December 2011, 'If the party took power in the country, we wouldn't stop people drinking alcohol in their houses or hotels. We wouldn't ban pornographic websites, we wouldn't apply *hudud* and we wouldn't intervene in how tourists behave on the beaches.'[109] Such promises were largely kept.

The Brotherhood's approach to the process of drafting the constitution was equally restrained. In its bid to placate all constituencies simultaneously, the Brotherhood found itself in the anomalous position of trying to rein in the Salafists, who were intent on binding the text of the constitution more directly to Sharia. The Salafists demanded that Article 2 of the 1971 Constitution be amended to specify that 'Sharia' rather than 'principles of Sharia' be stipulated as the source of legislation. The Salafists also called for the modification of Article 3 to read 'Sovereignty is for God and it is the source of authority', rather than 'Sovereignty is for the people alone and they are the source of authority'.[110]

Despite the Brotherhood's long held mantra, 'the Quran is our constitution', as well as Morsi's promise to 'reconquer' Egypt Islamically, the Brotherhood's approach to the constitution drafting process was far more pragmatic. The Brotherhood had always considered Sharia as something that should be applied gradually, meaning that so long as its general goals and core principles were upheld, details such as the application of *hudud* (punishments) could be postponed or reinterpreted to reflect the contemporary reality. Indeed, Morsi himself told the media prior to his election that *hudud* was part of *fiqh* (Islamic jurisprudence) rather than Sharia, which he described as the general framework.[111] Thus the Brotherhood had a much less rigid attitude towards those articles of the constitution that dealt with religion than the Salafists and complained that the Salafists' insistence on linking the constitution more closely to Sharia was an irritant that was hindering the constitution-drafting process.

The Brotherhood thus steered its usual middle course. While Article 2 remained unchanged, stipulating: 'Islam is the religion of the state and Arabic its official language. Principles of Islamic Sharia are the principal source of legislation', an additional article was added stating that senior Al-Azhar scholars were to be consulted in matters pertaining to Islamic law. More controversially, in what was seen as a sop to the Salafists, another article was added elaborating on what the principles of Sharia were. This article translates roughly as 'The principles of Islamic Sharia include general scriptural bases [the Quran and Hadith] and the main bases of jurisprudence and sources accepted by Islamic scholars.' Although there were many liberals who were deeply uneasy about this article, it served as enough of a compromise to convince the Salafists to support the unchanged wording of Article 2.

Despite the Brotherhood's long-cherished mantra, 'The Quran is our constitution', and Morsi's pre-election promise to 'reconquer' Egypt Islamically, the Brotherhood's Islamic project seemed to dissolve as it became subsumed in the reality of day-to-day politics. Indeed, the movement's lack of focus on Islamicisation was partly a result of the fact that it was very quickly overwhelmed by political challenges. It was also symptomatic of the Brotherhood's anxieties about how it was viewed by its own society as well as by the West, and its desire to be seen as a progressive party that could work within the framework of a modern state.

More importantly, though, its lack of focus on Islamisication also reflected the fact that its Islamic vision turned out to be as undeveloped as its political one. The Brotherhood never moved to contextualise its ideology within any meaningful political framework or model, seemingly believing its own rhetoric to the effect that Islam alone would be the solution. As a result, it stuck to slogans and used Islam primarily as a vehicle for mobilisation and a rallying cry to support its political objectives. But while this approach might have appealed to its core support base, it served to alienate others, bringing accusations that Morsi was the president of Islamists rather than a president for all Egyptians.

Within just a few months of attaining power, the Brotherhood was failing to deliver on almost every front, and Egyptian society was more polarised than ever. It had also alienated other political forces with whom it might have built a joint platform, and tied itself into a confrontation with the forces of the old regime, which proved able to outmanoeuvre it at almost every turn. From now on in, it was to be downhill all the way.

THREE

THE FALL

After just a few months in power, the Brotherhood was in trouble. It was still struggling to impose its authority, and found itself cornered at almost every turn. The movement had been unable to outmanoeuvre the SCAF, which was proving a far trickier 'partner' than it could have ever imagined; and while Morsi may have cleared out some of the old faces from the military leadership, the president was still not a free agent. Morsi's attempts to take on the judiciary had also backfired, and he was looking weaker than ever. Meanwhile the Brotherhood had failed to win over the institutions of the state or, as Egyptian analyst Kamal Habib put it, 'to understand the spirit of the state', and did not possess the tools to deal with it.[1] The Brotherhood therefore continued to sit apart from the state it was meant to be leading. The movement also seemed increasingly alienated. Its failure to break free from the mentality of a semi-clandestine opposition movement, trusting only its own rather than working in a truly consensual manner, meant that those political forces that had been willing to give it a chance when it came to power were increasingly turning their backs. The Brotherhood was starting to look like an island surrounded by very choppy seas.

The Brotherhood was proving incapable, too, of delivering on the basics. Despite the catalogue of promises Morsi had made in his election campaign, such as improving traffic, security and cleanliness within his first 100 days in office, the movement could point to few concrete achievements. As one young graphic designer complained in January 2013, 'This is not a revolution, they are fooling us. Nothing has changed since 25 January 2011. None of our demands have been met. Every day that passes we move three years back in time. Nothing has been changed.'[2] Such complaints were commonplace.

Not that one would expect miracles in such a short span of time, especially in such exceptional circumstances; but in its rush to achieve power, and with its inflated sense of self-belief, the Brotherhood had shackled itself with ambitious promises that it could not meet. It very quickly gave the impression, therefore, that it was incapable of delivering. It had become apparent that Morsi was 'just like any other person' and 'didn't have the magic touch'.[3] The few tangible achievements the Brotherhood could cite were piecemeal, and often rooted in the local.. When asked to list concrete policy successes, many Brotherhood members cited the local rubbish-collection schemes they had set up, often participating in such schemes themselves. Similarly, a Facebook page set up by the Brotherhood titled 'The Achievements of the Ikhwan' celebrated how, in a bid to deal with climbing food prices, the FJP, in conjunction with the Brotherhood, had launched a campaign in Assiut called 'Brothers against Price Rises', which entailed setting up special markets selling cut-price goods.[4] While such initiatives were certainly admirable, they were more akin to the work of a charitable organisation than a party in power.

The Brotherhood also gave the impression of being an organisational shambles. As well as the constant backtracking on policies, and switching between constitutional and revolutionary legitimacy, not to mention Morsi's own bumbling style, there was a general sense of muddle and chaos. Members of the movement, including those at a low level, started to appear in the media making seemingly arbitrary political statements; in the words of former deputy Murshid, Mohamed Habib, they kept 'talking about the president's affairs as if they were the ones who were planning and running things'.[5] The situation was made worse by the fact that decisions were sometimes issued at night and then cancelled the following day. All this contributed to the impression that the party was not up to the job of ruling, and that its elite members were behaving like amateurs, not statesmen.[6]

Rather than reducing the chaos, therefore, the Brotherhood seemed to be adding to it. Yet the movement did not switch tack or change its way of doing things. Instead it pressed blindly on while the situation continued to unravel before it. It also turned increasingly to mobilisation as its instrument of choice, so that Egypt increasingly took on the character of a battleground, as the various forces took to slugging it out with each other in the streets. Indeed, the Brotherhood had proved utterly incapable of working as a mature political actor, or even understanding the political environment it in which it was operating. For all its promises, holding onto power at all costs became the movement's primary objective. It was therefore little surprise that, when it came, the end was swift and merciless – and the Brotherhood seemed just as lost and stunned as it had been when the revolution first broke out in January 2011.

Descent into Chaos

If there was one moment during the Brotherhood's time in power that marked the beginning of the end, it was Morsi's explosive Constitutional Declaration of 22 November 2012. This declaration was an audacious attempt by Morsi to try to impose his authority in an arena in which he was feeling restricted. For all the Brotherhood's appeasement of the military, Morsi was still hemmed in by the SCAF, which was not ready to sit back and allow the movement free rein. As investment minister in Morsi's government, Yahyia Hamid noted, 'The military always sent the message: If you have the executive, I want the legislative. If you take the legislative, I will undermine your executive power and I will create problems in the state so you can't move on. You won't be able to achieve progress or real development.'[7] While these comments may be exaggerated, the SCAF certainly curtailed the Brotherhood's room for manoeuvre. It insisted, for example, on approving certain ministers before they could be appointed, and also blocked some of the Brotherhood's attempts to initiate development projects when its interests were under threat. This included the Brotherhood's proposals to develop the Sinai and the areas around the Suez Canal – both areas the army considered to be within its own domain.[8] The SCAF was thus still restricting the Brotherhood's freedom to operate.

Meanwhile the judiciary was hardly making things easy. On top of its dissolution of the lower house of parliament and its refusal to accept Morsi's attempted expulsion of the general prosecutor, the Judges' Club was now threatening to boycott monitoring of the referendum on the constitution, and also to launch an open-ended strike if its suggested changes to the judiciary section in the constitution were not considered. More importantly, in November the Constitutional Court announced that it had scheduled 2 December to address cases challenging the legality of both the Shura Council (upper house of parliament) and the Constituent Assembly. Given that the Constitutional Court had ruled against the lower house in June, the Brotherhood was convinced that it would issue similar rulings against these two bodies, triggering their dissolution. Morsi therefore struck out with this bold gesture, with which he was unwittingly to sow the seeds of his own downfall.

The Constitutional Declaration gave the president sweeping new powers, effectively placing him above judicial oversight. Most contentiously, Article 2 stipulated:

> Previous constitutional declarations, laws, and decrees made by the president since he took office on 30 June 2012, until the constitution is approved and a new People's Assembly is elected, are final and binding and cannot be appealed in any way or to any entity. Nor shall they be suspended or cancelled and all lawsuits related to them and brought before any judicial body against these decisions are annulled.[9]

Equally controversially, Article 6 stipulated: 'The President may take the necessary actions and measures to protect the country and the goals of the revolution.' Notably, however, the declaration did not elaborate on what these actions and measures might consist of, or how exactly the goals of the revolution were to be defined. Meanwhile, Article 5 declared that no judicial body could dissolve either the Shura Council or the Constituent Assembly. This declaration thus not only placed the president above the law but also those bodies that were dominated by the Islamists.

Morsi also used the declaration to get rid of the general prosecutor, Abdel Megid Mahmoud, who had resisted his ejection from office in October 2012. The declaration stipulated that the incumbent should be appointed by the president, and should serve a single four-year term only. This effectively disqualified Mahmoud, who had already served six years in office. Morsi lost no time in replacing Mahmoud with his candidate of choice, Talaat Ibrahim, a well-known proponent of judicial independence under the former regime. The declaration also ordered the reopening of cases against those accused of killing or injuring protestors during the revolution.

For a president whose rule had been characterised by dithering and backtracking, Morsi's declaration represented a strikingly radical gesture. Notably, it came at a time when Morsi was feeling particularly buoyant. He had just scored one of the few foreign policy successes of his rule by helping to broker a peace deal between Israel and Hamas – something that had brought him widespread international acclaim. Morsi seems to have been hoping that his Constitutional Declaration would not only show that he meant business on the domestic front as well, but would also meet the demands of the revolutionaries by striking right at the heart of one of the bastions of the old regime.

This proved to be a gross misjudgement. The declaration provoked immediate uproar and an outpouring of accusations that Morsi had staged a coup against constitutional legitimacy. 'An absolute presidential tyranny'[10] was how liberal politician Amr Hamzawy described it, while the former head of the International Atomic Energy Agency, Mohamed ElBaradei accused Morsi of having appointed himself as Egypt's new pharaoh, warning that the declaration was a major blow to the revolution and could have dire consequences.[11] Members of the judiciary were also up in arms, the Judges' Club calling for a boycott of the courts until Morsi rescinded the declaration. Widespread public protests erupted – not only in Cairo, where the crowds poured back into Tahrir Square, but in cities including in Alexandria and Assiut. Some of the Brotherhood's offices were attacked and set alight, and protestors called vociferously for Morsi's downfall. The public mood was boiling over, and things were threatening to get out of hand.

Shocked at the hostility of the response, a somewhat stunned Brotherhood justified its power-grab in revolutionary terms. Morsi, it argued, was simply trying to protect the revolution and drive it forward in the face of hostile forces. The FJP claimed that the declaration fulfilled 'many revolutionary goals demanded by all political, social and popular groups that participated in the January 25 revolution',[12] while Dr Mahmoud Ghozlan of the Brotherhood's Guidance Office asserted that it protected 'the original demands of the revolution'.[13] Prime Minister Hisham Qandil, meanwhile, told Al-Jazeera that the declaration had been issued to 'uphold what we have built and finish our revolutionary path'.[14] In fact the declaration does not appear to have been a deliberately tyrannical move on Morsi's part. Rather, it was a bungled attempt to deal with the latest round of challenges, including what he believed was the judiciary's intention to deal his administration another serious and potentially fatal blow by dissolving the Shura Council and Constituent Assembly. As Morsi's top legal advisor Fuad Jadullah explained, the Islamic current felt that the judiciary

> had it in for them ... I tried repeatedly to explain to these leaders [in the Brotherhood] that the judiciary didn't have it in for them ... When the Constitutional Court set 2 December to look at the cases of dissolving the Shura Council and the annulment of the standard law of appointing the Constituent Assembly, the belief started spreading among those in the presidential palace and the

> FJP and allied parties that the court was going to dissolve both in one session.[15]

The Brotherhood clearly saw in the judiciary a politicised entity that was intent on bringing it down at all costs. But that was not all. The Brotherhood also believed that the Constitutional Court's position was part of a wider conspiracy against it. Mohamed Habib has related how Morsi claimed that he had issued the Constitutional Declaration because there was a conspiracy to 'shatter him and bring him down'.[16] This reflected the fact that the Brotherhood still saw danger at every turn, as if it was still a repressed movement skulking in the shadows. Nursing a belief that there was a conspiracy against it became a default setting for the Brotherhood, and such a conspiracy was cited as its primary justification for all sorts of pre-emptive moves, including Morsi's Constitutional Declaration.

The declaration was therefore a panicked and frantic attempt on Morsi's part to prevent power from being snatched from under his nose. It was also a bid to try to protect the constitution-drafting process, which had been fraught with difficulties from the start. The first Constituent Assembly, elected by the Islamist-dominated parliament in March 2012, was criticised by opposition parties for being heavily dominated by the Islamist current. While the Brotherhood saw the Islamists' numerical superiority in this body as a natural reflection of its success in the parliamentary elections, other political players accused the movement of seeking to control the constitution-drafting process. Opposition figures therefore walked out of the assembly one by one, until it was ruled unconstitutional on the grounds that it was unrepresentative,. A second Constituent Assembly was elected in June. This was meant to be a more balanced and representative body – but it was not long before similar charges were being made against the Brotherhood, and secular and liberal forces started withdrawing. Mid November saw a notable exodus, with key forces including church representatives and members of secular parties, as well as influential political figures including Amr Moussa, walking out, complaining that their suggestions were being ignored by the Islamist camp. Given this exodus and the imminent ruling by the Constitutional Court, due on 2 December, the Brotherhood feared that its efforts to complete the drafting of the constitution were in mortal danger.

In many ways, therefore, Morsi's Constitutional Declaration was understandable within the context of the moment – but it was nevertheless a reactive and short-sighted move that once again highlighted the Brotherhood's inexperience and inability to understand the political environment in which it was operating. Despite the increasingly poisonous atmosphere that was gripping the country, Morsi had failed to comprehend how his actions would be perceived, and what kind of backlash the Constitutional Declaration would provoke. But this was a product not only one of a lack of understanding – it was also a function of a kind of arrogance. The Brotherhood may have talked a lot about dialogue and consensus, but it maintained the same dismissive attitude towards its opponents that it had shown the moment it had won power. Morsi had singularly failed to take on board the need to build a genuine consensus in this time of transition, apparently believing that including a handful of Copts and women in government institutions would be enough to demonstrate its inclusive credentials. Unsurprisingly, therefore, this earth-shattering declaration was made unilaterally, without consulting other political forces. More surprisingly, though, it was made without consulting of many of Morsi's own advisors. Despite his legal expertise, the deputy president, Judge Mahmoud Mekky, expressed his surprise at learning about the declaration while he was on a visit to Pakistan. Samir Marcos, Morsi's advisor on democratic transformation, commented: 'The constitutional declaration surprised me. I was never consulted about it.'[17] Meanwhile, Morsi's justice minister, Ahmed Mekki, revealed that he had only found out about the declaration on the day of its announcement.[18]

This almost contemptuous attitude towards others was also symptomatic of the Brotherhood's tendency to rely on majoritarianism, believing that its electoral victory had given it the right to do whatever it wished in the name of the people. As Brotherhood member and FJP MP Abdelmawgud Dardery reflected, the Brotherhood was fooled by its election victories into thinking that it had a popular mandate to 'move on and fix the country's problems', while 'the failure of the other parties in free and fair elections kind of emboldened the Brotherhood a little bit, which it shouldn't have done'.[19] This majoritarian mind-set was encapsulated in comments made by former Murshid Mehdi Akef, who declared in August 2012: 'To hell with anyone who does not accept the Islamic rule that the people want. Why? Because the people should.'[20] With the Constitutional Declaration, therefore, as with many other issues, the Brotherhood believed it was within its rights to impose whatever terms it saw fit.

This was to prove a fatal mistake. Not only did the Constitutional Declaration see protestors pour back into Tahrir Square to denounce Morsi and the Brotherhood, in what was to mark the beginning of a descent into chaos; it also prompted opposition parties to close ranks against the movement. Two days after Morsi issued the declaration, a wide range of political parties and figures pulled together under the banner of the National Salvation Front to demand that the president rescind the decree. It also called for the formation of a new, more representative Constituent Assembly and the issuing of a transitional justice law guaranteeing fair retrials for those responsible for the deaths of protesters during the revolution. The front was led by Amr Mousa, Mohamed ElBaradei and the Nasserite politician Hamdeen Sabahi, and included all the big opposition groupings, uniting what until then had been a largely fractured opposition. The Brotherhood was paying the high price of having alienated so many in such an extreme fashion.

In the face of such opposition, the Brotherhood backtracked. Morsi met with representatives of the Supreme Judicial Council on 26 November, and agreed that his declaration would be limited to decisions related to 'acts of sovereignty'. This was a rather vague term, but was generally held to mean that Morsi's power to act under the Constitutional Declaration would be curtailed. He also made clear that any retrials of Mubarak-era officials would depend on the discovery of new evidence. Yet, at the same time as he was negotiating with the judiciary to try to ease the crisis, the Brotherhood created another crisis of its own. Feeling cornered by events, and as though it could not trust the state, the Brotherhood turned once again to the street, calling on its supporters to rally behind Morsi and his declaration. On 24 November the Brotherhood called upon 'all national, revolutionary, Muslim and youth groups and movements to join protest marches in ... squares across Egypt's provinces ... to reaffirm their support for these decrees'.[21] It also called for a million-man march and demonstration in Abdeen Square on 27 November. It was as if the Brotherhood had forgotten that it was supposed to be in power, and had no other tools with which to deal with the unfolding situation.

In the event, the Brotherhood agreed in conjunction with the Salafist Al-Nour party to call off the 27 November protest, to avoid the inevitable bloodshed. It showed no such restraint on 1 December, when tens of thousands of its supporters, holding up Morsi's picture, rallied to its calls and massed near Cairo University. Although the Brotherhood had agreed to change the location of the protest, which had originally been planned for Tahrir Square where its opponents were gathered, it still encouraged its supporters to come out in a mass show of force. Brotherhood supporters also turned out in other cities, some of the protests turning violent as protestors clashed with their opponents. It was here that the Brotherhood came up with the slogan 'Al-Sharaiya wa Sharia', or 'Legitimacy and Sharia' – as if to give the impression that those demonstrating against the Brotherhood were against both.[22] This was divisive politics in the extreme, and only fuelled the polarisation that had already taken hold. It was also emblematic of the fact that, despite its talk of being inclusive and of Morsi being a president for all Egyptians, the movement had responded to the crisis by falling back on its own constituency.

By the early hours of 2 December, Brotherhood supporters had descended on the Constitutional Court chanting slogans against the judiciary, and gloating that Morsi had delivered it a 'knockout blow'. It was as if mobilisation had replaced politics altogether – in the words of Abdelmonem Abul Futuh, 'The Muslim Brotherhood tried to break the will of institutions by mobilisation. Getting people out into the street became an aim in itself.'[23] Egyptian analyst Dr Jihad Awda, meanwhile, commented that the Brotherhood used mass mobilisation 'because they lack experience, tools and political culture'.[24]

This lack of political culture was also evident in the Brotherhood's panicked efforts to finalise the constitution-drafting process before the court had a chance to rule against the Constituent Assembly, on 2 December. In a feverish session that began on 29 November and went on through the night, the Assembly – or what was left of it after all the walkouts and withdrawals – voted through all 234 articles, enabling Morsi to announce to crowds of rapturous supporters on 1 December that the job was complete, and that there would be a referendum on 15 December. All hope of a constitution built on consensus had been thrown out of the window, as a panicked Brotherhood sought to reach its end goal. Aside from the issues surrounding the role of Sharia (see Chapter Two), there were other controversial articles in the draft constitution that the opposition was uncomfortable about – not least those that gave leeway to the military. Article 197, for instance, provided for the creation of a National Defence Council that would be responsible for the military budget, while Article 198 upheld the principle of military trials. There were also questionable articles related to human rights, including those declaring: 'The state and society shall commit to preserving the true nature of the Egyptian family', and: 'The state shall protect ethics and morals and public order' – prompting concerns about how they might be interpreted.[25] To the Brotherhood, however, these concerns and inconsistences seemed to matter less than getting to the finishing line. Ensuring that the text was passed, and passed quickly, became more important than its content. As Lombardi and Brown have observed, Brotherhood members of the Constituent Assembly focused on 'simply getting a text – any text – in front of the voters'.[26]

The Brotherhood's railroading of the constitution in the face of objections from liberal and secular parties only fanned the flames of conflict. There were outbreaks of violence, and Brotherhood and FJP offices around the country came under attack. As one Brotherhood member recalled, 'In total, twenty-eight Muslim Brotherhood and Freedom and Justice Party headquarters were attacked. Most of them sustained damage, and there were attempts to set many of them on fire.'[27] By 5 December things had got completely out of hand. On the previous day, the opposition had called for a peaceful demonstration outside the presidential palace at Ittihadiya, to protest against Morsi's Constitutional Declaration. Some of the protestors declared a sit-in in front of the palace, erecting tents at the site. The Brotherhood responded in kind, calling on its supporters to launch a counter-demonstration outside the palace. On 5 December, Guidance Office member Mahmoud Ghozlan adopted hawkish tones, stating that Egyptian popular forces would show 'that they, the Egyptian people, chose this President and gave him full legitimacy through free and fair elections, and that they are able to defend that legitimacy, endorse the new constitution and protect state institutions'.[28] Ghozlan, it seems, did not see any irony in defending electoral legitimacy by relying on the street. In fact, both sides had descended into a politics of the lowest common denominator, slugging it out on the streets as if this was the only arena that mattered. Furthermore, the Brotherhood was still speaking in the name of the people, as if intoning a mantra that had been set in stone and sealed by the election results, regardless of how circumstances were evolving.

With tensions at fever pitch and the protests ongoing, a showdown was inevitable, and it was not long before clashes broke out between the two groups of protestors, leaving ten dead and more 700 injured. The details of exactly what happened are fiercely contested. As the opposition tells it, the anti-Morsi protestors were attacked by groups of Brotherhood supporters who set upon them in a blatant act of aggression. One protestor recounted, 'there were about 2,000 of the Brothers moving forward in a very fast pace towards us ... The Brothers ran towards us suddenly and very quickly with their poles, chanting 'Allah u Akbar ... Ila Al-Jihad' ['Allah is the Greatest ... To Jihad'].'[29] Graphic video footage certainly shows apparent Brotherhood supporters beating protestors and tearing down their tents. Allegations of torture also emerged, while, according to Egyptian novelist Bahar Taha, some Brotherhood supporters were chanting slogans such as 'Our dead are in paradise and your dead are in hell', and 'Morsi, give us a sign and we'll bring them all in sacks.'[30]

But the Brotherhood tells a different story. Fearful that the protestors were intent on breaking into the palace and assassinating the president, they moved in to dismantle the demonstrations. In FJP spokesman Walid Al-Badri's account, they had heard the protestors were about to force their way into the palace, 'So we went there, and we removed the tents.'[31] He also asserted: 'But those were not protesters. Those were thugs.' Indeed, the Brotherhood maintains that those responsible for the violence were *beltagiya*, or hired thugs, who had been a regular feature of the former regime. During a speech on 6 December, Morsi accused a conspiracy of Mubarak loyalists and foreign interests of having hired such *beltagiya* to attack his supporters. He also charged that some of them had 'direct links' to the opposition.[32]

More importantly, the Brotherhood accused the police and security forces of having deliberately stood aside and allowed these thugs to do their worst. According to some reports, Interior Ministry forces had pulled out from the area around Ittihadiya before the clashes erupted, and when Morsi contacted the interior minister, Ahmed Gamal Al-Deen, to ask him to intervene, he did not respond for four hours.[33] Meanwhile, a senior security officer told Reuters that there was no explicit order to disobey Morsi, but that they all acted 'according to their conscience'.[34]

Whatever the truth of these events, the incident left the Brotherhood severely shaken, and feeling more alone than ever. It was an indication of just how low things had sunk; as Abdelmonem

Abul Futuh commented in a tweet, 'Replacing security with the president's supporters represents the collapse of the state.'[35] It was clear, therefore, that the Brotherhood's honeymoon period was well and truly over. Although the constitution was passed by 63.8 per cent in the December referendum, indicating that the Brotherhood still retained some popular support, turnout was strikingly low, at only 32.9 per cent of the population. The Brotherhood was haemorrhaging support fast, and from this point on the only way was down.

Death Throes

The Ittihadiya events would also mark a watershed moment for the military, which started to intervene more overtly in political affairs. On 8 December the SCAF issued a statement declaring: 'The Armed Forces have been monitoring developments with growing concern ... The Armed Forces ... realise their responsibility to preserve the higher interests of the country and to secure and protect vital installations, public institutions and the interests of innocent citizens.'[36] The statement continued: 'The Armed Forces affirm that dialogue is the best and only way to reach consensus ... The opposite of that will bring us to a dark tunnel that will result in catastrophe which is something that we won't allow.'[37] A few days later, Defence Minister Abdelfattah Al-Sissi called for a meeting of 'national unity for the love of Egypt to bring together partners of the country in the presence of the president of the republic'.[38]

Not only was the military taking advantage of the Brotherhood's weakness to posit itself as protector of the nation and people, it was also attempting to direct the political arena in its own interests. This bold intervention threw Morsi into even more of a spin, not least because he had not sanctioned the meeting that Al-Sissi had proposed. The Brotherhood could feel that things were slipping out of its hands, and did not know how to arrest the process.

In desperation, Morsi announced a cabinet reshuffle in January, getting rid of the interior minister who it blamed for the Ittihadiya catastrophe. But this reshuffle ended up creating more problems, including with the opposition. The Brotherhood's unwillingness to engage in a complete overhaul of the government, as the opposition was demanding, as well as its injudicious appointment of three more FJP ministers to the cabinet, only raised the temperature further. Indeed, the Brotherhood's insistence on ploughing ahead in the same blind fashion regardless of what was happening around it provoked further resentment and fury. This was evident on the second anniversary of the revolution, on 25 January 2013, when tens of thousands of demonstrators gathered in Tahrir Square to call for an end to Brotherhood rule. There were violent clashes between police forces and protesters at various locations in Cairo, as well as in other cities, where Brotherhood offices were also attacked. In an echo of the revolution, protestors in Tahrir Square chanted 'Leave, leave!' and 'The people want the fall of the regime!' while others called for an end to 'rule by the Murshid'. This was a symbolic day, and the message was clear.

Things took another turn for the worse on 26 January, after a Cairo court handed down death sentences to twenty-one football fans from Port Said who had been accused of inciting football riots that had erupted a year before, leaving more than seventy-four dead. The verdicts against the Port Said fans provoked uproar in the town, not least because of how disproportionate they seemed to many – especially given that not one individual linked to the former regime had been brought to justice for the killing of civilians during the revolution. It was not long before police had lost control of Port Said, as protestors ran wild. Meanwhile, demonstrations and violent clashes erupted in Cairo, continuing throughout the following weeks and months. Sectarian violence also reared its head. In April a Muslim mob attacked the main cathedral of the Coptic Orthodox Church, as Christians were holding a funeral for four Christians who had been killed the day before; and in June four Shi'ite Muslims were beaten to death by a mob in Giza. The incident occurred just a few days after a conference in support of the Syrian uprising, attended by Morsi, had seen prominent Sunni sheikhs using sectarian language against Shi'ites.[39]

With trouble on every side and the whole country spiralling out of control, Morsi did not know where to turn. He tried to reach out to the opposition, but was rebuffed. The National Salvation Front boycotted his attempts to hold a national dialogue on 28 January, and again on 28 February, Mohamed ElBaradei making clear that his alliance had no intention of entering into what he described as a 'fake dialogue'. The opposition also refused Morsi's call for parliamentary elections to be held in April, shunning the whole process unless its own conditions were met. Morsi's gestures towards compromise were deemed to be too little, too late; through its past behaviour, the Brotherhood had already dug its own grave. The President and his movement were thus almost completely isolated, in a political arena filled with hostility.

In fact this antagonism towards the Brotherhood was such that it prompted a new alliance, as the opposition started to edge closer to the military. During March and April 2013 most opposition factions, including the Islamist Al-Wasat party, responded to Al-Sissi's overtures by attending meetings with the military to discuss the situation. According to some sources, ElBaradei refused to meet with Morsi at all, asking instead to meet only with Al-Sissi.[40] It suddenly felt as though ranks were closing against the Brotherhood.

Nevertheless, rather than move against Al-Sissi, who was clearly overstepping his role, the Brotherhood stuck to its familiar policy of appeasement. Although Morsi had been urged by some of his senior advisors to expel Al-Sissi and other senior military figures, the president preferred to avoid confrontation of this sort. On 22 February he publicly renewed his full support and trust in the army, and in April promoted a number of senior military officers, with the commanders of the air force, navy and air-defence forces all promoted from major-generals to lieutenant-generals. It seems, therefore, that, despite the army's increased meddling in the affairs of state, the Brotherhood remained locked into the idea that conciliation and pacification were the best means to manage it.

But even if it had wanted to tackle Al-Sissi, by now it was too late. As Mohamed Mahsoub reflected, 'President Morsi is dealing with institutions that are not loyal to the revolution and not consistent with him. He cannot restructure these institutions ... unless there is a national consensus.'[41] But this national consensus had been broken almost as soon as Morsi's rule had begun.

The situation was worsened by the fact that the Brotherhood's own allies were also now turning against it. The Salafists were starting to put more of a distance between themselves and the Brotherhood, and on 30 January the Salafist Al-Nour party went as far as to launch a joint initiative with the National Salvation Front calling for the formation of a national unity government. Meanwhile, Morsi's own advisors were peeling away from the Presidency one after the other. The list of resignations was long, as senior advisors began to recoil at Morsi's way of operating. Those who quit included Fuad Jadallah, Mahmoud Mekki, Samir Morcos, Mohamed Seif Al-Dewla, and many others. Morsi was looking increasingly alienated, therefore, even from his own associates.

Meanwhile, the Brotherhood was struggling to deal with other challenges, not least of which was the fact that Egypt's economic crisis was getting out of hand. In March 2013 a fuel shortage left the country blighted by blackouts and rising food prices. Yet Morsi's negotiations for a US$4.8 billion loan from the IMF had stalled. The IMF was insisting that the government introduce a package of tax increases and subsidy cuts linked to the loan, but, already fearful of the public mood, the Morsi government did not dare to introduce such crippling measures, which would be sure to spark further unrest. Instead, it paid lip-service to addressing the crisis, holding another cabinet reshuffle and claiming that this would resolve the problem. Deputy of the FJP and senior Brotherhood leader Issam Al-Arian told Al-Jazeera that the reshuffle that was carried out in May 2013 was intended to 'confront the economic crisis and to conclude the agreement with the IMF with new spirit and a new vision, and to confront the energy crises'.[42]

But this move was tantamount to fiddling around at the edges while Egypt burned. Worse, the changes to the government prompted further hostility, as the Brotherhood brought three more FJP members into the cabinet: Amr Darrag, a senior FJP official, as planning minister; Brotherhood member Yahyia Hamid as investment minister; and FJP member Ahmed Al-Gezawi as agriculture minister. This meant that the FJP now held eleven of the thirty-five government portfolios. Furthermore, Morsi's refusal to get rid of Prime Minister Hisham Qandil, despite the opposition's calls for a change of prime minister, only aggravated the situation. To many, this was yet another signal that the Brotherhood was incapable of even understanding the extent of the crisis in which it was embroiled.

Morsi stoked further tensions in this respect in June, when he appointed sixteen new governors – seven of whom were from the Brotherhood. Particularly controversially, among the new appointees was Adel Al-Khayat, who was appointed as governor of Luxor. Al-Khayat was a member of Al-Jama'a Al-Islamiya, the group that had been behind the 1997 attack in Luxor that had killed fifty-eight foreign tourists and four Egyptians. While Al-Jama'a al-Islamiya had since renounced violence, such a move – especially at a time when the whole country was boiling and the opposition was baying for the Brotherhood's blood – was extremely short-sighted, and displayed an astonishing lack of sensitivity.

Moreover, while the country was sliding into chaos the Brotherhood seemed still to be bumbling around in the dark, as if it had only just arrived in office. This was encapsulated by the debacle on 4 June, when the cabinet held a meeting to discuss Ethiopia's recent diversion of the course of the Blue Nile in preparation for the construction of a new dam. Unaware that the meeting was being broadcast live, ministers discussed options for dealing with the crisis in particularly undiplomatic tones. Saad Al-Katatni, FJP chairman, proclaimed: 'I say loud and clear that all options are available to us ... If diplomacy fails to change the situation, we shall resort to international law, and if this is unsuccessful, we shall resort to any option one can imagine in order to protect our water security.'[43] It was only when Magdi Ahmad Hussein, chairman of the Islamist-leaning Labour Party announced, 'I'm very fond of battles ... but this battle must be waged with maximum judiciousness and calm. Even though this is a secret meeting, we must all take an oath not to leak anything to the media', that the cabinet was informed the meeting was being aired live on television. This realisation prompted embarrassed laughter among cabinet members, while Morsi stepped in to proclaim his respect for the Ethiopian people, reassuring his audience: 'We are not about to start any aggression against anyone whatsoever, or affront anyone whatsoever. But we have very serious measures to protect every single drop of Nile water.'[44] This almost surreal episode gave the impression that Egyptian politics under the Brotherhood had descended to little more than a farce, and that there was no hope left for the country while it remained in power. If the Brotherhood had started out in power as if it were flailing around in the water, it was now most definitely a drowning man.

The Final Blow

It was not long before the situation exploded. In June the Tamarod movement, a youth activist group that had emerged in April promising to gather more than 15 million signatures for a petition calling on Morsi to resign, had called for a mass protest to mark the one-year anniversary of Morsi's assumption of power on 30 June. By the middle of the month it already claimed to have collected 7 million signatures, and the pressure was mounting. Meanwhile the opposition was calling ever more loudly for the appointment of a new government, the amendment of certain articles in the constitution, and – most worrying of all for the Brotherhood – early presidential elections.

In the meantime, Al-Sissi muscled onto the scene more directly, issuing an ultimatum on 23 June giving the political forces one week to reach an agreement. Al-Sissi's move stunned the Brotherhood, particularly because Morsi had somehow considered Sissi as his own man in the SCAF. It was Morsi who had brought Al-Sissi to the top of the SCAF and given him so much space to operate over the previous months. As senior Brotherhood member and speaker of the Shura Council Ahmed Fahmy commented, 'I never thought that a coup would take place by the military council, especially as they were appreciated by president Morsi and by us at that time. We never stood in the way of what they wanted ... to achieve.'[45] A furious Morsi met with Al-Sissi to protest at the ultimatum. When nothing came of the meeting, the Guidance Office sent the two Brotherhood powerhouses, Khairet Al-Shater and Saad Al-Katatni, to remonstrate with him. According to Al-Sissi it was not a pleasant meeting, and Al-Shater began threatening that if Morsi was ousted from power armed elements in the country would not just sit back and allow the legitimate power to fall.[46] Although Al-Shater's daughter has denied that her father made such threats, the Brotherhood was clearly outraged at Al-Sissi's audacity, and also shocked by its own realisation that there was a serious move afoot to dislodge it from power.

With few other options open to it, the Brotherhood turned once again to the street. On 24 June it announced an open-ended demonstration entitled 'Legitimacy Is a Red Line', to take place on 28 June at the Raba Al-Adawiya mosque in Cairo. Two days later Morsi made a speech to the nation lasting two hours and forty-five minutes. If ever there was a speech that demonstrated the Brotherhood's political naivety, this was it. Here was an adamant refusal to accept the reality of what was unfolding on the ground. In his characteristically long-winded fashion, Morsi employed his usual mixture of appeasement and condemnation, praising the police and the army while also lashing out at a whole host of constituencies, from former regime loyalists to the media, businessmen and judges.

But it was clear from the speech that Morsi had no intention of going anywhere. Adopting the tone of a revolutionary, the president announced that it was time for 'radical immediate reforms' to state institutions, and for corruption to be tackled. He also reached out to opposition forces, urging them not to undermine the revolution by making alliances with the remnants of the old regime, and expressing his belief that the presence of a 'strong opposition' was important in the democratic experiment. In some parts, therefore, this was the speech that Morsi should have made at the outset of his rule. But at this point such comments were ill-timed, and appeared crass. More importantly, Morsi's apparent determination to press on as if he was operating in a vacuum only hardened the opposition's resolve to take to the streets on 30 June.

Morsi's speech angered the military too – especially because the SCAF had instructed Morsi on what he should include in it. A senior military commander explained: 'We told him it has to be short, respond to opposition demands to form a coalition government, amend the constitution and set a timeframe for the two actions. Yet he came out with a very long speech that said nothing.'[47] Nor did the speech impress the Obama administration, which was adding to the pressure by pushing for some kind of reconciliation between political groups that might save the country.[48]

But, having attained power, the Brotherhood was not going to be pressurised into giving it up without a fight. Furthermore, the Brotherhood seems to have had a blind faith that its electoral legitimacy, as well as its supporters, would work as a shield to protect it from being brought down. As Yahyia Hamid commented, 'Morsi was betting on the Egyptians. Betting on those who came out on 25 January [2011] and sacrificed themselves, on those who came out to vote in five constitutional elections, those who queued in their millions for seven, eight, ten hours in order to vote. He was betting on all of that, on the awareness of the Egyptians.'[49] But Morsi had not understood the extent to which he had alienated those constituencies that did not make up part of the Brotherhood's core support base, and who, having experienced almost a year of Brotherhood rule, were not going to rally to his defence.

Indeed, by the time 30 June came around and millions of Egyptians flocked into the streets to demand an end to Brotherhood rule, Morsi and the Brotherhood remained in denial. The Brotherhood insisted that those protesting were mainly *beltagiya*, and, according to military sources, in a meeting with Al-Sissi on 1 July Morsi refused to accept the size of the demonstrations.[50] Morsi remained defiant in this meeting, and on the same day the Brotherhood insisted on the democratic right of the elected president to complete his term in office. Al-Sissi therefore upped the stakes further, this time issuing a forty-eight-hour ultimatum to Morsi to bow to the opposition's demands, failing which the military would impose its own solution. Foreign pressure was also mounting. President Obama telephoned Morsi on 1 July, and, according to Hamid, told the president that he should agree to early presidential elections, in which he should not take part.[51] Meanwhile, according to Amed Fahmy, both the EU and the United States tried to convince Morsi to step down and accept a new government led by Mohamed ElBaradei.

But even with Al-Sissi's ultimatum hanging over his head, Morsi still refused to back down. On 2 July the president met with his advisors, who informed him that a military coup was already underway. According to Hamid, who was present at the meeting, 'The president was sure that we were entering a conflict and confrontation, something he had been trying to avoid ... He could see it but he would be the first to confront it and to resist.' Morsi reportedly told those gathered: 'I don't want anyone to worry. I am steadfast. The people will defend their freedom and their legitimacy. I have no doubts in this regard.'[52]

Not that the Brotherhood was entirely averse to all compromise. During a meeting with Al-Sissi on 2 July, Morsi offered a number of concessions including a government reshuffle, the amendment of certain articles of the constitution, and the holding of parliamentary elections. The following day the Brotherhood went as far as to offer Al-Sissi the post of prime minister, as well as defence minister. But the Presidency was one thing the Brotherhood was adamant it would not give up. If the Brotherhood was going to be part of any solution, it would need to entail Morsi's retention of the most powerful office in the state.

Morsi continued, therefore, along the path of confrontation. At midnight on 2 July, a defiant president addressed the nation in a forty-five-minute speech, warning that Egypt risked descending into an endless spiral of violence if people continued to challenge his legitimate right to rule: 'There is no alternative to legitimacy, the constitutional legitimacy, legal legitimacy and electoral legal legitimacy that produced an elected president for Egypt for the first time in its history.'[53] Although Egyptians joked about the number of times Morsi used the word 'legitimacy' in this speech, his doing so reflected the fact that the Brotherhood had nothing else left to cling to. But Morsi's insistence only highlighted the fact that the Brotherhood had failed to understand that it was operating in a moment of transition, and that having won at the ballot box was not sufficient to justify clinging to power as the country fell apart. In its desperation to defend what it believed was its natural right, the Brotherhood had boiled democracy down to a single electoral victory.

On 3 July Al-Sissi's ultimatum expired, but still Morsi held fast. In a desperate bid to show that everything was normal, Morsi's communications advisor Yaser Haddara told the media one hour after the deadline, 'The president is still the president and he is still sitting in his office, with his team ... The general mood is actually quite comfortable. People are working, believe it or not.'[54] At around 7 p.m. that night, Al-Sissi called Morsi to ask him one last time if he would agree to a referendum on his staying in office, or to hand over power to the speaker of the parliament. This was Morsi's final chance to save the day and the movement. Predictably enough he refused, and at 9 p.m. Al-Sissi addressed the nation on live television, unveiling a new roadmap for Egypt that entailed Morsi's departure, his duties to be taken over by the head of Egypt's High Constitutional Court until presidential elections could be held; the suspension of the constitution; the formation of a new technocratic government; and the passing of an election law to hold new parliamentary elections. Morsi was placed under house arrest and detained in an unknown location, along with ten senior aides, while scores of other Brotherhood leaders, including the head of the FJP, Saad Al-Katatni, were arrested. In one fell swoop, it was all over for the movement that had waited so long to achieve power.

The Brotherhood's refusal to compromise during these final weeks was to have dire consequences for the movement. What came next was worse than the Brotherhood could ever have imagined, as the new regime embarked upon a brutal and bloody crackdown. On 8 July, military and police forces opened fire on hundreds of Morsi supporters as they demonstrated outside a military facility where the deposed president was believed to be being held, killing at least fifty-three and wounding more than 300. But worse was to come. On 27 July at least seventy-two Morsi supporters were shot dead and many more injured, when security officials attacked a protest camp at Raba'a Al-Adawiya.[55] On 14 August the military broke up the Rabba Al-Adawiya camp entirely, along with a smaller one in Nahda Square. Armoured bulldozers moved into the two camps shortly after dawn, and security forces proceeded to clear the camps using live ammunition.[56] The operation left more than 700 dead and scores more injured – although the Brotherhood maintains that more than 2,000 of its supporters were killed at Rabba Al-Adawiya alone. The new regime also embarked upon a campaign of mass arrests, detaining 1,400 in the aftermath of the break-up of the camps and thousands more over the course of the coming months.

The Brotherhood was left in tatters, with most of its senior leadership either imprisoned or on the run, while others fled the country – many seeking refuge in Qatar and Turkey. It was a sorry end for a movement that had come to power at a time of such hope and promise. In fact the Brotherhood's demise was so swift and so complete that it prompted some Egyptians to question whether the movement had deliberately sabotaged its own time in power as part of a grander strategic plan.[57] Although the movement may not have had any experience of ruling, its upper and middle ranks were stuffed full of middle-class professionals who, in the minds of many, should have been able to do a better job.

As for the Brotherhood itself, while it was stunned by the whole experience, it soon developed a narrative attributing its fall from grace to a grand conspiracy engineered by the military and the deep state in conjunction with Western powers. This was a theme that was to come up repeatedly in my interviews with Brotherhood leaders. The information minister in Morsi's government, Saleh Abdelmaqsoud, for example, commented: 'The armed forces saw that the president was succeeding, so they decided to get rid of him.'[58] A similar tone was taken by Gamal Abdelsattar, Morsi's deputy minister of awqaf: 'We didn't fail. The army staged a coup when it saw our achievements.'[59] The Brotherhood's secretary-general, Mahmoud Hussein, even speculated that the coup might even have been 'cooked up' during Mubarak's time.[60] Some Brotherhood members went further, situating the movement's experience within the context of some divine test. During the final days at Raba Al-Adawiya, Brotherhood members began invoking the language of a 'second ordeal' – the first being the movement's extreme repression under President Gamal Abdul Nasser in 1965. The whole experience was being elevated into near-metaphysical terms, as the Brotherhood sought to exonerate itself from what had occurred.

That the movement should have resorted to such a narrative is unsurprising. This was the discourse of self-preservation in particularly difficult times. Furthermore, having squandered the biggest prize in its history, deflecting the blame away from itself was always going to be easier than engaging in any kind of hard-nosed internal examination of what had gone wrong; the Brotherhood is an authoritarian movement by nature, and self-examination and self-criticism have never been part of its routine. Not that the Brotherhood has been unwilling to admit that it made mistakes. Another narrative also emerged alongside that of the conspiracy, Brotherhood leaders trotting out the same list of errors it had committed during its time in power. These included its failure to be sufficiently revolutionary; its striking of a deal with the SCAF when it should have been striking against it; its failure to engage in a radical overhaul of the state, or to explain itself adequately to other political forces with whom it should have worked more closely; the fact that its members were not experienced enough; and Morsi's unsuitability for the job. These criticisms of Morsi are often wrapped up in praise, Brotherhood members explaining that Morsi was too kind or too nice, or even too ethical in an unethical environment. Indeed, while the Brotherhood has been willing to acknowledge these errors, it continues to skim the surface, skirting around the real problems without getting to the heart of what went wrong.

The cold reality is that the Brotherhood was simply not up to the job of ruling, or of functioning as a modern political force in the contemporary age. That is not to suggest that its failure was entirely of its own making. There were certainly forces in place right from the start that were intent on undermining it, and that fuelled a narrative about the Brotherhood that was simply untrue. While the Brotherhood was condemned for Ikhwanising the state, it in fact never represented any sort of threat to the deep state, or even to the SCAF. Rather, it was dwarfed by the state and, in line with its non-revolutionary character, did not seek to implement any radical changes that might have turned the state on its head. Instead it was mostly timid and compliant, choosing appeasement over confrontation at almost every turn. Fears that it would embark upon a wholesale Islamisation of the state were equally unfounded. Notably, the Brotherhood chose to play the role of a restraining force when the Salafists were bent on tying the constitution more directly to Sharia. Indeed, throughout its time in power the Brotherhood did little to truly threaten the establishment. This is one of the reasons why it struggled so hard to digest the lessons of its own collapse. The move that the SCAF and the opposition made against the Brotherhood was therefore partly predicated on a fear of what the movement might do in the future, rather than of what it was doing in the present.

But the Brotherhood's fall was a result of its own failings, too. Its lack of any political or even real religious vision combined with its inexperience and inability to go beyond itself gave the impression that it was an empty vessel whose only interest was in taking and retaining control. Furthermore, the Brotherhood proved unable to reconcile the world of politics with its role as a socio-religious movement. Egypt's Arab Spring evolved, therefore, into a battle for control between the two old forces that had shaped the country's modern history. For the Brotherhood it was to be a battle that left it not only forced back underground but pushed out of the picture altogether.

PART TWO

LIBYA

FOUR

THE LIBYAN BROTHERS: OUT OF THE SHADOWS

If the Egyptian Brotherhood's experience of the Arab Spring was one of an old and unwieldy movement struggling to adapt to being a modern political actor, the Libyan Brotherhood's was more that of the new kid on the block. In contrast to the 'lumbering elephant' that was the Egyptian Brotherhood, the Libyan Brotherhood was a nonexistent force inside the country when the uprisings broke out in Libya's second city of Benghazi in February 2011. Such was Libyan leader Colonel Muammar Qadhafi's intolerance of any kind of political activity that fell outside the framework of his bizarre creation of a state, he ensured that no group, especially one of an Islamist hue, could exist, let alone endear itself to the population. While the Egyptian Brotherhood was able to build up its networks, conduct charity work and engage in the political process, the Libyan Brotherhood enjoyed no such privileges.

Although by the time of the Arab Spring the Libyan Brotherhood still operated as a movement in exile, it was very much in decline. It was so weakened and compromised that by the 2000s it had entered into a dialogue of sorts with Qadhafi's son Saif Al-Islam, who had been propelled to the fore as the reformist face of the regime following Libya's rehabilitation in the international community in 2003. While this flirtation with Saif Al-Islam was partly about trying to secure the release of some of its members from prison, it was also a desperate attempt to carve out space for itself inside Libya. Indeed, the Libyan Brotherhood was so emasculated by this point that its best hope was to be allowed to return to the country to operate as a charity or NGO – a hope that was unlikely ever to be fulfilled while Qadhafi was in power.

The Libyan uprisings in 2011, therefore, opened up a whole new world of possibilities for the Libyan Brotherhood, and it moved quickly to stand behind the revolution. Yet while the Egyptian Brotherhood was able to use its political and social weight to propel the Egyptian Revolution forward according to its own needs and desires, the Libyan Brotherhood could do no such thing. In fact the Libyan Brotherhood struggled to offer the unfolding revolution anything at all. With the uprisings quickly descending into armed conflict, there was little that the Brotherhood, which had a limited membership and lacked any real presence inside the country, could provide, other than some small-scale logistical support. Not that the Brotherhood was not involved in the conflict at all. Some of its members joined the fighting, but they did so in an individual capacity. But, as far as the Islamist scene was concerned, it was the jihadists who took to the front lines en masse, overshadowing any Brotherhood presence on the ground.

The situation was complicated further by the fact that the Brotherhood had always had a mantra of non-violence, and, like its Egyptian counterpart, had never considered itself a revolutionary movement. Like the Egyptian Brotherhood, the Libyan movement wrestled conceptually with shedding its long-held commitment to gradual reform and supporting the sudden overturning of the established order – so much so that, at the same time as actively supporting the revolution, it seemed to be almost reluctant to be part of it. Even after the conflict was well underway, the Brotherhood proved to be open to the possibility of striking some sort of deal with the very regime it was fighting, giving its blessing to attempts by the Islamist current to reach out to Saif Al-Islam to come up with some sort of negotiated solution. Yet even in this the Brotherhood was a minor player. The movement's limited size meant that it was forced to hitch its wagon to other more influential Islamist players, such as Dr Ali Salabi, a former Brotherhood member and Islamic scholar who, with the backing of Qatar, emerged as an informal leader of the various Islamist currents that came to the fore once Qadhafi's regime began to crumble.

Yet, despite the Brotherhood's limited role in the conflict and lack of depth inside the country, it succeeded in inserting itself into the emerging political structures being established by the rebels at the time. The Brotherhood gradually elbowed its way onto the National Transitional Council (NTC), established at the end of February 2011 as the political face of the revolution. It also came to dominate several local councils that were established at this early stage. Even before Qadhafi was killed, therefore, the Brotherhood had secured a political presence that far outweighed its power and influence inside the country. This was a pattern that was to continue into the transition.

The Brotherhood's ability to manoeuvre itself to the heart of these new political structures was partly a testimony to its universal organisational capacities. As soon as the uprisings began, the Brotherhood began organising its members and reactivating its old networks, however limited these may have been. However, its success was primarily the result of circumstances beyond its control. The Brotherhood's ability to put itself at the centre of things was largely a reflection of the hollow state of Libya's political landscape. The four decades of rule by Qadhafi had effectively depoliticised the country, leaving a population devoid of political experience and culture. Thus, when the uprisings erupted, there was no coherent movement or organisation, let alone any political force, that could step into the vacuum that opened up.

The Brotherhood was able, therefore, to rely on its relative experience and external connections to manoeuvre itself to the fore. Indeed, being part of a bigger transnational movement gave the Brotherhood additional clout, and helped to project it to the centre of the action (although this connection was to prove a double-edged sword later on). Given the fact that the Brotherhood had assumed a leading role in the Egyptian Revolution, and that the Islamists in Tunisia looked set to do well, there was a general expectation that the Libyan Brotherhood would play a major part in Libya's political future.

The result was that, by the time of liberation in October 2011, the Libyan Brotherhood appeared far more powerful than it really was. This meant that, in contrast to the Egyptian and Tunisian experiences, the Libyan Brotherhood's Arab Spring was essentially characterised by a struggle for relevance, both politically and Islamically, as it sought to anchor itself in a landscape it had been excluded from for so long.

Deep in the Shadows

Prior to 2011, the history of the Libyan brotherhood was largely that of a group in the shadows. It was also a history of stops and starts, and of disjointed activity. The movement was first implanted in Libya before it even became an independent country. Prior to independence, Libya comprised three regions – Tripolitania in the west, Cyrenaica in the east and Fezzan in the south. These regions were formally united in December 1951 in a federal system under a constitutional monarchy headed by King Idris Al-Sanussi. King Idris had previously been emir of Cyrenaica, and it was in this capacity that he gave refuge to a group of Egyptian brothers who had fled Egypt after they were accused of involvement in the assassination of Egyptian Prime Minister Mahmoud Nukrashi Pasha in 1948.[1] Idris welcomed these brothers to Benghazi, giving them asylum in his palace for six months. Around the same time the Brotherhood was also being introduced into Libya by Egyptian students and teachers who were in the country, and who formed a core part of its educational system. Libyans who had spent time in Egypt and been drawn to the movement's ideology also played their part in spreading this new message, while the establishment of Benghazi University in 1956 allowed for greater contact between Brotherhood adherents in the city and Libyans from other towns.[2]

Despite being given relative freedom to spread their message, however, these Brotherhood's devotees struggled to garner any real support among the population. This was partly because the Libyan monarchy had been born out of the Sanussi religious order – a Sufi revivalist movement that sought to reform and purify Islam, and by the nineteenth century had become the dominant religious and political force in the east of Libya. This meant that King Idris was imbued with a particular religious legitimacy that served as a buffer against alternative Islamist ideologies. In addition, being primarily a cultural and religious organisation, the Brotherhood's appeal was limited almost exclusively to the intelligentsia and elite, who represented a tiny proportion of Libya's still undeveloped state. More importantly, the Brotherhood's experience in Egypt had given rise to the belief that it had an overtly political agenda – something that put many people off.

Furthermore, Libyan society, with its closely guarded sense of tradition and conservatism, was wary of ideologies imported from outside. Thus, while the Brotherhood was flourishing not only in Egypt but also in Syria and elsewhere in the region, the Libyan Brotherhood struggled to grow beyond a handful of small cells of adherents. In the words of senior Brotherhood member, Haj Abu Sen, the Brotherhood at this time was 'just a group that had arrangements but that was not an organisation as such'.[3]

The 1967 Israeli defeat of Arab forces, and the Libyan government's limp response to the conflict, marked something of a shift in this respect, as it inspired Libyan Brotherhood enthusiasts to come together to try to set up a more formalised structure. But given Libya's uncompromising geography, with its main population centres separated by vast swathes of desert, what emerged were two branches, one in the west and the other in the east.[4] Although these two branches came together to agree on a leadership committee, and tried to co-ordinate with each other, they could hardly be called a movement. Their activities were limited mostly to making speeches and running cultural events – and according to former Brotherhood leader Mahmoud Nacua, who in 2012 was made ambassador to London, the group had 'no clear political vision or programme for how to deal with the daily political reality'.[5] Indeed, the Brotherhood represented more of an intellectual exercise than a push to create a political or socio-religious movement.

It was little surprise, therefore, that the group failed to grow into anything more substantial. There were at this time only forty *usrah* – Brotherhood 'families' or cells – each comprising just five people in Tripoli and other western towns.[6] And it was not long before the momentum declined and members stopped attending the meetings, which in Nacua's words had become 'routine and boring'.[7]

The seizure of power by a group of young army officers in September 1969 was to dampen the movement further. But it was the rise of Colonel Muammar Qadhafi as the head of this new Libyan Arab Republic in the early 1970s that was to set the tone for the coming decades. For Qadhafi, 1969 was not a coup or even an ordinary revolution; rather, marked the dawn of a whole new era for humankind that, by the late 1970s, would see him impose his bizarre revolutionary vision on the country. But even before this vision of the Jamahiriyah ('State of the Masses') that was laid out in his famous Green Book came to be articulated, the new nationalist regime was clear that it was not going to tolerate any challenge to its hegemony. In the interests of conformity, all political activity outside of the framework of the new state was banned, and punishable by death under Law No. 71 of 1972.

The Brotherhood soon ran afoul of this uncompromising approach. In 1973 the new regime targeted a number of political currents, including the Ba'athists and Marxists, but also the Brotherhood. Thirty Brotherhood members were arrested, and the movement's leadership committee was paraded on Libyan television, its members promising to dismantle the organisation and refrain from reconstituting its leadership. After eighteen months, the Brotherhood detainees were given two choices: either to stay in Libya but desist from engaging in any political activities, or to leave the country to work with Qadhafi's newly established Islamic Call Society to spread Islam in Africa. This move effectively finished off the movement inside the country, and it looked as though Qadhafi had nipped the Libyan Brotherhood in the bud.

However, within a few years this irrepressible movement was to reappear. At the end of the 1970s and early 1980s, the entire region was undergoing an Islamic revivalism prompted by the Iranian Revolution, which had seen a popular Islamist movement overthrow the western-backed shah, and by the defeat of the Soviets in Afghanistan by Arab jihadist fighters. It was a heady time that gave rise to the belief that, by going back to the roots of Islam, the region could regain its dignity and become master of its own destiny. Islam really did seem to be the solution to the challenges imposed by modernity.

Although these ideas were stirring inside Libya, the repressive nature of the state meant that they could not be translated into action. While some young Libyans went to Afghanistan to join the jihad, there was no space inside Libya for any real Islamic activism. However, it was in the late 1970s, when Libya was at the peak of its oil boom, that the government started to send Libyan students to pursue their studies abroad. It was in the West, and in the United States and UK in particular, that young Libyans came into direct contact for the first time with the kinds of Islamist ideas that were developing among Muslim students and dissident communities at this time.

It was not long before a number of Libyan students in the UK and the United States came together to form their own Brotherhood group, referring to themselves as the Jama'a Islamiya – Libia ('Islamic Group – Libya'). These students also started thinking about the difficult business of replanting the movement inside Libya. The challenges were enormous. According to senior Brotherhood leader Alamin Belhaj, there were no brothers left in the west of the country by this point, and only a handful of people who were prepared to identify themselves with the movement in the east.[8] Moreover, Qadhafi was not only utterly intolerant of all political activity outside the confines of his revolutionary state, the Libyan leader had developed a particular personal antipathy towards

Islamists, whom he described as *zinadiqa* ('heathens'). Libyans were at the receiving end of a discourse that castigated Islamists as the very embodiment of backwardness and evil. Qadhafi lambasted the Brotherhood as 'the servants of imperialism', 'members of the reactionary right wing', 'hooligans, liars, bastards, hashish smokers, drunks, cowards, delinquents ... '[9] He also warned that they were 'more dangerous than AIDS'.[10]

It was therefore a dangerous uphill struggle for the Libyan Brotherhood when it embarked in the early 1980s on trying to reorganise itself secretly inside the country. Nevertheless, it succeeded in making some progress on the organisational level. By 1987 it had connected up its members sufficiently well to establish a single Shura Council and an Executive Committee. But its activities on the ground were severely curtailed. As the movement's former general guide, Suleiman Abdelkader, notes, 'The grip of the governmental-security apparatus was extremely harsh at that time. There was no space for political activities or any tangible *dawa* work. All we could do was direct some of the youth educationally through work or family relationships or on social and religious occasions. The Muslim Brotherhood also collected some money to help the poor.'[11] During the 1990s the group managed to run a few student camps and to work discretely alongside some imams in the mosques, assisting people with their day-to-day problems. But this was a far cry from the bottom-up educational and *dawa* work the group's ideology had been founded on, and a million miles away from the kind of political activism or charitable work its counterparts in Egypt were engaged in at this time. The Libyan Brotherhood, therefore, had no means by which to create a proper base or to root itself in the social landscape, leaving it confined more to the realm of ideas than reality.

While many of these failings can be put down to the repressive nature of the Qadhafi regime, it is notable that the jihadist strand was able to expand considerably during this period. The Brotherhood's presence was notably smaller than, and overshadowed by, that of the more militant strand, which included the Libyan Islamic Fighting

Group (LIFG), the Libyan Martyrs' Group, and the Libyan Gathering – the last of which broke away from the Brotherhood in 1990 after becoming impatient with the movement's gradualist, non-violent approach, and what it considered to be its over-reliance on the Brotherhood in Egypt.[12] However, all these Islamist opposition groups were to meet with a similar fate in the mid-to-late 1990s when, having uncovered their existence, the regime moved to eliminate them.

In the Brotherhood's case, the blow was swift and deadly. In June 1998 the regime arrested 152 members of the movement, including almost all of its leadership. Those who escaped the clutches of the regime's security apparatus fled the country. This effectively finished the Brotherhood off inside Libya for a second time. But the regime did not stop there. In the mid 2000s, following Libya's rehabilitation within the international community after it agreed in 2003 to relinquish its WMD programmes, the regime saw in the Brotherhood an opportunity to prove its reformist credentials to the West. Qadhafi's son Saif Al-Islam embarked upon a 'Reform and Repent' programme, intended to de-radicalise and essentially co-opt Libya's Islamist prisoners. Although the main focus of this programme was to be the jihadist currents, Saif Al-Islam also worked on the Brotherhood, entering into a dialogue with imprisoned Brotherhood leaders. The deal offered by the regime was that, if these prisoners agreed to desist from political activities, they could secure their release from prison.

But the regime wanted to go beyond simply co-opting these prisoners, to neutralise the whole Libyan Brotherhood including its elements abroad. This was in line with its efforts at that time to lure back former dissidents if they agreed to make their peace with the regime. To this end, Saif Al-Islam opened channels of communication with the Brotherhood in Europe. In 2005 the young Qadhafi dispatched one of his representatives to the UK to deliver a recorded message to the Brotherhood on a cassette to the movement, expressing his desire to resolve their situation.[13] Although this was clearly part of the regime's effort to repackage itself and revamp its image, the Brotherhood was so compromised by this point that it had little choice but to respond. Libya's international rehabilitation had given the regime a new lease of life, and the Libyan leader had emerged stronger than ever. He had also been given a boost by the global war on terror, with Western nations now prepared to work with him to defeat Libyan militant Islamist networks. The Brotherhood thus appeared at this point to be doomed to dwindle into oblivion, and clearly saw in Saif Al-Islam its only hope in an otherwise bleak landscape.

Not that the Brotherhood complied completely with Saif Al-Islam's demands. Although some members of the movement chose as individuals to take up the regime's offer of return, the Brotherhood as a whole rejected it. As Suleiman Abdelkader explained, 'Saif Al-Islam's aim was that the Brotherhood and its leadership return [to Libya] and join the Libya Tomorrow current. We knew this would be a kind of political suicide. They offered us a lot of financial and political inducements. But the issue was clear for us: we needed genuine reform in Libya.'[14] Indeed, the main issue for the Brotherhood was to be allowed to return as a movement and to be given the space to operate. Mohamed Abdul Malek, the group's representative in Europe, explained that the group had been so emasculated that '[p]rior to 17 February 2011 our biggest hope was to be able to enter Libya as some sort of NGO. That was the ultimate goal.'[15] Only this would enable it to embark upon what it had always been denied – namely, the opportunity to carry out its project to try to reform the individual, the family, and by extension society, in order to bring about Islamic rule. It also sought to secure the release from prison of its members, some of whom had been sentenced to death.

With these aims in mind, the Brotherhood boycotted the large Libyan opposition conference that was held in London in 2005, justifying its absence by asserting that it sought real reform and practical solutions to Libya's problems. More interestingly, the Brotherhood's international website, Ikhwanonline, stated that the movement had boycotted the conference because it rejected some of the demands voiced there, including the demand for Qadhafi to go.[16] It looked therefore as though the regime had succeeded in at least neutralising what was left of the movement.

By March 2006, the regime was convinced enough to release its Brotherhood prisoners, prompting Suleiman Abdelkader to write a letter of thanks to Saif Al-Islam.[17] But this was to be no rebirth for the movement. These freed prisoners had been warned that they had to comply with the regime's conditions. Brotherhood prisoner Saleh Shamak described how, just two weeks prior to their release, Qadhafi and his intelligence chief, Abdullah Senussi, had visited them in prison. Senussi accused the prisoners of being agents of the West, while Qadhafi warned them against engaging in any political activities, threatening that the Libyan authorities were more than capable of fighting them if they returned to their secret work.[18]

These ex-prisoners kept to their word and did not reactivate their activities inside the country. Some returned to their jobs, while others simply kept their heads down. As Brotherhood member Saleh Shamek recalled, 'After they released us we didn't go back to underground work ... We didn't start restructuring ourselves. We didn't issue statements inside the country.'[19] In 2009, Abdelkader acknowledged to Al-Jazeera that the group consisted of 'no one inside the country and no more than 200 outside it'.[20] By the eve of the 2011 uprisings, therefore, the movement had been effectively eliminated inside Libya and all but neutralised outside it.

Edging into the Light: The Brotherhood and the Revolution

The uprisings that erupted in Benghazi in February 2011 were not the work of any particular group or revolutionary movement, let alone the Brotherhood. Although there were calls put out on social media sites by Libyan youth for a Day of Rage on 17 February, the Libyan protests were a largely spontaneous outburst of anger by ordinary Libyans who had been inspired by the events in Tunisia and Egypt to rise up and challenge the regime that had been repressing them for decades. Libyans were frustrated too because the regime's international rehabilitation had not brought the hoped-for reforms – and because, despite the country's vast oil wealth, the majority of Libyans were struggling to make ends meet.

But the fact that the protests erupted in Benghazi and spread to other eastern towns was no accident. Libya's eastern region had always had a particularly antagonistic relationship to the Qadhafi regime, perceiving itself as the victim of a deliberate policy of exclusion and marginalisation. This perception arose partly because Qadhafi had stripped Benghazi of what it viewed as its rightful status, making Tripoli – which had shared capital-city status with Benghazi, the government alternating its seat every two years – the heart of his highly centralised regime. This sense of injustice was compounded by a series of incidents during the regime's latter decades that became engrained in the collective memory and narrative. These incidents included the regime's brutal liquidation of militant Islamist networks in the region during the mid-to–late 1990s – as well as the Abu Slim prison massacre of 1996, in which scores of Islamist prisoners, most of whom were from Benghazi, were extrajudicially executed after they tried to rise up against the conditions they were being held in. In response to the discovery of these militant Islamist cells and support networks, the regime punished the east heavily, turning the area into a kind of security zone and starving the city of development infrastructure. Although many other cities, including those in the south, were also deprived of proper infrastructure – this being a reflection of the chaotic and arbitrary nature of Qadhafi's policymaking – Benghazi viewed its lack of services and facilities as the result of a deliberate ploy by the regime to keep it down.

Not that Libyans in the west or south of the country were necessarily more accepting of the Qadhafi regime. Although the regime had its fair share of supporters, including fervent ideologues and those tribes that had benefited from its largesse and patronage, the majority of Libyans across the country were fed up with four decades of Qadhafi's rule. However, it was in the east that this anger was concentrated enough to erupt into popular protest, and where people were far enough away from the core of the regime's security network to risk taking to the streets. In fact, there had already been an attempt at some sort of uprising in Benghazi, almost immediately after President Ben Ali had been toppled in Tunisia. At the end of January 2011, Libyans turned out in their thousands to occupy empty and half-finished blocks of flats in government housing projects across the country, to vent their anger at the regime's failure to allocate these housing units in a fair or timely manner. These were unprecedented scenes in Qadhafi's Libya, and although the protest was contained by the security forces, it was clear that there was further trouble ahead.

With unrest already brewing, the Libyan Brotherhood began to address what stance it should take towards the unfolding events. Just as for their Egyptian counterparts, the prospect of the revolution was conceptually problematic for the Brotherhood. Abdelrazzak Al-Aradi, a senior Libyan Brotherhood member, explained the movement's predicament at that time: 'As an organisation we don't believe in revolution. It is not our way to stage coups or revolutions. Our way is to change society, and that takes a long time. We don't believe that changing the head of a regime will change the people.'[21] While such deliberations may seem almost esoteric given what was developing on the ground, this was a serious issue for the movement, and went to the very core of its ideology.

In a bid to agree upon a position, the Brotherhood held a meeting of its general assembly in a Zurich Islamic centre on 30 and 31 January. According to Alamin Belhaj, the general consensus among the brothers was that the revolution was coming, and that the regime would respond with its typical brutality. Qadhafi was clearly no Ben Ali, and was not going to step aside so easily. More importantly, Libya had no armed forces to speak of. Qadhafi had long feared the Libyan military as a potential source of rebellion, and consequently had deliberately kept it weak and divided, relying instead on a complex hierarchy of security services drawn largely from his own tribe, the Qadhadhfa, and from allied tribes such as the Werfella and Marqarha. Thus, where the Tunisian army had been able to step in as a relatively neutral force in the Tunisian uprisings, and the Egyptian army was able to play a major role in directing events, in the Libyan case there was no comparable institution that could intervene. It was clear, therefore, that it was going to be a case of Qadhafi and his security forces against the people. As Belhaj commented, 'We agreed first that the revolution would take place; secondly that Qadhafi will suppress the revolution; and thirdly that the uprising may start, but because of Qadhafi's repression would not succeed immediately and would take a long time.'[22] The movement was also doubtful about whether the Libyans would go as far as to demand Qadhafi's departure, and believed the protestors might limit themselves to calling for reform only.

Given its problematic relationship to the idea of revolution, the Brotherhood seems to have decided at this point that it would support the uprisings but not a full-scale revolution. As Belhaj told the *Al-Hayat* newspaper, 'We thought it more likely that the demands would be to increase reforms but not to bring down the regime. And frankly we entered the revolution with the aim of raising the ceiling of the demands but not of changing the regime. That was our stance at the end of January.'[23] Indeed, the movement seems to have decided to play it safe, agreeing that it would focus its efforts on 'how to help people, the fleeing and the injured.'[24] It also decided to open two 'operation chambers', one in Tunisia and the other in Egypt in order to get medicines and humanitarian aid into the country.[25] The Brotherhood began buying satellite thuraya telephones, too, that it could smuggle them into the country, believing correctly that the regime would cut communication lines once the uprisings began.

But at the same time as positioning itself to support those who chose to rise up against Qadhafi, the Brotherhood seems to still have had some hope that something could be worked out with the regime. This appears to have been driven in part by its desire to avoid bloodshed but was also tied up with its natural aversion to revolution. To this end the movement turned once again to Saif

Al-Islam and tried to impress upon him the need to adopt a proper reform programme for Libya. According to senior Brotherhood member, Salim Sheikhi, three weeks before the revolution the movement sent a letter to Saif Al-Islam laying out a 'genuine reform agenda' for the country and asking him to 'call for elections, write a constitution and amend laws and other things.'[26] On 5 February the Brotherhood published a statement arising out of its general assembly meeting in Zurich, calling on the regime to 'hold a comprehensive national conference adopting the demands of the Libyans' and to 'respect the people's rights in deciding their fate'.[27]

It is clear, therefore, that even at this late stage the Brotherhood's instinct was to try to avert rather than initiate or encourage revolution, even if this meant providing oxygen to one of the most authoritarian regimes in the region. For all that Saif Al-Islam may have been genuinely more open and reform-minded than his father, there was little doubt that his commitment to reform had been skin-deep at best. By the late 2000s, Saif Al-Islam had effectively abandoned his reformist projects, including his initiative to write a constitution for Libya, declaring in 2007 that there were four red lines that could not be crossed – one of which was Muammar Qadhafi.[28] But the regime's lack of real commitment to reform, let alone democratic principles, did not seem to matter to the Brotherhood, which clearly felt more comfortable striking some kind of deal with Saif Al-Islam than it did with full-blown revolution, and for whom securing space to operate was the paramount concern. This was all the more surprising given that the conditions seemed ripe to overthrow Qadhafi. Not only had a kind of dress-rehearsal been carried out through the housing protests mentioned above: both of Libya's neighbours had gone down the revolutionary path, successfully overthrowing dictatorial regimes. Even so, the Libyan Brotherhood was still reticent about striking a deadly blow to the regime that had suppressed it so brutally for so many decades.

As it was, the Brotherhood's overture to Saif Al-Islam did not achieve the desired results and, according to Sheikhi, 'Saif Al-Islam responded to the messenger with sarcasm and rejection and looked down his nose.'[29] But this did not deter another key figure associated closely with the Brotherhood from making another appeal to the young Qadhafi. This figure was Dr Ali Salabi, an Islamic scholar who resided in Qatar, having escaped from Libya. The exact nature of Salabi's relationship to the Brotherhood remains ambiguous, some arguing that he was once part of it and others insisting that he has always been independent. However, Salabi's way of thinking was certainly close to the Brotherhood's, and he came from the same reformist Islamist current.[30]

On 4 February Salabi travelled from Qatar to Tripoli, where he held a meeting with Brotherhood member Abdelrazzak Al-Aradi, and former higher education minister, Aqeel Mohamed Aqeel (who was one of Al-Aradi's relatives). Salabi impressed upon Aqeel the importance of meeting Saif Al-Islam to convince him to do something to avert the crisis, urging him that '[p]reventing Libyan blood from being spilled is a necessity. If he [Saif Al-Islam] doesn't respond then no one can blame us.'[31] Aqeel agreed, and arranged a meeting for Salabi at which he put a number of demands to Saif Al-Islam. These were very similar to the demands already put to the young Qadhafi by the Brotherhood in its earlier letter. They included a demand that a proper constitution be drafted; that Libyans be permitted to form NGOs and carry out political work; and that opposition parties and currents be accepted. Salabi also told Saif Al-Islam that he had encountered a degree of acceptance among some Libyan opposition currents, including those in Western countries, and that these currents wanted him to take over from his father.[32] Once again, therefore, the driving force behind this overture to the regime seemed to be to find a solution that would allow the Islamist current to operate inside Libya, rather than any genuine desire for reform or democratisation.

Although Salabi emerged from the meeting declaring it to have been a success, he was called back the next day. This time Saif al-Islam was in the company of a group of members of the Qadhafi regime. Most rejected Salabi's demands outright, while some shouted at him to 'get out', and others emphasised that they would have no problem in killing off a revolution if one started.

But this was not to be the last of the Islamists' attempts to reach out to Saif Al-Islam. On 15 February the families of the victims of the 1996 Abu Slim prison massacre gathered in Benghazi to protest at the arrest of their lawyer, Fathi Terbil, who had been seized by security forces earlier that day. They were joined by hundreds of other protestors, and it looked as though the uprisings that had been planned for 17 February were erupting ahead of schedule. This clearly prompted panic on the part of Al-Aradi, who rushed to Aqeel's house to plead with him to make another appeal to Saif Al-Islam. Aqeel has noted how Al-Aradi was agitated, remarking that he drank only one cup of green tea rather than his habitual two, and how he begged, 'Please Dr Aqeel, contact Saif [Al-Islam] Qadhafi and speak to him about stopping the blood that will be spilled in Libya if he doesn't do anything to reform. If he doesn't stop it I swear that Libya will be destroyed and anyone who survives being killed directly will drown in the blood.'[33]

But such pleading was in vain. By 17 February Benghazi was gripped by protests, and, as the Brotherhood had predicted, things very quickly turned violent. Thirteen people were killed and more than 200 injured in Benghazi's Jamal Nasser Street on that day alone, as security forces opened fire on protestors. There were deaths in other eastern towns, too, where locals had also risen up. On 18 February more people were killed, including some who were shot dead when security forces opened fire on mourners attending the funerals of those killed the previous day. But the more the regime attacked, the more defiant the crowds became, and it was clear that the protests were going to continue. There were also signs that the west of Libya might follow suit. On 19 February there was a protest in Zawia to the west of the capital, as well as clashes in Misrata and a limited attempt at a demonstration in Tripoli itself.

With things moving so quickly, the Brotherhood held another meeting in Switzerland on 19 February. This time the stakes were higher. The revolution it had felt so ambivalent about had begun, and the regime had started attacking its people. With all hopes of the regime responding positively to its demands for reform now abandoned, the Brotherhood concentrated its mind on whether to stick with its traditional reformist stance or to throw in its lot with the revolution. According to Belhaj, the outcome was a resounding: 'We are with the revolution.'[34] Or, in the words of Salim Sheikhi, the Brotherhood decided, 'We are joining the people.'[35] Belhaj also explained that it was when the regime had resorted to violence that the movement decided it could no longer demand reform only, but had to 'join the people'.[36]

At this stage, some of the thinking inside the movement was running even further ahead. As Mohamed Abdulmalek recalled, 'Suddenly one day, the 17 February, we started actually thinking about the possibility of ruling Libya, of gaining power in Libya. That was a big jump.'[37] Yet it was too early for such thoughts at this stage, and the Brotherhood instead focused its energies on supporting the uprisings as best it could. Brotherhood-aligned preachers urged Libyans to join the protests, while the movement set up more operations cells in Britain and Switzerland. It also turned to its external allies for assistance. Most importantly, it looked to Qatar. Shortly after the uprisings broke out, Belhaj travelled to Doha to establish a media office in co-operation with the Al-Jazeera channel. According to Salim Sheikhi, much of the material aired on Al-Jazeera as the revolution unfolded came directly from the movement. 'If any videotape that came from Libya wasn't from the Muslim Brotherhood' he explained, 'then Al-Jazeera had to check that it was genuine. But anything from us they put on immediately.'[38]

From Qatar, Belhaj travelled by military plane to Egypt, from where he went on into Benghazi, arriving on 1 March 2011, ready to start distributing humanitarian assistance.[39] But it was not only humanitarian aid that the Brotherhood was supplying. Once the uprisings had turned violent, the Brotherhood also sought to send weapons to the rebels on the front lines. As Belhaj explained, 'We found a way to buy weapons in the east', justifying its actions by asserting that, while it was uncomfortable about using violence, it 'knew Qadhafi's brutality'.[40] Indeed, having spent decades trying to distance itself from violence, this was a difficult call for the movement. However, it also worked to try to get weapons into Tripoli, which was still under tight control. As Belhaj recalled, 'It was very risky especially inside Tripoli ... We had weapons coming from everywhere. From Qatar, the UAE and others. But how to send these weapons to Tripoli?'[41] The movement ended up smuggling stashes of weapons into the capital by boat – often using small fishing boats that moved at night.

Immediately after his arrival in Benghazi, Belhaj was tasked with chairing a meeting of the Brotherhood in the east, at which the question of whether or not to join the front lines – which by now had shifted outside Benghazi to other towns and areas – was the main point of discussion. He explained, 'We left the question open and let individuals decide for themselves. Whoever wants to fight, let him fight and we can help. Whoever wants a different role, let him do it too. We thought that helping people with aid or with fighting, both were of equal importance.'[42] This is exactly the same stance that the Muslim Brotherhood took in the Afghanistan jihad of the 1980s. Former Egyptian brother Kemal Helbawy, who was in charge of the Brotherhood's activities in Afghanistan and Pakistan at the time, explained that the Brotherhood did not fight en masse as an organisation, but that '[i]f any Muslim brother decided to fight on his own, then no one would stop him'.[43]

So it was that some Libyan brothers took part in the fighting, but, as Belhaj explained, 'They did not go as a group, and we did not set up our own military brigade. We did not set up a brigade, as we didn't have a military mentality.'[44] According to Saleh Shamek, Brotherhood members joined rebel brigades in Benghazi, Ajdabia and Tobruk.[45] They also joined the front lines in Misrata, where, because of the ferocity of the fight, local residents pulled together and took up arms against the regime. Indeed, at this stage things were not yet really divided along ideological lines, and Libyans from their own towns came together to try to defeat the regime. As

Belhaj explained, 'In the beginning there were no specific brigades that followed any particular ideology. People were united, and so you join to fight the regime.'[46]

But the Brotherhood became closely linked to one military force that was to evolve into one of the most prominent Islamist brigades in the east. This was the Martyrs of the 17 February Brigade, led by revolutionary commander and Brotherhood member Fawzi Abu Katif. Abu Katif, an oil engineer in the Arabian Gulf Oil Company (Agoco), established this brigade at the end of February after he and a group of revolutionary leaders and officers who had defected from Qadhafi's military came together to try to secure Benghazi.[47] As Belhaj tells it, he and a group of brothers were having a meeting in Benghazi when Abu Katif and three men entered the room. Abu Katif told the group that he had been through the whole of Benghazi and found it to be devoid of security, and was therefore setting up a security force to protect the city.[48] When the Brotherhood asked him what he needed, Abu Katif responded: 'I have my car and three men with me. I have one Kalashnikov, but I need three.'[49] This prompted Brotherhood member Ounis Mabrouk to make a phone call to inquire about the price of a Kalashnikov. After being quoted 3,500 Libyan dinars (US$2,500), the Brotherhood proceeded to purchase three Kalashnikovs for the brigade.

This brigade was to expand considerably after Ismail Salabi, Ali Salabi's brother and a member of the LIFG, joined along with a group of jihadist elements. Despite starting out with the aim of protecting Benghazi, the force soon moved to the front lines. But the 17 February Brigade cannot be considered a Brotherhood brigade. Rather, it comprised an array of individuals of different orientations, and also operated independently. Or, in Abu Katif's words, 'No one gave us orders.'[50]

But toppling the regime was to be a far harder and longer battle than anyone could have predicted. The initial euphoria was soon dashed when, in early March, Qadhafi's forces launched a major counter-offensive, succeeding in retaking a number of towns and areas in the east, including Ajdabia. As Qadhafi's forces began to close in on Benghazi, it was looking as though it would be only a matter of time before Libya's attempt to join the Arab Spring would be quashed. It was at this point that Qadhafi gave his famous blood-curdling speech, threatening to hunt down the rebels in Benghazi street by street.

But it was also at this point that the international community stepped in. On 17 March the UN Security Council voted to impose a no-fly zone over Libya and to take 'all necessary measures' to protect civilians. Two days later, French, British and US military forces launched Operation Odyssey Dawn, aimed at enforcing the no-fly zone, and started hitting regime targets. On 24 March, NATO announced that it was taking over the operation, and at the end of the month declared that it had started Operation Unified Protector, which included an arms embargo, a no-fly zone, and 'actions to protect civilians and civilian centres'. Although many Islamist elements, including Ali Salabi, were openly hostile to such intervention, the Libyan Brotherhood did not oppose it, emphasising that it was being carried out to protect civilians.[51] However, it was the entry of NATO that would shift the balance of power back towards the rebels, although there was still to be a long-drawn-out battle before Qadhafi was finally overthrown.

Brotherhood as Political Actor

From the earliest days of the uprisings, the rebels realised that they needed to establish some sort of political body that could run the areas that had already been liberated from Qadhafi's forces, but could also steer the political transition. More importantly, this new body could serve as a conduit for dealings with the international community. On 5 March, therefore, the rebels announced the creation of the National Transitional Council, which they had established at the end of February. This council was headed by Mustafa Abdeljalil a former justice minister in the Qadhafi regime who defected to the rebels almost immediately after the uprisings began. Despite having been part of the regime, Abdeljalil was considered an appropriate choice to head up this new body, not least because, with his traditional and conservative outlook, as well as his tribal roots in the east, he was widely viewed as being quintessentially Libyan. He had also clashed publicly with the regime on a number of occasions, including over its refusal to release militant Islamist prisoners who had served their sentences.

Aside from Abdeljalil, the thirteen initial members of this new NTC (whose names, for security reasons, were not all revealed) comprised mainly academics, lawyers and human rights activists, the majority of whom had been active in and around the margins of Saif Al-Islam's reformist project. Notably, the NTC included a number of defectors from the Qadhafi regime, such as Mahmoud Jibril, who had been head of Libya's Planning Board and who was chosen to head up the NTC's Executive Board, which was also announced in March; and Ali Al-Issawi, a former ambassador to India, who was made deputy of the same board. The NTC was therefore a hotchpotch of individuals, many of whom had no real experience of running anything, let alone what was starting to look increasingly like a government in waiting.

But what was particularly striking about this new body was that it did not contain a single Islamist in its ranks, but was composed largely of those with a more liberal orientation. Jibril noted that, until the middle of April 2011, 'no one in the NTC even had a relationship with the Islamic current'.[52] The Brotherhood's exclusion from this new body came as a shock to the movement itself. As Sheikhi commented, 'When the NTC was formed we had no idea about it.'[53] Being excluded in this way was a major blow, given that the Brotherhood had assumed it would be part of the country's political future. The movement had already issued a statement at the end of February declaring that any new government should comprise those who were leading the revolution on the ground, and stating that its composition should not be influenced by tribal or regional considerations. The statement also asserted that those who had taken part in the 1969 coup with Qadhafi should be excluded from office. The Brotherhood was therefore already laying down who should and should not be part of Libya's political scene before it had even evolved.

The announcement of the formation of the NTC therefore left the Brotherhood feeling as though it had been the victim of some kind of coup by liberal forces, many of whom had links to the former regime. It therefore pulled together with other Islamist strands, including Salabi, to try to formulate a united response. In March the Islamist current issued a 'National Charter', laying out its vision for the future of Libya and its transition. This was a direct response to the NTC's issuing of a document titled 'Vision of a Democratic Libya' in the same month. The NTC document, which was meant largely for Western consumption, set out the NTC's commitment to creating a modern, pluralistic and free Libya. But this vision was notably silent on what role religion should play in the new Libyan state.

Unsurprisingly, the Islamist charter that was signed by Brotherhood member Salim Al-Sheikhi was forthcoming on this issue, including the assertion: 'The religion of the state is Islam and the principle of Islamic Sharia is the source of its legislation.' Aside from this, however, there was little to distinguish the document in terms of its overall aims and principles from the NTC's vision, and both stressed their commitment to pluralism and the peaceful alternation of power. But the Islamists' charter was clear about one thing. It specified that the NTC, which by this point had already been recognised by France, should be dissolved upon liberation and replaced by a General National Congress, which would include representatives from all local councils – an area in which the Islamists, and the Brotherhood in particular, had already moved to implant themselves.[54]

From this very early stage, therefore, the Islamists were clear that the group of liberal elements who had formed the NTC should not be in the driving seat once the regime was toppled. Salabi, meanwhile, appeared on Al-Jazeera on 28 March, the day before the NTC was due to present its vision to the major London conference on Libya, and condemned the NTC, accusing it of being illegitimate because it had not been formed according to 'allegiance' – or in other words, it had not been chosen by the Libyan people.[55]

A few days later, fifteen Libyan Islamists convened in Istanbul for a three-day meeting led by Ali Salabi, to discuss how they should proceed. Present at the meeting were Brotherhood representatives Alamin Belhaj, Abdelrazzak Al-Aradi and Nizar Kawan, and a number of LIFG representatives, including Muftah Dawudi. Although the participants agreed that 'secular' elements were trying to take over the political framework of the revolution,[56] they determined that the best course of action would be to 'support the NTC and not to confront it'.[57] However, they agreed that they should push to get themselves represented inside this new political body. They agreed, too, to establish their own civil society organisation, the National Gathering, which they expected would later become a political party.[58] Indeed, at this point the Brotherhood, with its limited strength, was more than happy to link itself to these other Islamist currents, and to consider establishing a political party with them.

But this National Gathering did not get very far, mainly because the different strands of the Islamist opposition were too preoccupied with other things – not the least of which, as far as the more militant elements were concerned, was the fight to topple the Qadhafi regime.[59] More importantly, it was not long before the Brotherhood had succeeded in elbowing its way onto the NTC. As it turned out, it did not have to work very hard in order to do so. The NTC was having problems being accepted as a truly representative body, including by some of the Western powers to which it looked for support. This was partly because, with Tripoli still in Qadhafi's grip, the NTC was inevitably an eastern-dominated body. This was something to which the towns of Misrata and Zintan, which by this point had also broken free of Qadhafi's hold, had objected. But it was also because the NTC was lacking Islamist representation. According to Belhaj, Western nations 'wanted to trust the NTC, and in order to recognise it they wanted a representative body for

Libya. There were no Islamists in the NTC, and therefore it did not represent Libya.'[60] Jibril, meanwhile, has argued that the West 'got the idea that the presence of a moderate Islamic power in North Africa is the main guarantee and the most active weapon to confront extremism ... That formula is very attractive, and it helps shift the suspicion that the West is hostile to Islam.'[61]

Sometime around the start of May, therefore, Abdeljalil informed the Brotherhood that he wanted two representatives from the movement to join the NTC. As one of the Brotherhood's most senior leaders, Belhaj was an obvious choice. He was also attractive to the NTC because he came from Tripoli. Belhaj therefore joined the NTC on 17 May along with Al-Aradi, who also represented Tripoli.

The Brotherhood also succeeded in securing some representation for itself on the NTC's Executive Board, which acted like a government, and was reformulated in May. Abdullah Shamia, a senior Brotherhood member and economics professor, took charge of the economy portfolio, while Salim Sheikhi was appointed to head up the Awqaf (religious affairs and endowments) portfolio. Thanks partly to pressure from external powers, but also to its belief that it had the right to play a role in the transition, the Brotherhood thus ended up securing a presence in the country's new political structures that far outweighed its influence on the ground.

This was not all. Having initially been excluded from the NTC, the Brotherhood worked to secure a foothold in the local councils that were being formed in some of the towns that had broken free from Qadhafi's rule. Through its organising power, the Brotherhood succeeded in taking the majority of seats in the Benghazi local council, and more than half in Misrata. As Belhaj explained of the setting-up of the Benghazi local council, 'Our brothers participated in that. Half of the local council were brothers. We were there right from the beginning.'[62] The Brotherhood also proved itself to be adept at working through these councils. As one observer at a local council in the west of the country observed, 'The Ikhwan would come to the meetings of the council and vote as a single bloc. They were the single most powerful grouping present.'[63]

But what is striking is that, for all its involvement in these emergent political structures, even at this stage the Brotherhood appears still to have been open to the possibility of striking some sort of deal with the regime. Sometime in June, in a reflection of the regime's increasingly desperate situation, Qadhafi's general secretary (prime minister) Baghdadi Mahmoud stated at a press conference that the regime was 'ready for dialogue with all structures that represent the whole of Libya'.[64] Controversially, Mahmoudi also revealed that the regime was already in dialogue with the opposition, and that a series of meetings had taken place in Egypt, France, Norway and Tunisia.[65]

Mahmoudi's revelations came as a bombshell. Abdeljalil moved quickly to deny the claims, as did Suleiman Abdelkader, who in a statement to the *Asharq Al-Awsat* newspaper accused Mahmoudi of trying to 'drive a wedge in the national ranks'.[66] Abdelkader also insisted that there could be no dialogue without the 'departure of Qadhafi, his sons, and his henchmen from Libya', adding that 'any call for dialogue must be through the legitimate representative of the Libyan people, namely the NTC'.[67]

Yet, despite the denials, Ali Salabi had in fact been engaging with the regime. In May he had held a meeting in Cairo with two regime representatives, Aqeel and Abu Zeid Dorda, a former Libyan ambassador to Italy. Among the topics discussed was the possibility of establishing a joint national committee between the regime and the rebels that would run the transitional period. Discussions also focused on trying to launch a dialogue to work out a new political system and constitutional framework.

The extent to which this and other similar meetings had been sanctioned by the NTC remains unclear. Aqeel asserts that, during the Cairo meeting, he asked Salabi whether he had been entrusted by the NTC to enter into such talks. Salabi responded that he had indeed been given the go-ahead by the NTC, and that Abdeljalil had given his consent to the meeting. Salabi also claimed that he had the consent of Suleiman Abdelkader, as well as Brotherhood members Nizar Kawan, Ismail Gritli and Abdullah Zwai.[68] He claimed, too, that the meetings had been approved by other parts of the Islamist current, including members of the jihadist faction including Abdelhakim Belhaj and Muftah Dawadi (LIFG).[69] However, this dialogue had certainly not been sanctioned by some elements within the NTC. Mahmoud Jibril claims that he only learned of it when Baghdadi Mahmoudi gave his press conference, and that he rushed to Abdeljalil to ask whether he knew anything about it – which the NTC leader acknowledged that he did.[70] This initiative was thus looking decidedly like an Islamist attempt to reach out to the regime that had the backing of Abdeljalil.

Although the extent of the Brotherhood's role in this dialogue is still not entirely clear, the movement seems at the very least to have had no serious objections to the principle of seeking a compromise with the regime. The Brotherhood appears to have felt no contradiction in its being part of the NTC, which had been explicit in its aspirations for a modern democratic state, while at the same time being open to striking a deal with a regime that represented the very antithesis of these principles. Although it would be unfair to ignore the Brotherhood's seemingly genuine desire to prevent further bloodshed, one cannot help but wonder whether this dialogue, and the exclusion from it of liberal forces inside the NTC, was a bid by the movement to manoeuvre itself to the centre of some sort of transitional deal that would place it in the driving seat. Just as the Egyptian Brotherhood was more than willing to cut short the revolution in order to position itself advantageously for the transition, the Libyan Islamist current, including the Brotherhood, could arguably be accused of attempting something similar. This was certainly how it appeared to some of the more liberal elements in the NTC, who accused the Islamists of using these talks to try to take over.

But this was not to be. After Mahmoudi's revelations to the press the dialogue broke down, and the fighting continued. At the end of August Tripoli finally fell to rebel forces, and as Libyan army units melted away, Qadhafi and his family fled the capital. This came just a few weeks after the NTC announced its Constitutional

Declaration, which was to serve as a legal framework for the transition. This declaration, issued on 3 August, stipulated that after liberation the NTC should be reformulated to include representatives from all local councils, and that it should oversee elections to a 200-seat General National Congress. While the NTC agreed on this formula, there were some disgruntled elements who saw in it echoes of the Islamists' National Charter, which had first proposed the establishment of such a congress to replace the NTC.

Indeed, the polarisation between liberal and Islamist currents inside the NTC was already deepening. This was partly because the Islamists had bolstered their presence through the inclusion of local council representatives, who joined the NTC as and when their towns were liberated. It was also because the Brotherhood had found some Islamist-leaning allies inside the NTC, thereby bolstering its stance. There were also accusations that Abdeljalil had a strong sympathy for the Brotherhood and its ideology. Jibril claimed that Abdeljalil was 'biased and sympathised with the Muslim Brotherhood', explaining how he and other liberal-minded figures in the NTC had tried unsuccessfully to open his eyes to the fact.[71] However, at this point the divisions between the two camps were still relatively contained, and had not yet reached the cataclysmic levels of antagonism that were to develop as the transition progressed, and would leave Libya with two competing centres of government authority.

For the Brotherhood, though, re-entry into Libya had been a success. By the time of Qadhafi's unceremonious killing in October 2011, the movement had come almost out of nowhere to position itself as a key political actor. More importantly, the terrain was now open to the Brotherhood for the first time in more than four decades, and the traditional nature of Libyan society, which was conservative even by regional standards, made it seem ripe for the Brotherhood's reactionary ideology. The fact that the whole region seemed to be 'going Islamist' only added to the sense that it would be only a matter of time before Libya could fill in the blank between Egypt and Tunisia to create a bloc of Islamic republics that would change the face of North Africa and beyond. It seemed, therefore, as though the Brotherhood had not only emerged from the shadows, but transformed itself into a serious political player that would have a major role in steering Libya's transition.

FIVE

OUT IN THE OPEN

The end of more than four decades of rule by Qadhafi was a momentous occasion for Libya and its people. For the Brotherhood it was particularly moving. For members of a movement that had been repressed and forced out of the country for so long, the toppling of the Qadhafi regime marked the start of a whole new era, in which it could finally operate freely on Libyan soil. The Brotherhood was clear from the beginning that it wanted to play a part in Libya's political future, and moved quickly to establish a political party, the Justice and Construction Party (JCP), in order to contest the country's first democratic elections in decades. Although the movement was realistic enough to know that it would not sweep the board, as its counterparts in Egypt and Tunisia had done, the Brotherhood's unifying ideology made it appear able to transcend the chaos and fragmentation that had taken hold. In contrast to the other political forces and alliances that were being hurriedly cobbled together at the time, the Brotherhood, with its history and tradition, looked to be the only force that could offer a truly national solution in a broken landscape. The time appeared even more propitious for the Brotherhood, which finally seemed to have achieved international acceptance. At long last, the international community, despite its misgivings, was ready to engage with the Brotherhood as a mainstream political actor. In addition, the Brotherhood had the backing of two key external powers, Qatar and Turkey, bolstering it further through their political and financial support. The Brotherhood, it seemed, was ready, if not to ride the crest of a wave, at least to become a major force in Libya's future.

But, when it came to it, the July 2012 elections were to prove hugely disappointing for the Brotherhood. The JCP secured only seventeen of the eighty seats allocated to political parties in the 200-seat General National Congress (parliament), while the more liberal-leaning grouping of more than fifty NGOs and political forces, the National Forces Alliance (NFA), took thirty-nine seats, putting it in first place. Being outflanked by the liberals – and in particular by the Brotherhood's rival, NFA leader Mahmoud Jibril – was a very bitter pill for the Brotherhood to have to swallow.

These election results meant that the Brotherhood had to face up to the fact that it lacked any real popular mandate inside the country. For many Libyans, the movement was still considered an outsider – a force to be wary of rather than embraced. While An-Nahda leader Rachid Ghannouchi had returned to Tunisia, after decades in exile, to a rapturous hero's welcome, the Libyan Brotherhood appeared to have returned to Libya by the back door. And in contrast to An-Nahda, which had banked up significant symbolic capital over the decades, the Libyan movement was widely regarded with suspicion rather than as a symbol of purity, authenticity and salvation. Libya's new heroes were not members of the Brotherhood, but the conflict-hardened revolutionaries who had risked their lives on the battlefield to bring about change.

But it was not only in the political arena that the Brotherhood found itself outflanked. Even in the religious field it struggled to assert itself, and almost from the start was dwarfed by other Islamic forces. The array of jihadists in their different hues, the various Salafist currents that had sprung up, and the ultra-orthodox official religious establishment and its hard-line mufti, Sheikh Sadiq Al-Gharianni, were all brought to the centre of the political stage, leaving the Brotherhood as just one link in a long chain of Islamist factions. At the same time, there was no space for the kinds of ideological debate over identity politics that were polarising societies in Egypt and Tunisia, and had been harnessed by the Egyptian Brotherhood and An-Nahda, respectively, in the service of their own cause. Given the conservative nature of the Libyan population, such debates hardly even raised their heads. The

Brotherhood therefore struggled to distinguish itself ideologically, while its Islamicisation project appeared to be moot.

The Brotherhood therefore had to digest the fact that Libya's future was not going to rest in its hands, and that it was just one political and religious actor among many. Yet it was not about to let the moment of political opportunity slip through its fingers. It continued to believe that it should play a powerful role in the newly emergent political arena, and, on the basis of the election results, clearly considered itself to be the county's second political power. It therefore ploughed on in the political realm, still trying to punch above its true weight.

But the Libyan Brotherhood proved just as inept at politics as its Egyptian counterpart. If the Egyptians failed to come to terms with consensus politics, the corresponding failure of the Libyans was spectacular. The Libyan Brotherhood's aversion to the liberal or so-called 'civil' political current was so intense that it preferred to enter into a marriage of convenience with the most radical of Islamist and revolutionary elements rather than work with these liberal components in any constructive fashion. Its reasons for doing so were complex, and related to a host of factors – including the liberal current's association with individuals linked to the Qadhafi regime. But they were also a product of the fact that the Brotherhood placed the desire for power as well as ideological affiliation above the kind of pragmatic politics that the movement had gained a reputation for internationally, and that An-Nahda was to go on to employ with such success. Indeed, the Libyan Brotherhood's trajectory after the revolution showed no causal relationship between inclusion in the political process and moderation. Rather, having an open playing field in which to operate led the movement to ally itself with some of the most extreme elements, for whom revolutionary legitimacy was all.

Singling out the Brotherhood in this way is somewhat unfair, given that other political players acted little differently. Its more liberal opponents also played dirty politics and aligned themselves with armed groups and antidemocratic forces. In fact, there has been little in the way of 'normal politics' practised across the board in Libya since the fall of the Qadhafi regime, reflecting the absence of political culture resulting from his forty-year rule. All sides have indulged in the crudest form of zero-sum politics, using the country's new political institutions as little more than arenas to press for their own demands. Both sides have also slipped into employing crude narratives, the Islamist camp castigating their liberal opponents as 'Azlam Qadhafi' ('Qadhafi's men') and the liberals denouncing the Islamists as 'terrorists'. Politics in the new Libya has been boiled down to the crudest sort of struggle for territorial and institutional control.

But, perhaps most importantly, none of the political institutions created since the fall of the Qadhafi regime has been able to gain any real control on the ground. When Qadhafi fell, the centre of power fell with him, and the thousands of brigades and militias that sprang up during and in the aftermath of the conflict continued to be the country's real powerbrokers. Right from the start, therefore, these revolutionary forces dwarfed the emergent political structures, rendering them all but impotent before they had even begun to operate. The Libyan Brotherhood's experience beyond the Arab Spring has continued, therefore, to be one of a struggle for relevance and recognition.

Into the Political Arena

In November 2011 the Libyan Brotherhood held its first public meeting on Libyan soil. More than 700 individuals attended the gathering in a large wedding hall in Benghazi. As if to press home the point that this was a movement that was part of something bigger than just Libya, guest speakers from An-Nahda as well as the banned Syrian Muslim Brotherhood gave speeches at the event. Hosting these international speakers was also the movement's way of portraying itself as being part of the revolutionary spirit that had gripped the region with the Arab Spring.

The mood was optimistic and the talk was promising. 'Rebuilding Libya is not a task for one group or one party but for everyone, based on their ability', declared Suleiman Abdelkader.[1] He also affirmed: 'We don't want to replace one tyranny with another. All together, we want to build a civil society that uses moderate Islam in its daily life ... our shared task is to protect Libya, to talk to each other instead of fighting.'[2] The Libyan Brotherhood was clearly keen to show that it was fully on board with the Brotherhood's latest global discourse, which portrayed the movement as fully committed to democracy and a civil state and as ready to work with others for the common good.

Such talk belied the very real struggle that was already being played out behind the scenes in Libya's political arena. As Belhaj explained, 'After liberation we were faced with running a state. ... We started to talk about elections, and here every side started fearing the others. That means whatever you propose may be misinterpreted by others. We had aggressive people from both sides, and so the temperature started rising.'[3] Salabi had also already caused a storm of controversy in September when he publicly accused Mahmoud Jibril and his followers of being 'extreme secularists', and Libya's 'tyrants' in-waiting.

Yet this was a moment of celebration, and also a chance for the Brotherhood to get its house in order. The movement decided to renew the activities of its Shura Council, and as a reflection of the new openness expanded it from eleven members to thirty.[4] It also elected a new leader, Bashir Al-Kebti taking over from Suleiman Abdelkader. An accountant by profession, Al-Kebti, who was born in Benghazi and had spent over thirty years in exile in the United States, was hardly a well-known personality.[5] If the Egyptian Brotherhood was lacking in scholars and charismatic leaders, the Libyan Brotherhood was even more deficient in this respect. However, the Brotherhood made much of the fact that it was now operating out in the open, presenting its new leadership to the public.

The Brotherhood also announced that it was intending to set

up a political party, prompting a major debate on what kind of party to establish. Some brothers favoured transforming the *jama'a* ('movement') into a political party as An-Nahda had done decades before; others preferred the idea of following the Jordanian example and setting up a separate political party, but with the movement retaining overall control of its decisions; while a third group wanted to do as the Egyptians had done, and create what purported to be an entirely separate party. After lengthy discussions, almost 70 per cent of members present at the November conference supported the last option, and called for establishing a separate party that would be open for anyone to join.[6] As Al-Kebti explained, 'The Muslim Brotherhood, in partnership with others, can form a national political party with an Islamic reference.'[7]

However, Al-Kebti added that 'this partnership should be on an individual basis and not on a bloc basis'[8]. This was not quite what others in the Islamist camp had been expecting. At the April meeting in Istanbul (see Chapter Three), Libyan Islamists had come together under Salabi's leadership, creating the 'National Gathering' as a precursor to an Islamist political party. Although this National Gathering had all but dissolved as the various groups had become tied up with their own preoccupations, the idea that these groups would pool their resources to create an Islamist political party with which to contest the elections retained some currency. But Al-Kebti's comments were to shatter this possibility. It was evident from his remarks that the movement was now intent on having its own party, which other Islamists would be welcome to join only on an individual basis. Thus, while the Brotherhood had, out of necessity, harnessed itself to a bigger Islamist force during the revolution, now that the revolution was over, it was ready to drop these other forces, in the belief that it should be the dominant force. Despite its long absence from the country, the movement seems to have believed that politics was its own domain, and that it was somehow the mother group of Islamist political movements, and should thus go it alone.

This attitude provoked serious resentment among other Islamist groups, including those who had been part of the Libyan Islamic Fighting Group (LIFG), which had established the Libyan Islamic Movement for Change, and who in January issued a statement claiming that the Brotherhood was trying to control the process of establishing a political party. This did not go down well with the Brotherhood. Alamin Belhaj recounts how he confronted two LIFG members during a meeting, telling them: 'If this statement is true it means that we cannot work together ... A party should not be created if there is already a suspicious air.'[9] One former LIFG member claimed that the Brotherhood was more explicit, telling Al-Salabi something to the effect that its party was like a car that other Islamists were not going to get the chance to drive, but in which they could have a ride in the back seat only.[10]

The Brotherhood, therefore, proceeded to create its own party, Belhaj explaining: 'I invited people [to join] but not the LIFG, as we could not work with them.'[11] In March 2012 the Brotherhood duly launched the Justice and Construction Party (JCP), electing Mohamed Sawan as its leader. A sociology graduate and former political prisoner from Misrata, who had been released from prison under Saif Al-Islam's 'Reform and Repent' programme in 2006, Sawan was little known inside Libya, though he was the head of the Brotherhood's Shura Council when he left prison.

Under Sawan's stewardship the JCP issued its political programme. The platform was typical, trotting out the usual phrases about establishing a civil state that 'guarantees the rule of democracy and peaceful transfer of power'.[12] As with the Egyptian movement, it was as if the Brotherhood had swallowed a dictionary of all the latest governance buzzwords and bolted them together, without any real substance to underpin them.

Notably, however, the programme stressed that the democracy it sought was based on the constitution being drafted in accordance with 'the beliefs of the Libyan people and community values ... which consider Islamic Sharia as the main source of legislation'. Such an assertion was hardly controversial in the Libyan context. Unlike in Egypt or Tunisia, where the role that Sharia should play was a major point of debate, in Libya the subject caused hardly a ripple. The almost complete absence of nationalist or secularist forces, the lack of a significant non-Islamist minority, and Libyans' innate conservativism all meant that there was a broad acceptance inside Libya that Sharia should be the main source of legislation. In his first public speech in Tripoli, in September 2011, the head of the NTC, Mustafa Abdeljalil, confidently declared: 'We seek a state of law, prosperity and one where sharia is the main source of legislation'.[13] His assertion provoked no real response inside Libya. Even the liberal-leaning NFA campaigned on a platform that called for legislation to be based on Sharia. Thus, while in neighbouring countries the Brotherhood could present itself as a defender of Islam and as the voice of authenticity, the Libyan Brotherhood had no comparable role to play.

But the Brotherhood's programme still displayed the movement's traditional preoccupation with reforming the individual and the family. It reiterated, for example, the importance of 'paying special attention to the family and protecting it from disintegration' and 'facilitating access to marriage by spreading Islamic values and norms, fighting social corruption, and promoting social institutions that sponsor this aspect'.[14] Just like the Brotherhood in Egypt, the Libyan movement clearly equated being a political actor with safeguarding morality through intervention in the private sphere.

As to the nature of the relationship between the party and the movement, the Brotherhood insisted that the two entities were separate and that its members made up only 10 per cent of the overall membership of the party.[15] The movement was certainly aware of the need to ensure that the JCP could not be accused of being the Brotherhood's political arm. As the Brotherhood's representative in Europe, Mohamed Abdulmalik, explained, 'a large number of the leadership [of the Brotherhood] became members of the political party. But because we were serious about the independence issue we saw this as a conflict of interests. Therefore, some individuals were asked to leave the leadership of the party and others were asked to leave their leadership positions in the *jama'a*.'[16]

But members of the Brotherhood have conceded that the issue was not unproblematic. As Abdulmalik himself acknowledged, 'The relationship is not clear and we are still working on that ... the problem we are facing is where the role of the *jama'a* ends and the role of the party starts, and vice versa.'[17] Meanwhile, Brotherhood leader Abdelrazzak Al-Aradi admitted that, while the JCP was administratively, financially and organisationally separate from the *jama'a*, the Muslim Brotherhood was 'a source of strength to the JCP'.[18] Belhaj has also acknowledged that Brotherhood elements were the most active within the party:

> We have found the [local] branches that are headed by Ikhwani members are more active than the others, as we have more experience in organisational skills. So, on the branch level, most of them are Ikhwan. Members elect the Ikhwani to these posts as they are the most effective ones ... The reason why it appeared as though the Ikhwan was in control, though they made up just 10 per cent of all membership, is because they were more effective. You cannot compare somebody who was involved in the organisation for twenty to thirty years with somebody who just joined in.[19]

Thus, despite its efforts to dispel the impression that the JCP was the Brotherhood's party, in reality things could not work in any other way.

But the Brotherhood's rush to establish a political party was arguably misguided. In its haste to try to replicate the Brotherhood's success in Egypt, the movement appears not to have fully comprehended that Libya was not ready for political parties, let alone those based on ideology. Many Libyans retained a deep suspicion of political parties and of multi-party politics. This was partly a hangover from Qadhafi's relentless rhetoric castigating political parties as 'the modern instrument of dictatorial government',[20] but was also a reflection of the general lack of political culture and experience arising from forty years of repression. These attitudes were evident in the 2012 election law, in which only eighty of the 200 seats in the General National Congress were reserved for parties, with the remaining 120 allocated to individual candidates. Although the push to limit the number of seats available for parties was partly a misguided ploy by some of the more liberal elements in the NTC to ensure that the Brotherhood could not sweep the board, it demonstrated a general unease about the political party as an instrument of governance. It seems, therefore, that in its hurry to try to achieve power the Libyan Brotherhood overlooked the particular characteristics of the country in which it was operating.

Indeed, on the eve of the elections the Brotherhood appeared positively jubilant. With Mohamed Morsi's recent victory in Egypt, it looked as though the region was turning Islamist and that this was the Islamists' long-awaited moment. A confident Mohamed Sawan predicted that the Islamist current would take at least 60 per cent of seats in the Congress.[21] Not that the movement was completely unaware of the challenges involved. Some members acknowledged beforehand that the party was not well known in Libya, and that Libyans were much more likely to give their backing to individuals they knew from the Brotherhood than to the party itself.[22] To this end the movement, like many other political forces, fielded a number of its members as individual candidates. However, the movement was still anticipating a victory of sorts.

When they came, therefore, the results were a serious blow. Not only had the JCP won only seventeen of the eighty seats allocated to parties (as opposed to the NFA's thirty-nine), the gap between the number of votes cast for the JCP and the NFA in some constituencies was staggering. In the constituency comprising Tobruk, Al-Qubbah and Derna, the NFA took 62,061, votes as opposed to the JCP's 8,828; in the one incorporating Shahhat, Al-Baida, Marj and Qasr Libya, the NFA took 48,846 votes, while the Brotherhood took only 6,572.[23] A similar pattern was replicated in many other constituencies.

The Brotherhood has attributed its poor showing to a number

of factors. Al-Aradi, for example, flagged up the fact that, unlike the NFA, the Brotherhood had failed to open a dialogue with those Libyans who were either 'upset with the revolution' or were neutral towards it.[24] Others believed that the Brotherhood had spent too much time focusing its campaigning on issues such as identity, while the NFA had offered more practical solutions. One Tripoli resident explained that NFA head Mahmoud Jibril 'was very clever. He listened to what the Libyans were saying, gathered it together, repackaged it, and then sold it back to them. This is why he won.'[25] Moreover, the NFA had a strong advantage. While characters like Mohamed Sawan were all but unknown to Libyans, Mahmoud Jibril had already made a name for himself. Although he had been part of the former regime, Jibril had been prominent in the political arena right from the start of the revolution, and was credited with being instrumental in securing international approval for the NTC and rebel forces. Jibril was also viewed as a technocrat, whose reformist credentials were well known, even during Qadhafi's days. Furthermore, Jibril was astute enough to downplay his liberal credentials, openly rejecting the label 'secular' – something that prompted the Brotherhood to accuse him of having deliberately tricked Libyans.

Yet the Brotherhood's problem went far deeper than the way in which it had gone about running its campaign. The Brotherhood had never been able to root itself effectively in the fabric of Libyan society (see Chapter Four), and was therefore an unknown quantity. To make matters worse, Qadhafi had spent almost forty years railing against the Brotherhood, warning repeatedly of its plots to subvert the country. Some of this propaganda had clearly hit home, and many Libyans saw no distinction between more moderate forces like the Brotherhood and more radical jihadist elements. Moreover, more liberal elements sought to play up the idea that the Brotherhood was alien to Libya. Ali Tarhouni, the head of the National Centrist Party and former oil minister on the NTC's Executive Board, publicly slated the Brotherhood in December 2011, accusing them of being 'foreigners' and of having 'a foreign ideology'.[26]

In addition, after forty years of being subjected to Qadhafi's uncompromising and all-encompassing ideology, Libyans were naturally suspicious of ideology-based parties. Thus, many rejected the Brotherhood on the grounds that they did not need a party or ideology to define their identity. As one Libyan graduate explained, 'It is offensive to tell me that I have to vote for an Islamic party ... In Libya, we are Muslims. They can't take away my identity and claim that it's only theirs.'

But there was another issue muddying the waters for the Brotherhood. The movement's links to Saif Al-Islam were still unclear. Its attempts to downplay these connections, and failure to come clean about them, were troubling for some. It was as if the Brotherhood had deliberately kept one foot in the camp of the regime and one foot in that of the revolution, thereby fuelling suspicion about the movement and its real intentions. Thus, while Ghannouchi returned to Tunisia with what was widely viewed as a clean slate, the Brotherhood returned to Libya with a large question-mark hanging over it.

These factors had the combined effect that, when it came to the elections, the Libyan Brotherhood was unable to fill in the blank between Egypt and Tunisia to complete the Islamist line-up in the region. Not that one should dismiss the Brotherhood's performance altogether. It should be remembered that, despite being largely unknown, having no real roots inside the country, and having only a very short time to campaign, the Brotherhood still managed to take seventeen seats out of the eighty reserved for political parties. Furthermore, its true showing in the new Congress was greater, because some of its members who had stood as individual candidates were successful, giving it more like forty seats in total. The Brotherhood also did significantly better than other Islamist parties, such as those set up by former LIFG members, which barely scraped any seats at all.

More importantly, while clearly nowhere near the outcome the movement had been hoping for, the election results still gave the Brotherhood a base from which to propel itself into the heart of the new political arena.

Brotherhood in Government

Despite the fact that the Libyan people had not given the Brotherhood a resounding endorsement in the polls, it still seems to have believed that it should play a major role in the political process. It clearly considered itself to be the country's second political power, and assumed that it should have almost equal status with the NFA. It still had a strong sense of entitlement, seemingly born out of the movement's history and reach as a global movement. As a result, when the NFA, which did not have a big enough majority in the Congress to take the lead by itself, set about negotiating who should take on the leadership posts in the new transitional institutions, the Brotherhood came forward with all guns blazing, ready to secure all that it could for itself.

But as Libyan politics descended immediately into deal-making, the Brotherhood very quickly took umbrage at the way things were unfolding. In particular, it resented the fact that, rather than prioritise negotiations with the Brotherhood, Jibril treated the movement in the same way as he did other political players. Belhaj's response to Jibril's inviting the Brotherhood to a meeting to discuss the new leadership posts, along with other political currents, was telling: 'What's this? I am the second bloc and wanted to be a partner and you tell me to come along with others? ... In fact, that was a shock to us ... Jibril wanted to humiliate us, dealing with us as [though] we were nothing.'[27] It seems, therefore, that despite Al-Kebti's assertion at the November 2011 conference of the need to rebuild Libya together, what the Brotherhood really wanted was for it and the NFA to divide up the main posts between them.

The Brotherhood was equally infuriated at the NFA's attempts to monopolise the top jobs. Al-Aradi explained:

> We sat with the NFA. We tried to reach an agreement, but we couldn't ... They insisted on Ali Zidan [a liberal from the National Party for Development and Welfare] for the head of the Congress and Jibril as head of the government. So we said this is unfair. We

> said, if you want Ali Zidan to be the head of the Congress and his first deputy to be a woman from the NFA, and you want the second deputy to be Dr Jiuma Attigha [from the liberal current] and Jibril to be the head of the government, why are you sitting with us?[28]

Such was the Brotherhood's fury that it cut all meetings and contact with the NFA, putting forward its own candidates for the different posts instead. It also rejected Jibril's nomination for prime minister, Belhaj asserting: 'When Jibril put his name forward we rejected him. That's politics.'

Yet this rejection of Jibril was related to more than just the Brotherhood's sense of being slighted and marginalised. The movement was also distinctly uncomfortable with Jibril as an individual, partly because of his liberal orientation but also because of his links to the former regime. Al-Aradi commented, 'As a matter of fact we didn't want Jibril to win because we saw him as a controversial figure, and a controversial personality shouldn't be heading the political scene.'[29] Despite its own dealings with the former regime, the Brotherhood seemed bent on flagging up Jibril's connections to the past as if they made him unfit to rule, irrespective of the fact that he had just been handed a popular mandate through his party's achievement of first place in the elections.

The Brotherhood therefore determined to block Jibril from taking on a leading position. In doing so, it put itself in the same camp as many revolutionary forces on the ground, who were equally keen to prevent Jibril from heading up Libya's new political institutions. As Jibril himself explained, 'I was told that the Congress building would be hit by missiles if the Congress voted for me as prime minister. Because of the threats the NFA couldn't have its own man.'[30] Thus, even before the political process was properly up and running, the Brotherhood was already standing with those forces on the ground who believed that revolutionary legitimacy should trump political or electoral legitimacy.

With Jibril out of the running, the Congress voted on who it wanted to lead it. The post went to Mohamed Al-Magarief, the leader of the National Front party. This party, which had won just three seats in the elections, had been born out of the National Front for the Salvation of Libya, which had been one of the most active Libyan opposition groups abroad during Qadhafi's rule. Although not explicitly Islamist, this front had what could be described as a moderate Islamist orientation – something that prompted a number of Brotherhood members to join when it was established in the early 1980s. The Brotherhood was thus not unhappy with Al-Magarief as a compromise choice. In order to back him, however, it wanted something in return. The movement struck a deal with the National Front, therefore, agreeing to give its vote to Al-Magarief as head of the Congress on the condition that the Front would, in return, vote for Brotherhood candidate Awad Al-Barassi when it came to electing the prime minister. Despite its repeated protestations that it was not seeking power, the Brotherhood was intent on putting its candidate forward for the post.

But things did not go the Brotherhood's way. The National Front broke its promise and, rather than voteing for Al-Barassi as prime minister, backed its own candidate, Mustafa Abu Shagur. This knocked Al-Barassi out of the race in the first round of the vote, marking another blow for the Brotherhood. The second round was therefore a choice between Abu Shagur, who was also from the National Front, and Jibril, who was the NFA's candidate, despite the threats that had been made against him. Although the Brotherhood was infuriated at the National Front, it no choice in this round but to support Abu Shagur, as failing to do so would risk Jibril's election. The Brotherhood's support was decisive, and Abu Shagur received ninety-six votes to Jibril's ninety-four, opening the way for him to become prime minister. Libya's new political arena was therefore already thrown into the anomalous position of having its two most senior posts held by a party that had won only three seats in the elections, while the leading party was left out in the cold.

Although backing Abu Shagur was the Brotherhood's way of blocking Jibril, once again the movement demanded a price for its support. Abu Shagur claims that, prior to the second round of the vote, the JCP made its backing for him conditional upon his giving the party eleven portfolios in his government.[31] Although he told them that he would consider the proposition but would only accept those who were qualified, he also recounted, 'As soon as I won I contacted the party to ask for their nominations. They sent me their first list seven days later. They asked for the [post of] deputy prime minister and ten ministries.'[32]

Some members of the Brotherhood have tried to downplay this apparent power-grab. Al-Aradi insists that the party 'didn't demand any portfolios from Abu Shagur', claiming that it had been the head of the JCP's bloc in the Congress, Abdelrahman Al-Dibani, who had 'asked Abu Shagur for certain portfolios as a condition to give him confidence'.[33] Yet, given that this was such an important moment, it is difficult to believe that the JCP, and the Brotherhood, were unaware of the kinds of negotiations that were ongoing at the time.

Not that the Brotherhood was the only party to make such demands. The NFA duly demanded nine portfolios from Abu Shagur, and also called on him to adopt its political platform as a roadmap for the country.[34] A whole host of independents and other parties also demanded posts. Abu Shagur was therefore to be the first in a succession of Libyan leaders faced with the challenge of producing a government that would appease a host of different constituencies. In the event, he failed. When it came to putting forward his proposed government list to the Congress, the key players, who had realised that they were not going to get what they had demanded, had already closed ranks against him. This included the JCP, which was given just four ministries in the final list. As Abu Shagur explained,

> When I was reading out the names of the government, even before I had finished reading out the list a large number of Congress members walked out. Clearly there was already a decision not to accept it. When I came back on the second day, supposedly to

discuss the government, the discussion had moved on to holding a no-confidence vote [in me].[35]

This no-confidence vote delivered Abu Shagur a resounding rejection, with 144 members voting against him.

With Abu Shagur out of the picture, the search for an alternative began. Knowing that there was no chance for Jibril to become prime minister, the NFA decided to back Ali Zidan. Zidan had been elected to the Congress as an independent, although he had been a member of the National Front for the Salvation of Libya in the 1980s. He was a liberal, however, and as such was not liked by the Brotherhood. More importantly, the JCP was still intent on taking the post of prime minister for itself, and once again put forward its own candidate, this time fielding Mohamed Al-Harari. But it failed yet again, as Zidan won by ninety-three votes to Al-Harari's eighty-five. Notably, a number of JCP Congress members from the south had broken ranks and backed Zidan rather than Al-Harari, seemingly because Zidan was from Libya's southern Fezzan region, suggesting that in this instance regionalism triumphed over ideology. Al-Aradi has also explained that some members of the JCP were on pilgrimage in Mecca at the time of the vote, and were therefore unable cast their ballots.

Zidan emerged, therefore, as the new Libya's first elected prime minister, despite his having no real power base of his own. Another compromise figure, Zidan, like Abu Shagur before him, was forced to pull together a government that appeased not only the various political currents, but also the different regions of Libya. In fact this latter point came to dominate all other considerations, as, in line with the fragmentation that was already characterising post-Qadhafi Libya, different towns and regions were all demanding their share of the pie. Zidan also had to satisfy the revolutionary forces on the ground, some of which stormed the Congress to protest at some of his proposed choices because of their links to the former regime. Zidan's government was duly cobbled together through a process of fraught bargaining and unhappy compromise, and was not grounded in any solid political platform or real expertise.

As for the JCP, it got nowhere near as many ministries in Zidan's government as it would have liked. However, it still ended up with the post of deputy prime minister, which went to Awad Al-Barassi, as well as four additional ministries – including the all-important oil ministry which went to Abdul Bari Al-Arusi. This was not a bad result for a party that had had such a disappointing showing in the polls. Once again, the Brotherhood had succeeded in pushing itself forward and securing a political representation for itself that far outweighed its popular footing in the country.Despite having manoeuvred itself into the government, the Brotherhood started grumbling almost immediately that it was being marginalised. It complained that Zidan was deliberately blocking Brotherhood members from taking up senior positions in the administration, and that he was bypassing those JCP ministers who were in government. As Adbulmalik explained,

> Ikhwani ministers were undermined. For example, in Al-Arussi's Oil Ministry decisions were taken outside the ministry. They were taken by Zidan and other people in a farm. Decisions were not made in the cabinet ... If a minister suggested appointing a deputy, Zidan would ask 'Is he Ikhwan or JCP?' If he was [either], then the deputy would not be appointed.[36]

Abulmalik put this down to Zidan's having what he described as an unexplained 'personal animosity' in his heart towards the Brotherhood. Thus, almost from the start there was a polarisation within the political arena.

However, it was over the controversy of the political isolation law – legislation to ban those with links to the former regime from public life – that this division became really solidified. The idea of banning individuals who had been part of Qadhafi's regime was already well-established, reflecting the mood of revenge that had taken hold in the country, and was evident in the killings and abductions of suspected Qadhafi loyalists that were taking place, the victims often picked up off street corners or outside cafés, and held incommunicado by the various revolutionary forces that controlled the street. Revenge had even been exercised during the revolution itself, most notably with the killing of Colonel Abdelfatah Younis Al-Obeidi, a senior figure in Qadhafi's regime who defected almost as soon as the uprisings began, and who went on to head up rebel forces, but who was killed in July 2011 by Islamist elements in revenge for the leading role he had played in suppressing Islamists in the east of the country in the 1990s. Defecting to the opposition was not enough to wipe the slate clean.

In April 2012, more formalised measures were introduced when the NTC set up a High Commission for the Implementation of the Standard of Integrity and Patriotism, otherwise known as the Integrity Commission, which was tasked with vetting individual candidates for the 2012 elections, as well as for key state posts.[37] This commission worked tirelessly to bar nominees who did not meet its stringent standards. But this was not deemed sufficient for many, and once the Zidan government had been formed there were forceful calls for the Congress to implement something more far-reaching, and to enshrine it in law. These calls came not only from ordinary Libyans but also from the array of revolutionary forces, some of whom had staged protests demanding the speedy introduction of a political isolation law. Libya's ultra-orthodox grand mufti, Sheikh Sadeq Al-Gharianni, was also calling for such a law – something he later referred to as 'a collective duty'.[38] Indeed, the desire for political exclusion dwarfed all talk of rebuilding the country, which was shattered after months of civil war.

Yet the concept of political exclusion was considerably more complicated in Libya than it was in other countries where dictatorships had been overturned. This included not only Iraq, which had undertaken a de-Ba'athification process, but also Egypt and Tunisia, where the idea of a political isolation law had been toyed with, although not followed up. The highly personalised nature of the Qadhafi regime meant that, in Libya, there was no comparable ruling party to the Ba'ath party in Iraq – or the NDP in Egypt, or RCD in Tunisia – to ban, and no comparable ideology to fight against. Unlike Ba'athism, which had some ideological substance, Qadhafi's quirky ideology comprising his 'Third Universal Theory' and 'Green Book', was so thin and so tied up with its author that it died with him. Libya's purge of the past, therefore, could only be carried out against individuals rather than against members of a particular party or ideology. This posed particular challenges such as deciding whether those who had been part of the former regime but who had defected to the revolution should be considered contaminated or not.

But such concerns did not deter the Congress, which turned its attentions to enacting a political isolation law almost as soon as it was established. The Brotherhood was a strong and vocal proponent of such legislation from the outset. Keen to tap into the public mood, the movement began to equate support for a political isolation law with defence of the revolution. Mohamed Sawan told the media: 'We are honoured as the JCP to be demanding the political isolation law. We are part of a societal consensus on the principle of this law.'[39] Saleh Makhzoum, the second deputy of the Congress, used even more emotive language, describing the law as representing the 'demands of the blood of the martyrs'.[40] A movement that had shied away from revolution throughout its existence, the Brotherhood was now calling forcefully for a law to overturn the vestiges of the old order.

But this law was not only about tapping into the popular mood or fulfilling the genuine desire among Brotherhood members to exclude those who had been part of the apparatus of the Qadhafi regime. A political exclusion law would have the added advantage of eliminating some of the Brotherhood's most powerful opponents from the political scene. Many key figures in the liberal current, and in the NFA in particular – including its leader, Mahmoud Jibril – had held senior positions under Qadhafi. The passing of a law would not only bring the Brotherhood popular and revolutionary legitimacy, but also skew the political arena to its advantage.

The JCP was quick, therefore, to take the lead in proposing

the political isolation law to the Congress. On 25 December the Congress duly voted in favour of the principle of political isolation, and established a committee comprising Congress members and legal experts to draft the law. This prompted various parties, including the National Front and the NFA, to put forward their own drafts. The drafts drawn up by both of these parties were strikingly draconian, as all sides began a process of intense political manoeuvring dressed up as a bid to cleanse Libya of its past.

The National Front's draft was clearly an attack against the Brotherhood and other Islamist groups, since it proposed isolating not only those who had held leading positions in the former regime, but also former opponents who had engaged in dialogue with Qadhafi and who had reached some sort of accommodation with the regime.[41] Given the Brotherhood's dealings with Saif Al-Islam in the 2000s, such a draft would clearly include it in the ban. The NFA, meanwhile, proposed to extend the period covered by the law so that anyone who had held a position in the regime, dating all the way back to 1969, would be barred – regardless of whether or not they had defected during Qadhafi's rule or during the revolution. This would mean that the law would target many thousands of state personnel, including some of the most seasoned of Qadhafi's opponents. It is not entirely clear why the NFA opted for such an extreme draft, but it seems to have been an attempt to widen the net of exclusion so far as to render the law unworkable. It was also a way to ensure that many Islamists and Brotherhood figures, as well as those from the National Front, would be targeted along with its own members.[42] In other words, if the NFA was going down, it was going to take its political rivals down with it, in an act of collective political suicide.

Unsurprisingly, the Brotherhood reacted against the extreme nature of these drafts. Mohamed Sawan explained: 'The National Front came with a proposal; the NFA came with a proposal ... What we came up with was certain principles, i.e. the law shouldn't be expanded and shouldn't apply to certain people ... Expanding the law would abort the law.'[43] Sawan also declared: 'We are the elite and we need to explain to people that we can't make the law absolute. We need to narrow it to those who were really part of the regime. Otherwise, it will verge on revenge, and we don't want that.'[44] The JCP therefore came up with its own proposal that exempted all who had taken part in the 17 February Revolution. Yet, aware of the need to be seen to be defending the cause, Sawan also made clear that the party was not going to oppose the more extreme draft, and suggested that its own proposal should only be used as a backup if the former could not be passed.[45]

The law had thus become like a political football tossed between the different parties in their bid to outdo each other in demonstrating that they were the true defenders of the revolution, and therefore the most qualified to lead the transition.

It was little surprise, then, that the draft that was eventually presented by the Congress committee, which seems to have been an amalgamation of the various different proposals, was uncompromising in the extreme. It not only targeted those who had held senior political, diplomatic or military positions dating back to 1969, but also barred those who had worked in the state media, had held senior positions in state companies and universities, and even those who had worked with charities run by the Qadhafi family. The Congress had therefore ended up proposing a law that, by its very nature, would see large numbers of its own members banned from the political arena.

Yet these Congress members were not free agents. There was a far more powerful force on the ground, in the form of the revolutionary brigades and militias that were determined to pass the political exclusion law at all costs. These military forces that had formed during and after the revolution had become a serious problem for post-Qadhafi Libya. All hopes that these forces would hand in their weapons and become part of an official armed force had been dashed as these bodies, reluctant to abandon their newfound power and prestige, refused to oblige. Instead, Libya was left with a morass of thousands of armed brigades and militias whose ultimate loyalty lay with their own local area, town or tribe, or in some instances with a militant Islamist ideology. With no strong army of their own, there was little the country's newly elected authorities could do to rein them in.

The situation was made worse by the fact that there was a strong resistance among revolutionary forces to rebuilding the country's new military bodies around the remnants of the official armed forces, because of the latter's associations with the former regime. The Brotherhood shared this approach. The movement had already demonstrated its objections to the Qadhafi-era military in its political programme, which listed the '[p]urification of the security apparatus of corrupt leaders and the remnants of the former regime' as its first priority under the heading: 'The Establishment of Security and Stability'. Like the revolutionary forces themselves, the Brotherhood held that the armed forces should be constructed around revolutionary brigades such as the Libya Shield forces that had been brought, nominally at least, under the Defence Ministry in 2012, and had become a kind of parallel defence force. As Mohamed Abdulmalik asserted, 'The [Libya] Shields are a must. We want a strong army but we want it to stay in the brigades.'[46]

Yet these revolutionary forces and the power they wielded were to prove disastrous for Libya and its transition. The Congress was subjected to ongoing intimidation at the hands of these forces as they staged sit-ins or stormed the Congress to force the political outcomes they desired. But it was over the political isolation law, which some revolutionaries referred to as the 'security valve of the revolution',[47] that these forces really came to assert their dominance over the political arena. The Higher Council of Libyan Revolutionaries, one of the revolutionary bodies in the capital, warned that any Congress member who voted against any article in the law would be committing 'high treason against the revolution and its noble aims'.[48] On 5 March, 500 revolutionaries stormed a congressional session being held supposedly secretly in a meteorological institute in one of Tripoli's southern suburbs, to press for the law to be passed. The twenty-six Congress members who had dared to turn up to the session were held hostage for the day and subjected to threats and physical violence, while Al-Magarief's car came under a hail of bullets when he was finally allowed to leave.[49]

It was under such pressures that the Congress voted in April 2013 for a series of measures to ring-fence the political isolation law before it was even passed. These included amending the Constitutional Declaration of August 2011 so that individuals barred under the law had no right of appeal, and reducing the number of votes required in order for the law to be passed from 134 to 101 (half the Congress plus one). While many in the Congress were horrified at the changes, there was little they could do given that, as one Libyan journalist noted at the time, 'The air is charged and the threat of weapons hovers constantly.'[50]

At the end of April the situation worsened, after some 200 revolutionaries, many of them from Misrata, surrounded the Foreign Ministry in pickup trucks loaded with anti-aircraft missiles, putting it under siege. Misratan revolutionary forces, who were some of the most powerful in the country, had had such a horrendous experience during the revolution, when Qadhafi's forces put the town under a brutal three-month siege, that they, along with the Misratan representatives in the Congress, were among the strongest proponents of political isolation. These revolutionary elements who had surrounded the Foreign Ministry raised banners calling for Qadhafi's men to be purged, while their commander told the media that the ministry would remain closed until the political isolation law was passed. Shortly afterwards the Finance Ministry was broken into, and the Justice Ministry also placed under siege. It was thus all but inevitable that, when the vote finally took place on 4 May, the Congress approved the law in its most draconian of formats almost unanimously.

Despite the Brotherhood's earlier objections to the extreme nature of the draft, when the law was actually passed the movement appeared euphoric. Brotherhood member Omar Bu Shah described the passing of the law as 'a historic day and the day that the Qadhafi regime really fell'.[51] Yet this law was to do more than simply ban individuals with links to the former regime. It served a far more insidious purpose, formalising a division that was already polarising the country and hampering the transition. This law fed directly into a discourse that separated revolutionaries from those who were now being labelled 'Azlam Qadhafi' – Qadhafi's men. This division took on almost sacred dimensions, the revolutionaries being classed as 'pure' and as 'martyrs' while those who had links to the former regime were dismissed as impure or corrupt, even if they had defected at the time of the revolution.

Despite its obvious engagement with the regime through Saif Al-Islam, the Brotherhood chose to place itself firmly in the former camp, positioning itself as defender of the revolution alongside the most potent and powerful forces operating in the country. Indeed, the movement's interests came increasingly to converge with those of the revolutionaries, who Belhaj praised as 'good' and 'willing to die for their country',[52] as both sought to play on the issue of revolutionary legitimacy so as to further weaken their opponents. This included their opponents in the Congress, which had been turned upside-down by the political isolation law. One of the first casualties was Congress head Mohamed Al-Magarief, who stepped down in anticipation of being excluded. Although Al-Magarief had been one of the most well-known and active of Qadhafi's opponents, he had served as Libya's ambassador to India for a brief period in the 1970s, meaning that he fell foul of the legislation. He was replaced by Nouri Abu Sahmaine, who was from the Islamist-dominated Al-Wafa for Martyrs' bloc, which contained a number of jihadist and former jihadist elements. Abu Sahmaine was elected by the Congress at the end of June 2013, reflecting the fact that the political isolation law had also resulted in the expulsion of a number of NFA members, putting the already fragmented alliance into further disarray.

Full of self-righteousness derived from their sense of being on the side of good and purity, the Islamists were therefore able to tighten their hold over the Congress. Next they turned their attentions to the prime minister, who the revolutionaries were already demanding should step down. Zidan had proved to be firmly part of the liberal camp, and during his time in office had increasingly made common cause with the NFA. Like Al-Magarief, he had also served as a diplomat in the 1970s. As far as the revolutionaries were concerned, therefore, he was part of 'Azlam Qadhafi', and should be excluded. As for the Brotherhood, it had never liked Zidan or wanted him to be prime minister, and saw him as an obstacle to its own political ambitions.

Although Belhaj and other senior Brotherhood leaders, including Mohamed Al-Hirazi, asserted that the Brotherhood had deterred the revolutionaries from staging a coup against Zidan around this time, claiming that the movement had served as a 'mediator between the government and the revolutionaries',[53] the Brotherhood effectively sought to achieve the same objective through political channels. The movement began attacking and undermining Zidan at every turn. In June 2013 it accused the prime minister of being weak, and announced that it was withdrawing confidence in his government because of its 'successive failures to perform its duties'.[54]

By the summer of 2013, therefore, it looked as though the Brotherhood and other Islamist elements were on a roll and, with the backing of the revolutionaries on the ground, were poised to bring Zidan down, thereby consolidating their control over the political arena.

An Unexpected Blow

In July 2013, however, the Brotherhood was dealt an unexpected blow in the form of the toppling of Mohamed Morsi in Egypt. This blow was primarily psychological, in so far as it struck right at the heart of the Islamist project and put an end to the prospect of a Brotherhood-dominated North Africa. Yet the Egyptian Brotherhood's downfall also sparked real fears inside the Libyan Brotherhood that it would face a similar fate, the movement warning that that there were 'political forces inside Libya that want to exploit what is happening in Egypt and they are trying to force the same outcome inside Libya, hence their call to bring down the congress and the government'.[55] The Brotherhood believed that a conspiracy was being cooked up against it. This was partly because of the accusations that were increasingly being hurled at it, including allegations that it had deliberately teamed up with revolutionary elements to pass the political isolation law, with the specific aim of seizing control. Despite all the Brotherhood's protestations that it was not seeking power, it could not dispel the belief that, because it had been unable to dominate the political arena through the ballot box, it was intent on doing so by whatever means were possible.

At the same time the Brotherhood, along with all Islamist forces, was being blamed for the violence that was still gripping the country. This included the assassinations and attacks taking place in Benghazi, as well as incidents such as 'Black Saturday', in which the Islamist-oriented Libya Shield 1 Brigade opened fire on unarmed protestors outside its base in Benghazi, leaving thirty-two people dead. Although the Brotherhood was not directly implicated in any of these attacks, many Libyans did not distinguish between the movement and the more militant Islamist forces suspected of being behind them. There was serious disquiet, too, at the Brotherhood's connections to external powers, most notably Qatar. Although a discussion of the role played by Qatar in the Libya crisis is outside the scope of this book, the movement's perceived closeness to Doha stoked up further suspicion towards the Brotherhood and its agenda. By the time of Morsi's fall, therefore, the Brotherhood was already the target of growing hostility and resentment at the power it was perceived to wield. Somewhat ironically, therefore, while the Brotherhood's capacity to punch above its weight may have assisted it in its bid to win power, this inflation of its influence was now coming back to haunt it.

Fearful of a major backlash, the Brotherhood's initial response to Morsi's fall – aside from denouncing it as a coup against legitimate authority – was to temper its language and distance itself from the Egyptian Brotherhood. Al-Kebti told the media: 'Our principles are not like our brothers in Egypt. Our principles are to be partners, not to take over. We are a harmonious society and we are all Muslims and no one is trying to outdo each other over who is following Islam.'[56] Hisham Krekshi, a senior Brotherhood member in Tripoli, stressed that the Egyptian Brotherhood had been mistaken in 'not sharing enough with other parties', asserting: 'we have to be sure that we are open, to say, "We are all Libyans and we have to accept every rainbow colour, to work together."'[57] In an attempt to demonstrate that it was not power-hungry, on 5 July the JCP announced that it was freezing its work in the government and the Congress – although, confusingly, also stated that its members would continue serving in both bodies, but as individuals rather than as party members. Both the JCP and the Brotherhood were thus vague as to exactly what role they would continue to play in the political arena. This was partly due to internal disagreements over whether or not to pull out of the government. But it also reflected the Brotherhood's efforts to have its feet planted in different camps at the same time, reassuring the public that it was not interested in political domination, while at the same time ensuring that it would not lose the gains it had made in the political sphere.

At the same time as it employed its conciliatory rhetoric, the Brotherhood continued in its efforts to carve out more space for itself by trying to get rid of Zidan. In July 2013, deputy prime minister, Al-Barassi, suddenly announced his resignation, launching a scathing attack against the prime minister and his government, accusing them of dealing with the country's problems by dispensing only painkillers.[58] Al-Barassi also accused Zidan of deliberately curtailing the powers of his own deputy prime ministers.[59] Al-Barassi issued another statement on 26 August accusing Zidan of taking 'all decisions in his own hands', and of having achieved nothing towards establishing the army or the police.[60] Such accusations were telling, given that the Brotherhood knew full well that Zidan was in no position to do anything on this front, given the general impotence of the country's political institutions. But in the same month the JCP issued a number of other statements against Zidan, reproaching his government on a whole host of issues, including its failure to remedy poor service-provision and the dire security situation.

But it was in September 2013 – the same month in which the Brotherhood condemned Zidan for making a visit to Egypt's new rulers – that the JCP launched a more determined attack against the prime minister, calling on the Congress to question the government over its performance and arguing that, if the Congress was not satisfied, then it should hold a no-confidence vote in the government. Bashir Al-Kebti proclaimed at this time that there was 'almost a national consensus in Libya that Zidan is not suitable for this phase. The focus now is on finding a replacement for him.'[61]

Yet, for all that Zidan may have been struggling, getting rid of him would not be that easy, and the JCP struggled to secure the 120 votes needed for a no-confidence vote. Undeterred, it refused to give up and continued to call for such a vote at every opportunity, repeatedly tabling congressional sessions that were postponed or scuppered by what was left of the liberal current. However, in March 2014 the Brotherhood and the Islamist camp saw their chance in another crisis that was gripping the country. Federalist commander and head of the central branch of the Oil Facilities Guards, Ibrahim Jedhran, who had been blockading a number of Libyan oil ports over previous months, provoked uproar when he made an attempt to sell oil independently of the state, loading up a North Korean–flagged tanker with crude at the blockaded Es-Sider port. Zidan responded by ordering navy vessels and Misratan revolutionaries to block the tanker and escort it to another Libyan port. On 10 March Zidan announced that the operation had been successful, and that the tanker was under the 'complete control' of state forces. The following day, however, the government was forced to admit that the vessel had broken free overnight, and that bad weather conditions had prevented state forces from recapturing it. In a humiliating development, the tanker was eventually apprehended by US Navy Seals off the coast of Malta.

The Islamists seized upon the incident, which had provoked considerable public anger, and rushed to push through the no-confidence vote. This time they were successful, and on 11 March the no-confidence motion was passed by 124 of the 145 members present in the Congress, prompting Zidan, who had already endured the indignity in October 2013 of being kidnapped by revolutionary elements from a Tripoli hotel room, to flee the country in fear for his life.

For all intents and purposes, therefore, the Islamists had staged an internal coup and removed the final obstacle to their takeover of the political arena. It was as if they had learned nothing from the Egyptian experience; with the chance to seize power so close at hand, they rushed at it without thinking of the consequences. This is certainly how things seemed when it came to the election of Zidan's replacement. The Brotherhood (along with other Islamist players) was clearly determined to complete its hold over the political arena, even if that meant trampling over the democratic process promoted by its own rhetoric. When the Islamists' candidate of choice, Ahmed Meitig – who was not an Islamist but was sympathetic to the Islamist cause, and was also supported by the powerful Misratan lobby in the Congress – was unable to secure enough votes to become prime minister, his supporters in the Congress turned to unorthodox methods to ensure his victory. When Meitig received only 113 votes – seven short of the minimum number to enable him to take up the post – his supporters frantically started telephoning absent Congress members calling on them to come and cast their votes. Such tactics provoked outrage among liberal elements, including the Congress's first deputy, Izzadine Al-Awami, who was presiding over the session and who, amid raised fists and raucous shouting, stormed out declaring the session to be over, and insisting that any additional votes for Meitig were invalid.

But, with victory so near, the Islamists were not going to back down now. The JCP's Saleh Makhzoum, who was the Congress's second deputy, jumped in and took over the session, allowing the late votes to be included until the final count for Meitig had been nudged up to 121. Unwilling to give his opponents the slightest space to challenge what had occurred, Makhzoum immediately declared Meitig the new prime minister, and gave him two weeks to form a new government. Once again, the Brotherhood's mood was jubilant and triumphant. Nizar Kawan applauded the decision: 'Meitig is the prime minister regardless of whoever wishes it or rejects it.'[62]

Some of the desperation of this act was related to the fact that the country was already gearing itself up for elections for a new body to replace the Congress. The Congress's mandate was meant to have ended in February, but there had been resistance inside the ruling body, particularly among Islamist elements, to stepping aside and holding new elections. This unwillingness to put an end to what by now was a limping body (given that large numbers of liberals had withdrawn) prompted widespread public anger, based on a belief that those inside the Congress were hanging onto power at all costs. Under public pressure, therefore, the now discredited Congress passed amendments to the Constitutional Declaration allowing for elections to a 200-seat House of Representatives to take place in June.

With the Islamists sensing that the tide was turning against them, they feared that these elections would deal them a bad hand and leave them in a weaker position than before. The Islamists wanted to ensure, therefore, that there was at least an Islamist-dominated government that would remain in place while the newly elected legislative body installed itself and dealt with the initial tasks assigned to it, including deciding on whether to hold direct or indirect elections for the newly created post of president.

But, once again, the Islamists were to be thwarted in their ambitions. In early June Libya's Supreme Court ruled that Meitig's election had been unlawful, forcing him to step aside, with the effect that the acting prime minister, Abdullah Al-Thinni, who had taken over from Zidan and was also part of the liberal current, was to remain in his post. Despite all the Islamists' efforts, therefore, they had failed to clear the way for their own take-over of power.

But by this point, a far more potent threat was brewing. This came in the form of a retired military officer who had been a senior commander in Qadhafi's army, before defecting in the early 1980s while fighting in Libya's disastrous war with Chad. Khalifa Haftar, who had been in exile in the United States for many years, joined the revolution from the start, but seemed to court controversy wherever he went. In February 2014 Haftar caused a stir when he appeared on Libyan television calling for the Congress to be brought down, in what appeared to be an attempted military coup. It was in May, however, that Haftar really made his mark, when, with the backing of a number of retired military officers, he launched his Operation Dignity campaign. This campaign was aimed at eliminating Islamist militants from Benghazi, who had been tightening their grip on the city, where they were suspected of carrying out the almost daily assassinations and killings of liberals and security personnel. But Haftar targeted not only militant Islamist groups, but also those revolutionary brigades in Benghazi that were allied to the Congress, some of them forming part of the Libya Shied forces that were in the pay of the state. Haftar went even further, making no bones about his desire to 'cleanse' Libya of Islamists of all hues, including the Brotherhood, which he described as a 'malignant disease that is seeking to spread throughout the bones of the Arab world'.[63]

It was little wonder, therefore, that the Brotherhood soon came to view Haftar as a Libyan Abdulfattah Al-Sissi. The Brotherhood also saw Haftar as the very embodiment of the counter-revolution and of 'Azlam Qadhafi'. In a statement issued on 21 May, the Brotherhood denounced Haftar's Operation Dignity campaign as a 'desperate coup attempt' by someone 'who has shunned legitimacy'.[64] The Brotherhood's attitude towards Haftar was also encapsulated in a Facebook post by Mohamed Abdulmalik, who wrote in May 2014:

> Oh Allah, Oh Allah, save Libya from the war criminal Haftar ... This

> criminal will not hesitate to kill thousands of Libyans if he manages to take control of the country … I hope my fellow esteemed revolutionaries in the eastern region learn the lesson and cleanse Libya from these carrion who constantly try to pull the rug from under the 17 February revolution.[65]

The Brotherhood feared also that Haftar was intending to extend his campaign to the capital. In May a number of revolutionary brigades from Zintan, who were linked to the liberal camp, stormed the Congress, demanding its dissolution and proclaiming their support for Haftar. The move was deemed serious enough for the head of the Congress, Nouri Abu Sahmaine, to call on revolutionary forces to come from Misrata to Tripoli to help secure it. Thus, although Haftar's campaign was still in its infancy, the Brotherhood and other Islamists feared that it might spell their end. To make matters worse, the June 2014 election results delivered a worse result than the Islamists could have predicted. Reflecting the public's growing disillusionment with the Islamist camp, the Islamists and the Misratans won no more than thirty seats combined in the 200-seat body, which was clearly going to be dominated by the liberal or so-called civil current. It looked to the Islamists, and to the revolutionaries, therefore, as though Libya was about to fall back into the hands of the forces of the counter-revolution – both militarily, through Haftar, and politically, through the establishment of the House of Representatives.

This threat prompted a major reaction on the part of the revolutionaries. The powerful Misratan brigades came together with an array of revolutionary brigades in Tripoli, many of them Islamist in orientation, to launch Operation Libya Dawn. This operation, which was meant to put the revolution back on a straight path, sought to force those brigades that were allied to Haftar and the liberal camp out of the capital once and for all. Operation Libya Dawn forces began attacking the Zintani brigades that had been in control of Tripoli International Airport since the revolution. The situation soon escalated, and a bloody conflict ensued, with other towns in the west of Libya lining up behind Operation Libya Dawn. By August the militarily superior Operation Libya Dawn forces had succeeded in pushing their Zintani opponents out of the capital, securing revolutionary and Islamist domination of the capital and most of the west of the country.

Unsurprisingly the Brotherhood, along with other Islamist political forces, sided with Operation Libya Dawn and backed the assault against the Zintani brigades. Mohamed Sawan is reported as having told the Associated Press that the assault was a 'legitimate' response to Haftar's campaign to eliminate Islamists.[66] Notably, the Brotherhood also proved more than willing to give Operation Libya Dawn political cover, working with other Islamist political forces to reinstate the Congress in Tripoli and to appoint a National Salvation Government in the capital, despite there being no legal mandate for them to do so. According to senior Brotherhood member Mohamed Al-Harizi, the JCP not only supported Operation Libya Dawn 'politically and materially', but also played the 'biggest role in bringing members of the national Congress back and voting on the formation of the salvation government'.[67]

This reinstated Congress insisted that it was Libya's sole legislative power, and refused to accept that the House of Representatives – which had holed itself up in the remote eastern town of Tobruk and inaugurated itself there despite there having been no official handover ceremony and several members boycotting it – had proper legislative authority. Indeed, this was the start of the country's division into two competing authorities, each claiming sole legitimacy and struggling to control the country's resources and institutions, as Libya gradually ground to a halt. Over the coming months the split became even more pronounced, as the House of Representatives, backed by Egypt and the UAE, adopted Haftar, formalising his position as general commander of the Armed Forces in March 2015, while the Tripoli camp looked increasingly to countries such as Turkey and Qatar to provide it with legitimacy and backing – especially after the international community chose to recognise the House rather than the Congress.

The Congress thus came to lose credibility, and was increasingly seen as one of the main obstacles to the UN-sponsored peace process that had been launched in 2014 (the other big obstacle being Haftar). But by this point the Brotherhood had already aligned itself with some of the most extreme and anti-democratic forces operating in Libya. For all its talk of consensus and of rebuilding the country together, the Brotherhood teamed up with those elements that represented the very antithesis of state-building, and that were convinced that the country's most pressing need was to complete the revolution. Like these elements, the Brotherhood had no compunction in going for the kill where eliminating those with links to the former regime was concerned, and banked its future on revolutionary legitimacy above all else. It was as if the Brotherhood failed to distinguish between the politics of revenge and what was needed in a time of transition.

In addition, these revolutionary elements to which the Brotherhood had allied itself in its struggle for legitimacy and relevance were prepared to use violence in order to achieve their objectives. The Brotherhood's failure to distance itself from such actions and groups, and its willingness to piggyback on them in order to make political gains, served to alienate it from a population, already suspicious of its motives. Indeed, the Brotherhood's ideological ambiguity did it no favours with most Libyans.

Furthermore, the Libyan Brotherhood articulated no solid political programme or vision, and its politics appeared both reactive and opportunistic. Of course, the Brotherhood was operating in extremely challenging circumstances; the country had fragmented beyond repair, and the political arena was powerless and held hostage to the more powerful forces on the ground. But, despite its decades of experience as part of a transnational Islamist movement, the Brotherhood was just as unable as all the other political forces operating in Libya to rise above a zero-sum politics that was about little more than control.

Even in the religious sphere, the Brotherhood had little to offer. The movement was dwarfed by other Islamist forces, including those of a militant bent, which succeeded in implanting themselves far more effectively in the social terrain. Ansar Al-Sharia, a newcomer on the scene, for example, was able to attract thousands of recruits, in Benghazi and other cities, in a very short time. As Mohamed Abdulmalik ruefully noted, 'They stayed on the periphery involved in charity work. They are doing what we should be doing. As a result they gained a lot of popularity.'[68] Indeed, it seems that the Brotherhood had channelled its efforts in the wrong direction, working as neither a religious movement nor an effective political party, turning the story of the Libyan Brotherhood beyond the Arab Spring into a dismal tale of dashed hopes and missed opportunities.

PART THREE

TUNISIA

SIX

AN-NAHDA AT THE HELM

'I managed to democratise Ghannouchi, but he didn't manage to Islamicise me.'[1] So Tunisia's first post-revolution president, Moncef Marzouki, is alleged to have quipped about Sheikh Rachid Ghannouchi, the founder and leader of the An-Nahda movement. Whether or not Marzouki ever made such a comment, the words are revealing nonetheless. An-Nahda's experience after the Tunisian Revolution, in which it found itself catapulted out of the shadows and into power as the head of a troika government, certainly forced the movement to adopt a number of democratic norms and principles that were a far cry from the Islamic goals that had been at the core of its ideology for decades.

Not that its adoption of these norms and principles represented a complete change of direction. Prior to the revolution that erupted in December 2010, after young street vendor Mohamed Bouazizi set himself alight, An-Nahda was already considered to be at the more progressive end of the Islamist political spectrum. This was largely because of the figure of Ghannouchi himself, who during his years of exile in the UK moderated his approach, and began arguing that Islam was not incompatible with Western democracy, the latter of which, he asserted, perfectly encapsulated the Islamic concept of *shura* ('consultation').[2] Indeed, Ghannouchi was among the leading proponents of what he referred to as 'Islamic democracy' – a concept that incorporated Western democratic principles into the specificities of a Muslim society.

An-Nahda's more enlightened stance was not only due to the figure of Ghannouchi. It was also a result of the fact that the movement was not shackled by being part of the global Muslim Brotherhood movement. Although An-Nahda was born out of the same reformist Islamist tradition as the Brotherhood, sharing a broad ideological platform with the movement as well as many of its spiritual references, it always guarded its independence. As senior An-Nahda member Walid Bannani commented in 2013, 'Our affiliation is Ikhwani but we don't intervene in others' affairs. We have co-ordination and contacts and we share the same references. But we don't intervene in each other's affairs or agenda.'[3] An-Nahda was never constrained, therefore, by the Brotherhood's heavy sense of tradition or duty to the global movement's core ideological principles. An-Nahda had also freed itself from the Brotherhood's obsession with loyalty and obedience, enabling Ghannouchi not only to develop his ideas independently of the movement, but also to become a personality in his own right. Thus, while An-Nahda certainly has strong links to the Brotherhood, it has always forged its own distinct path.

Prior to Tunisia's revolution, therefore, An-Nahda, had already marked itself out as one of the most open and progressive of Islamist political movements. Yet it was also a movement in disarray. On the eve of the revolution, An-Nahda was riven by divisions and contradictory stances, some of which were the result of circumstances and some of which were more of its own making. Firstly, there was a split between those members who were inside the country, where the movement was banned and heavily repressed, and those in exile, with the two groups unable to communicate because of the security situation. Secondly, relations between exiles in Paris and those in London were becoming increasingly tense. Things were so bad that there was a growing push by some elements to get rid of Ghannouchi, whose days as leader appeared numbered.

The 2011 revolution, therefore, presented itself as a gift to both An-Nahda and Ghannouchi, and breathed new life into an ailing body. As one former An-Nahda member explained, 'Ghannouchi was on his way, out but the revolution saved him ... If it wasn't for the revolution history would have ignored him.'[4] Although this statement is perhaps somewhat harsh, Ghannouchi was certainly looking increasingly irrelevant and unable to hold the various factions of the movement together.

After Ghannouchi returned to Tunisia like a prodigal son in January 2011, An-Nahda came to political prominence, riding to victory in elections to the Constituent Assembly – the body tasked with writing the new constitution – in October 2011, in which it won 89 out of 217 seats. Like its Brotherhood counterparts in both Egypt and Libya, An-Nahda seized upon the opportunity to take power, forming a troika government with two secular parties, the Congrès pour la République (CPR) and the Forum Démocratique pour le Travail et les Libertés, known as Ettakatol. The scene was now set for An-Nahda finally to achieved what it had been pursuing for decades.

But it soon became clear that, like its counterpart in Egypt, An-Nahda had bitten off more than it could chew. The movement, which after so many years of dislocation had not had sufficient time to consolidate its own identity or ideological stance, let alone any meaningful coherent political or economic vision, immediately faced a morass of complex challenges. As well as having to manage a state in transition and an economy that was tanking, An-Nahda also had to contend with a secular opposition that was determinedly hostile from the outset, as well as a burgeoning Salafist movement that was unwilling to be tamed.

Indeed, it quickly became apparent that An-Nahda was unprepared for power. Despite its seemingly progressive credentials and ideological sophistication, once it actually got the chance to lead, An-Nahda proved almost as politically inept as its Brotherhood counterparts. It rushed at power before it was ready, struggled to work in a truly consensual fashion, and could not fully shake off the mentality of an opposition movement. It also turned out to have no concrete political or economic ideas or programme, while its Islamism seemed to dissolve almost as soon as it made contact with the realities of rule. For a movement which, like the Brotherhood, believed itself to be a force of salvation and authenticity, An-Nahda struggled either to articulate or respond to the hopes and aspirations of a large section of Tunisia society.

Before the Revolution

An-Nahda has its roots in the Jama'a al-Islamiya (Islamic Group) that was formed in Tunisia in the 1970s, when Islamic revivalism gripped the whole region. The group consisted primarily of students and pupils who had gravitated around the figure of Ghannouchi, who in his words were brought together by 'general ideas, thoughts and the trend of preaching about Islam'.[5] The movement quickly attracted a strong following, tapping into feelings of alienation prompted not only by modernisation but also by President Habib Bourguiba's aggressively secularising approach. Bourguiba's entire political project in the wake of independence was to establish a modern state that emulated Western secular traditions – something that left whole swathes of the population feeling marginalised. As Ghannouchi explained, 'I remember we used to feel like strangers in our own country. We have been educated as Muslims and as Arabs, while we could see the country totally moulded in the French cultural identity.'[6] Tunisian academic Moncef Ouanes has argued that, although the Bourguiba regime created modern institutions and promoted secularism, it was not able to create the social forces, let alone the mental structures, to support them.[7] While this statement is not entirely correct, as evidenced by the fact that Tunisia has a robust middle class that has continued to defend the secular nature of the state, large sections of society nonetheless felt alienated by Bourguiba's approach.

The primary preoccupation of these young Tunisian Islamists at this time was around issues of religion and morality. As Hmida Ennaifer, a former member of the group, remarked, 'At the beginning the religious side was essential, on the other hand the political side was very vague ... We didn't really know what we wanted. We were not in a general fashion in agreement with the government, but we did not have a line of actions that was well determined.'[8] However, the evolution of the Brotherhood, particularly in Egypt, was to have a profound influence on the movement, shifting more towards political activism. As Ennaifer explained, President Sadat's freeing of members of the Brotherhood in the early 1970s was instrumental, and 'was to influence us and push us to engage more directly in political action, as well as in a certain underground formation ... We read everything concerning the formation of a brotherhood, how the Egyptian brothers had conceived their first cells, etc.'[9] In October 1979, galvanised partly by the Iranian Revolution, the group established a nationwide structure for the movement that was modelled on that of the Brotherhood, comprising clandestine cells at the base that were overseen by a tight hierarchy of councils and executive committees.

This organisational structure did not mean, however, that the movement was ideologically cohesive. It comprised several different strands that were broadly divided into three wings: those who represented traditional Tunisian religiosity; those who were of a more Brotherhood–Salafist orientation; and those who Ghannouchi described as being 'rational' religionists, although this latter group constituted by far the smallest element. Many of this last group were to move away from the movement during the 1980s, objecting the closeness of the links that the party was forging with the Egyptian Brotherhood. As Salehedinne Jourchi, a progressive who moved away from the movement at this time, explained, 'When we spoke of doctrinal crisis that meant before anything else that there were doubts about the school of thought of the Muslim Brothers, which had been a model for us.'[10] Ennaifer, who also left at this time, commented that he and the more liberal elements favoured a more Tunisian approach that was tied to the nation rather than the text.[11] Indeed, this group of progressives started to advance the idea of a specifically Tunisian Islam that was rooted directly in the national experience, and free from the cumbersome burden of the Egyptian model. This was not well received by Ghannouchi. As Ennaifer recalls, 'I began to use a notion that was entirely taboo: "Tunisian

Islam". "Tunisian Islam?" What is that? There were some very hard discussions with Ghannouchi: Islam is Islam. There cannot be a "Tunisian Islam!" "One God! One Prophet! One Islam!"'[12] Thus, while after the 2011 revolution Ghannouchi came increasingly to talk about an Islam that was rooted in the national experience (as opposed to that of Salafist groups, inspired by a foreign agenda), at that time the An-Nahda leader clearly subscribed to a more transnational, Brotherhood-type ideology.

But, unlike the Brotherhood, Ghannouchi had no qualms about establishing a political party, which was something the Egyptian Brotherhood had always wrestled with (see Chapter One). A shift in the political environment at the start of the 1980s, in which the Bourguiba regime briefly liberalised the one-party system, prompted the group to declare its own existence on 6 June 1981, though under a new name: the Mouvement de la Tendance Islamique (MTI). It also announced its intention to be recognised as a political party. This move was not supported by the more radical elements within the movement, who in the words of one former member were in favour of 'political mobilisation and confrontation'.[13] This radical wing, led by Saleh Karkar, objected strongly to the request for recognition as a legal entity on the grounds that it conferred legitimacy on the regime. But Ghannouchi and other forceful personalities such as Abdelfatah Mouru pressed ahead, viewing this slight opening by the regime as the movement's chance to impose itself in the political arena.

But the regime clearly viewed this as too much of a threat. It unleashed a wave of repression against the group, carrying out mass arrests that swept up the movement's leadership. In 1984, however, the MTI's fortunes were to change again, after the regime switched tactics and began employing a policy that mixed repression with co-option and containment. Scores of MTI members were released from prison and granted clemency, while the then prime minister Mohamed Mzali entered into a dialogue with the MTI leadership. This did not mean that the harassment came to an end. Ghannouchi may have been released from prison, but he was forbidden to speak in mosques or at public gatherings, to publish his writings, to teach, or to travel abroad, while there was also a more generalised clampdown against Islamism.[14]

Despite these restrictions, the MTI moved quickly to capitalise on this new period of relative tolerance. It issued a tract on the third anniversary of its establishment in which it proclaimed its acceptance of democratic principles, asserting: 'For the first time in our knowledge, in the Arab world the Islamists are taking for their part, a clear position in favour of democracy, which they demand, and the defence of ... the right of expression and organisation for all parties, even when they represent on the ideological level – as is the case with the Communists – an opposite extreme.'[15] It was presumably the movement's having taken such a stance that prompted Ghannouchi to boast in his first interview after Tunisia's 2011 revolution: 'We drank the cup of democracy in one gulp back in the 1980s while other Islamists have taken it sip by sip.'[16] Such a comment is a little disingenuous, given that, in the year when the MTI issued this tract, the Egyptian Brotherhood contested parliamentary elections – albeit under the banner of the Al-Wafd party.

More importantly, for all its talk of democracy, when the MTI realised that Bourguiba was not going to cede it the space it craved but was instead bent on further repression, the movement adopted an increasingly confrontational stance towards the regime. According to Salehedinne Jourchi, 'Democratic thought was weak inside the movement and that is why some elements in the leadership were thinking of using the military to seize power.'[17] Indeed, the MTI had already established a secret group – the 'National Salvation Group' – inside the movement, which incorporated military and security elements, and by 1987 was considering staging a coup against an increasingly ailing Bourguiba.[18] As one of the founders of the MTI's student wing explained, 'We thought a military coup was a normal thing in 1987. We thought people would support any group that did it – this was the only way to change the regime.'[19] Moreover, in stark contrast to the Muslim Brotherhood's traditional aversion to revolution, the MTI urged in an internal document issued in 1986: 'We have to make the theory of revolution more rooted. At the same time we have to make the political, cultural and social contradictions explode so the revolutionary climate is there ... Revolution requires that the confrontation is not just between us and the regime; we have to bring the people into it.'[20] It is not clear how aware Ghannouchi was of these kinds of activities at this time, but the MTI's increasingly confrontational stance did not sit comfortably with its own stated support for democracy, which appears to have been mainly about trying to secure recognition for itself within the political sphere.

In the event, the MTI was beaten to it by Interior Minister Zine Abedinne Ben Ali, who staged a coup himself in November 1987, impeaching Bourguiba on medical grounds. The new president immediately adopted a slightly softer stance towards the Islamists than his predecessor, releasing many from prison and opening up the political arena. Once again the MTI grasped at the opportunity presented to it, and in 1988 changed its name to An-Nahda ('Renaissance') – as the regime still refused to allow parties based on religion – and sought recognition as a political party in order that it could contest the parliamentary elections in April 1989. But the regime was not ready to go that far; while it was willing to allow the Islamists to stand as candidates, it insisted that they did so as independents.

The official results showed that these 'independent' candidates had won around 13 per cent of the vote, while the ruling RCD party took over 80 per cent. An-Nahda accused the regime of foul play, claiming that the results had been rigged, and that its candidates had won closer to 60 or 70 per cent of the vote.[21] While such figures are likely to be exaggerated, An-Nahda clearly believed it had won a majority, and should be permitted to take power. As Jourchi explained, An-Nahda 'saw in itself the ability and the legitimacy to declare that it had the majority in the parliament. It was as if power was in its hands and it had to pluck it like a fruit that was about to ripen.'[22]

But An-Nahda was stopped in its tracks yet again. The regime decided that its experiment with political liberalisation had gone far enough and executed a speedy retreat, clamping down heavily on the movement once more. On 8 June 1989 An-Nahda was refused a licence, and in November the movement was banned. A long and bleak period of brutal repression was to follow, with further mass arrests. Ghannouchi, who had been released from prison in 1989 but had fled to Europe, was sentenced in absentia to life imprisonment. Although as the years dragged by the regime loosened up slightly, releasing An-Nahda prisoners in several waves from 1997 onwards, those released were not permitted to engage in any kind of political or religious activism, and were closely monitored. Thus, while there were still An-Nahda networks inside Tunisia, the movement could only operate openly in exile.

Even in exile, however, An-Nahda appeared increasingly fragile, and by the time of the revolution serious cracks had begun to emerge. The movement struggled to agree on its past, and was reluctant to engage in a proper review of what had happened. When former An-Nahda member turned Salafist preacher, Sheikh Khamis Majeri, who was in exile in France, tried with the encouragement of some other leaders to embark upon a review of the previous period, An-Nahda 'confronted the idea with harshness'.[23] According to Majeri, his attempt to inaugurate such a process resulted in his being expelled from the movement on the pretext that he worked for the French intelligence services. Majeri reflected, 'They didn't even accept having an internal dialogue in the country of freedom [France].'[24]

Such was the hopelessness of their situation that some An-Nahda exiles began toying with the idea of reconciling with the regime. This view was rejected by others, including Ghannouchi, and caused serious rifts among exiled members. As An-Nahda Shura Council member Rida Idris explained, there was one view which held that the regime was weak and had no future, meaning that the best course of action was to stand firm with other opposition forces to work against it.[25] This was the view adopted by Ghannouchi, who still believed that a social movement could break the regime. The other view, shared by what Idris described as 'elitist members' of the movement, held that there was a difference between the authorities and the state, and that a dialogue could be opened with the latter.[26] Amar Larayedh, who went on to become the head of An-Nahda's bloc in the Constituent Assembly, explained that there was one view in the party that wanted to work with other political and human rights groups to push the regime to adopt a 'comprehensive reconciliation based on freedom and that respected Arab and Islamic identity'.[27] The other view, he said, held that pressurising the regime, even very modestly, would force it to close its doors, and that the best approach was to 'build bridges, knock at doors and to give up on oppositional discourse and refrain from provoking the regime'.[28] Proponents of this view concluded that, if they planted one foot in the camp of other opposition parties and the other in that of the regime, much could be achieved.[29]

Tied up with this split was a growing feeling among some parts of the movement, particularly those in Paris, that Ghannouchi's time as leader was up. While Ghannouchi was busy making a name for himself in European circles, where he was being hailed for his progressive theories of 'Islamic Democracy', some of those around him were complaining with increasing bitterness that he had been at the helm of the movement since its inception in the 1970s, and that it was time he stood aside.

By the time of the revolution, therefore, An-Nahda was divided and disenchanted, looking very much like a movement that was on the verge of breaking apart.

The Revolution and Beyond

Few could have predicted the events that would unfold in Tunisia after twenty-six-year-old Mohamed Buazizi set himself alight in the impoverished town of Sidi Buzid. In no time at all, the angry protests that erupted in Sidi Buzid spread along the belt of poverty running from the interior up to Jendouba in the north, which had long suffered from underdevelopment compared to the wealthy coastal towns of Sousse and Monastir, which had traditionally supplied Tunisia's ruling elite. Indeed, Tunisia's revolution was initiated by Tunisia's poor and marginalised, and was fuelled in the early stages primarily by discontent over unemployment, rising prices, and the difficulty of making a living. But it was not long before the protests reached the capital, where they became much broader-based and were carried forward by the middle classes as much as by the poor. The middle classes were particularly frustrated at the corruption that had pervaded Tunisia's political and economic life, and at the mafia-like way in which Ben Ali ran the state. The revolt was assisted, too, by the support of the powerful trades unions and political parties, which mobilised their supporters to join the demonstrations, and by the Tunisian army, which refused from the outset to defend Ben Ali.

Just like the revolutions in Egypt and Libya, therefore, this was a revolution driven not by any particular ideology or movement. It was another broad-based and spontaneous expression of frustration with the status quo and a desire to see a change for the better. With much of its leadership in exile, An-Nahda, which was as taken aback by this sudden show of people power as the rest of the world, did not take part in the revolution as an organisation. While some individual An-Nahda members inside the country joined in the protests, others refrained from getting involved because they were still under security monitoring, and were unsure of exactly what was happening.[30] Indeed, there was a general hesitancy within the movement, deriving from a fear of the consequences of what was unfolding and how it might relate to its own situation.

But, like its counterparts in Egypt and Libya, once the ruling power had gone, with Ben Ali's exit on 14 January 2011, An-Nahda moved quickly to reap the benefits. On 29 January 2011, Ghannouchi returned to Tunis to a hero's welcome, thousands of supporters and well-wishers flooding Tunis airport to welcome him back. Although some Tunisians described Ghannouchi's return as almost messianic,[31] such descriptions are a little overplayed. Ghannouchi was not Ayatollah Khomeini returning to Tehran from Paris in 1979; unlike Khomeini, he could claim no revolutionary legitimacy. But it was clear from the public response that Ghannouchi retained significant symbolic capital inside Tunisia. And contrary to speculation by some who were close to the movement – who asserted in the years preceding the revolution that Ghannouchi's time was over and that he would not be recognised by Tunisian youth[32] – the An-Nahda leader clearly still commanded respect, and was viewed by many as a clean and noble figure who represented a kind of salvation.

After Ghannouchi's return, An-Nahda set about organising itself, reconnecting its members and mobilising its networks, which had been all but dormant over the previous two decades. It was a challenging task given the conditions the movement had endured. After it was legalised as a political party by the interim government in March 2011, however, it began to establish offices and charities across the country. It also began preparing for the October 2011 elections to the Constituent Assembly. In September 2011, An-Nahda launched its political programme. An ambitious document comprising 365 points, it was launched at a large conference attended by more than one thousand adherents, under the theme of 'freedom, justice and development'. The programme certainly offered a more comprehensive and sophisticated vision than the election programmes of its Brotherhood counterparts in the region, however hurriedly it had been put together. It listed three major objectives, including establishing a democratic system founded on the basis of 'freedoms, dignity, the supremacy of the Constitution, rule of law and all standards of good governance'; implementing an economic and social plan aimed at 'providing jobs for all Tunisian men and women, offering all the amenities of a dignified life, achieving balanced regional development and promoting investment in all economic sectors'; and building a 'modern, balanced society, steeped in solidarity and rooted in its identity as well as contemporary culture'. It also contained a raft of concrete measures in both the political and economic fields. In fact, the document was so comprehensive that it went as far as to detail proposed tax rates, development models, and reductions in public transport costs for graduates. This was a thoroughly modern text that seemed to cover all of the required bases.

What it shared with the platforms of its Brotherhood counterparts, however, was that it was a decidedly over-ambitious document that promised the earth. It undertook, for example, to create 590,000 jobs between 2012 and 2016, and to achieve an average annual growth rate of 7 per cent during the same period. Indeed, for many, An-Nahda's programme may have been slick, but it represented little more than a long list of promises that were detached from realities on the ground, and whose primary purpose seemed to be to draw in voters.

In striking contrast to those of the Egyptian and Libyan Brotherhood, however, An-Nahda's electoral programme was not presented as a project of moral salvation. Rather, it was a distinctive example of 'Islam-lite'. Although it listed Islam as 'a supreme point of reference' and stipulated its desire to affirm Tunisia's Arabic and Islamic identity, there were few overt references to Islam or the identity of the state in the document. Even the section on culture stressed the need to protect cultural freedoms, and to develop Tunisian culture without so much as a mention of doing so within any particular moral framework. In the section on the child, the pledge to 'Bring up children within Arab and Islamic values and character' was almost buried among the articles about the need to protect children's rights and enhance day-care and nursery provision.

Significantly, however, the programme did include a clause stating that An-Nahda considered itself to be

> an extension of the reform school elaborated in our country in the nineteenth century, aiming at political, social and cultural reform and opposing colonialism and subservienceIn this context, the Movement considers that Islamic thought is in need of constant

> innovation so that it can keep up with progress and contribute to it, stemming from its belief that Islam accepts anything that is beneficial and encourages it, such as the International conventions on human rights, which are generally compatible with Islamic values and objectives.[33]

While, on the face of it, there was nothing particularly controversial about this point, it contained an implicit dismissal of the entire period since independence as some sort of aberration from Tunisian identity.

In general, though, it was clear that, with this programme, An-Nahda was positioning itself as a progressive, reformist Islamist party that was more akin to the AKP in Turkey than to the Brotherhood in Egypt. This was a comparison Ghannouchi himself had made, telling Al-Jazeera in February 2011 that the 'closest comparison to An-Nahda would be the AKP'[34] – though Ghannouchi also made a point of stressing that the AKP had taken his books and articles as its reference, rather than the other way around!

While such comparisons were certainly heartfelt, they were also an attempt to placate those secular elements inside Tunisia who were already accusing An-Nahda of double-speak, and of secretly wishing to impose an Islamic state. They were also meant to reassure an international audience that An-Nahda was not intent on seizing power or embarking upon a wholesale project to Islamicise the Tunisian state. In what appeared at times rather like a carefully crafted PR strategy, Ghannouchi stressed on numerous occasions that he was not seeking to put himself forward for the presidency, and that he believed Tunisia required a national unity government that included all trends and currents. He also told the international media that, if An-Nahda came to power, it would not ban alcohol or prevent women from sunbathing on Tunisian beaches.[35] He placed a heavy emphasis, too, on the fact that An-Nahda had no intention of amending or cancelling Tunisia's liberal personal status code. In an article for the *Guardian*, Ghannouchi explained:

> We have long advocated democracy within the mainstream trend of political Islam, which we feel is the best system that protects against injustice and authoritarianism. In addition, it provides institutions and mechanisms to guarantee personal and public liberties, most importantly the peaceful transfer of power through the mechanism of elections, respect of the popular will, protection of the rights of women, separation of powers, independence of the judiciary, press and media freedom and protection of minority rights.[36]

But the organisation's progressive stance and seemingly coherent programme did not tie in with what was going on inside the movement at the time. As well as physically reconnecting its members and rebuilding its eroded networks, An-Nahda was struggling to reconcile the various ideological strands and currents that it had always contained. Riyadh Chaibi, a Shura Council member who defected from An-Nahda in November 2013, explained that after the revolution there were 'big differences' in vision inside the movement between those who wanted to separate ideology out from politics and those who did not. This was an issue that continued to haunt the movement. Although on the surface An-Nahda seemed not to have the same dilemma as its Brotherhood counterparts, given that it had already turned itself into a political party years before the revolution, the reality was that it was still struggling to reconcile its dual identities of political party and religious movement.

But An-Nahda made no attempt to wrestle with these differences. As Bannani explained, 'We set up a civil party according to the constitution. As for the relationship between politics and *dawa*, we left that for the exceptional conference.'[37] Yet even at this conference, in March 2012, An-Nahda remained unable resolve the dichotomy. The party also failed to update its somewhat rigid ideological platform, which had been in place since the mid 1980s and which, in keeping with when it was written, was that of a very conservative religious movement, and was light years away from the election programme the party had laid out.[38]

Thus, as Chaibi complained, the movement made no real attempt to revise its ideas despite the immense changes that had taken place on the ground: '[T]he revolution didn't have any deep impact on the [ideological stance of the] movement'.[39] Indeed, An-Nahda's desire to triumph in the elections overrode any sense of the need to put its own house in order, or to resolve its own pressing internal issues.

The choice to focus on the elections paid off. An-Nahda's taking 89 seats in the Constituent Assembly, representing just over 37 per cent of the vote, put it streets ahead of the other parties. The CPR, led by a veteran human rights campaigner who had also spent years in exile, Moncef Marzouki, came second, but took only twenty-nine seats, corresponding to 8.7 per cent of the vote. An-Nahda swept the board, far outstripping the other parties, many of which managed to gain only one or two seats each.

The result was no surprise. With the Ben Ali regime collapsed, there was no real alternative to An-Nahda. Although an array of political parties rushed to set themselves up in order to contest the polls, it was only An-Nahda that had real reach. More importantly, An-Nahda was the only party that was not elitist in nature – with the sole exception of the Popular Petition Party, headed by Islamist media personality and former An-Nahda member Hachmi Hamdi, which took twenty-six seats in the elections. Indeed, it was not An-Nahda's progressive programme or elevated ideals about the compatibility of Islam and democracy that enabled it to triumph at the polls; rather, its success was assured by the unbridled energy it had invested in grassroots campaigning, reaching out directly to people in towns and villages across the country. In contrast, the other parties had focused their campaign efforts in the big cities and urban centres. Most importantly, however, Ghannouchi had made the effort to visit twenty-two of Tunisia's twenty-four provinces before the elections took place, often being greeted at local rallies like a celebrity.[40] Indeed, Ghannouchi's charisma and status were a special bonus for An-Nahda, enabling it to distinguish itself quite easily from its electoral competitors.

But An-Nahda was careful not to forget the secular bourgeoisie either, and succeeded in winning over some sections of this constituency. This was largely because, during the 2000s, An-Nahda had managed to win the trust of some parts of the elite through its membership of the 18 October Coalition for Rights and Freedoms – an alliance of opposition parties that came together to challenge the regime. Not only was An-Nahda's willingness to join with leftist and other parties reassuring to parts of this elite; its readiness to put its signature to texts issued by the Coalition that advocated a civil-democratic state and the peaceful rotation of power, and that also made a commitment to uphold the existing personal status code, worked to build trust between the movement and some of the Tunisian elite. In addition, prior to the elections An-Nahda made a particular effort to reassure those associated with the former regime that it would not go after them or target them, asserting that the revolution would 'forgive what went before it'.[41]

An-Nahda also enjoyed a particular legitimacy born out of the years of its struggle against the former regime. As Chaibi observed, 'An-Nahda won the election not because of Ghannouchi, despite the importance of his presence. No, it was because of the struggle of An-Nahda members. People looked at them as victims, so they gave them their vote ... They didn't vote for programmes, they voted for sentimental reasons.'[42] More importantly, it was this struggle that enabled An-Nahda to differentiate itself from the former regime in a way that those parties that had formed the opposition during the Ben Ali years could not. Shortly after his return to the country, Ghannouchi declared knowingly: 'I was proud that I came back holding my head high, not having submitted to anyone but my creator and not having to offer any compromises or anything to the toppled dictator.'[43] With the euphoria of the revolution still fresh, such claims counted for a lot, enabling An-Nahda to come to the political scene already in credit.

An-Nahda's experience, combined with its focus on issues of morality, the fight against corruption, and the rule of law, enabled it to posit itself as the clean and new alternative that would enable

Tunisia to regain its self-respect. An-Nahda, as Tunisian journalist Jamel Dridi commented, 'whether rightly or wrongly, represented in the eyes of some of the population a return to morality, righteousness, and justice ... And it's not even a matter of religion, but rather a matter of seeking direction and values.'[44] All these factors, on top of the long list of promises about how it was going to improve life on every level, were sufficient to convince enough Tunisians that the country's future should lie in its hands.

But An-Nahda was clear from the outset that it did not want to bear the burden of ruling alone. This was partly because it was keen to uphold the impression that it was a consensual party that had no interest in dominating the political scene; but it was also a product of its realisation of the enormous scale and scope of the challenges that lay ahead. At the same time, while it may have come first in the polls, An-Nahda did not have a large enough majority to press ahead without bringing others on board. It therefore invited other parties to join it in a coalition, hoping that it might end up co-operating with a broad-based group of parties. This would not only mean it would face no real opposition, but would also be able to share the burden of responsibility with others.

But, while it may have won the goodwill of large swathes of the electorate, for many opposition parties An-Nahda was already tainted by its ideological orientation. While some of these parties were more than willing to work with An-Nahda as part of the shared opposition platform of 18 October, working with it as a mainstream actor was something they were unwilling to contemplate, and most refused An-Nahda's advances. In the end, therefore, An-Nahda agreed on a troika arrangement with the CPR and Ettakatol. This was a somewhat unlikely alliance from the start, given the diverging ideological orientations of these parties. Indeed, it was an artificial coalition built upon a marriage of convenience between inexperienced parties, two of whose leaders had been in exile for most of the preceding decade, rather than an alliance grounded in shared values or goals.

Nonetheless, An-Nahda had finally achieved what it had been

craving for so many long and miserable years, and the movement seemed poised to embark upon a new and resplendent phase in its history.

An-Nahda in Power

Despite the euphoria, however, it was not long before the cracks began to appear. From the outset, An-Nahda came under fire for its attempts to dominate the political arena. This began with the appointment of the government, in which it became apparent that, despite all An-Nahda's talk of consensus, there was going to be only one party in the driving seat. Although the troika agreed on a power-sharing arrangement in which CPR head Moncef Marzouki was president, Hamadi Jebali, a veteran An-Nahda member who had spent long years in prison, was prime minister, and Ettakatol's Mustafa Ben Jafar was head of the Constituent Assembly, the focus of power rested firmly with An-Nahda. In December 2011 the Constituent Assembly had passed a mini-constitution to legislate for the period until a permanent constitution had been adopted. This mini-constitution was the subject of much fractious debate as, in accordance with An-Nahda'a preference for a parliamentary system, it invested significant new powers in the prime minister at the expense of the president, whose role was reduced considerably. This mini-constitution was fiercely debated in the Constituent Assembly, with some secular parties boycotting the vote on the grounds that they believed it marked the start of a bid by An-Nahda to dominate the political process.

Jebali's assumption of the role of prime minister therefore left An-Nahda with the most powerful post in its hands. While it was only natural that the leading party in the elections should take up this post, An-Nahda's arrogation of other cabinet positions was less easy to explain. In what appeared to be the very antithesis of the kind of consensual politics that An-Nahda had been promoting since the revolution, the party took almost all the sovereign portfolios. Although Abdelkarim Zbidi, the defence minister in the outgoing interim government, retained his post, the Interior Ministry went to senior An-Nahda member and former political prisoner Ali Larayedh; the Justice Ministry to senior party figure Nourredine Bhiri; and the Foreign Affairs Ministry to Rafik Abdessalem, Ghannouchi's son-in-law. Indeed, these posts went not to just any An-Nahda members, but to senior figures within An-Nahda's leadership – many of whom had no qualifications whatsoever for the posts they had been given. The rest of the posts were divided up between An-Nahda members, its troika partners, and independents. Thus, while it had made some concessions to consensus, An-Nahda was accused of capitalising on the weakness of its partners to manoeuvre itself into power.

An-Nahda was also accused of packing the administration with its own members, and of only trusting its own. Abu Yaareb Marzouki, an advisor to Jebali who resigned in 2013, complained bitterly that despite his entreaties to Jebali to bring others on board, the prime minister listened only to those advisers who were from An-Nahda, with whom he had surrounded himself.[45] Abu Yaareb Marzouki also accused An-Nahda of treating power as if it were a 'spoil of war', distributing government posts among 'its friends, its allies and others who were close to it', despite the fact these individuals had 'no competence'.[46] An-Nahda Shura Council member, Jalal Ouerghi, levelled similar complaints against his own movement: 'An-Nahda chose to give priority to its members when appointing posts. This was in order to use its own people and to secure loyalty.'[47] Ouerghi also commented that An-Nahda dished out positions as a kind of compensation for those who had been political prisoners, regardless of the fact that many of them had lost touch with the outside world, had no proper experience, and were suffering from all sorts of psychological problems on account of their experiences. Jebali's culture minister, Mehdi Mabrouk, concurred, explaining that ministers from An-Nahda were 'not the best qualified in the party' but were chosen 'because of personal relationships and the need to uphold a regional balance, as well as the compensation principle, i.e. the number of years spent in prison'.[48] It seemed therefore that, in spite of its years of exile in Europe, An-Nahda did not have the sense to adhere to its own rhetoric about consensus politics and share power in a more equitable fashion. Instead, it handed the opposition an own-goal, justifying its power-grab by reference to its election victory, and a sense that it was somehow entitled to take senior positions in the state because of what it had suffered under the former regime.

All this combined to give the impression that An-Nahda was a closed party that could not shake off the past and saw hostile forces at every turn. It also fuelled the belief that An-Nahda prioritised its own interests above those of the state. Even Jebali acknowledged the problem, explaining in 2014: 'What I take against An-Nahda is the fact that they are not sufficiently interested in public affairs. The ruling party has to be open, not to close itself. It has to change its organisational mentality, i.e. the concept of affiliation. All Tunisians are our people.'[49] Indeed, for all its talk of becoming a party for all Tunisians, An-Nahda struggled to go beyond itself, or to dispel the impression that it was a closed private members' club that those of different ideological orientations were not welcome to join.

This mentality was to have a detrimental effect on the troika, which very quickly started to unravel. Members of the troika baulked at An-Nahda's insistence on appointing its own members in the administrative, political and diplomatic architecture, and accused it of trying to dominate the government. Some CPR and Ettakatol MPs also turned against their own leadership, condemning them for having given in to An-Nahda's demands too easily. CPR Constituent Assembly member Souhir Dardoui complained bitterly that Marzouki had given An-Nahda 'a blank cheque', and that the party did whatever it wanted.[50] Such behaviour was exemplified in An-Nahda's decision to extradite Qadhafi-era Libyan prime minister, Baghdadi Mahmoudi, to Libya in June 2012. This controversial deal, allegedly brokered at a meeting in Paris between Libyan intelligence chief Salim Al-Hassi and Ghannouchi's right-hand man and then advisor to the justice minister, Said Ferjani, reportedly for a large sum of money,[51] was made without the blessing or knowledge of An-Nahda's troika partners. The incident provoked uproar inside the troika, An-Nahda's partners accusing it of bypassing the state. Senior presidential advisor Ayoub Massoudi, who resigned in protest at the incident, complained:

> I wonder whether An-Nahda recognises the state ... The fact that it used all the tools of state institutions (the Ministries of Defence, Justice, Interior and Foreign Affairs) to extradite the former Libyan prime minister from Aouina airport on a private Libyan plane and in the company of a Libyan staff colonel, is a betrayal of the legal representative of the state and the supreme commander of the armed forces.[52]

Incidents such as this placed real strain on the troika, fuelling the perception that An-Nahda was trampling over its partners.

For many, therefore, it looked as though An-Nahda had donned a mask of compromise and consensus before the elections that it had dropped as soon as it had achieved power. Indeed, like the Egyptian Brotherhood, An-Nahda was unable to dispel the impression that it was a party that could not work in a truly consensual fashion, whose real intent was to take over the country's institutions with the longer-term aim of Islamicising the state. Its failure to correct this apprehension and to try to reach out to other constituencies damaged the party. As Salehedinne Jourchi commented, 'An-Nahda have excessive confidence in themselves ... They got it wrong. They didn't understand that this phase requires both electoral legitimacy and consensus legitimacy.'[53]

Equally damaging was An-Nahda's failure to dispel the idea that, regardless of what was occurring inside the government, it was Ghannouchi who was running the show. The local media frequently drew attention to Ghannouchi's ambiguous role, as well as his habit of making pronouncements on state policies, such as his announcement to the Moroccan media in early 2012 that, in order to attract investment from the Gulf, visa requirements were going to be scrapped for investors from Gulf states.[54] This pronouncement prompted one Tunisian journalist to ask: 'Who out of Ghannouchi and Marzouki or even Jebali is really running Tunisia? ... this question is still being asked because the leader of the An-Nahda movement gives the impression that he is guiding the actions of the government, the head of which seems to obey him completely.'[55] One of Ghannouchi's neighbours in the upmarket Menzah 9 district of Tunis certainly complained that, every morning at 6 a.m., the cars of cabinet ministers were parked outside Ghannouchi's villa before they set off for their day's work. It seemed to some, therefore, as though Ghannouchi, this unelected advocate of democracy, was the real power behind the scenes

Revealingly, Hamadi Jebali admitted that he was not free to make decisions for himself:

> The head of the government should be for all Tunisians. An-Nahda as a party entrusted me as head of the government not to put the state in the service of the party ... So I wanted all ministers, especially those from An-Nahda, to respect the rule of the state, its laws, institutions, the auditing institutions, administrative courts. And I saw that it was difficult for the ruling parties to accept that ministers should follow the head of the government and not anyone else. The party can expel the head of the government, but when it trusts someone to head it he has to be in the service of the state, not the service of the party. So I wasn't free to choose ministers. I also wasn't free to do what I wanted. I felt the ministers belonged to their own parties more than the government. I wanted to reform that. I couldn't.[56]

Thus, whether in relation to Ghannouchi or the party leadership, it was clear that there was no proper separation of powers between An-Nahda and the state.

An-Nahda was also unable to dispel the impression that it was completely out of its depth as a party – that, in its rush to achieve power, it 'did not give itself the chance to learn'.[57] An-Nahda had already revealed its inexperience in November 2011 when Jebali proclaimed at a rally in Sousse that the present time was 'a divine moment in a new state, and in hopefully a 6th Caliphate', and that 'the liberation of Tunisia will, God willing, bring about the liberation of Jerusalem'.[58] The uproar that followed forced the party to make a speedy retreat, claiming that the comment was a misunderstanding. But such a slip-up was a gift to the media, while the secular parties hailed the comment as proof of An-Nahda's double-speak.

Once An-Nahda was in power and found itself naked in front of the people, things deteriorated further. An-Nahda's grandiose political and economic programmes, which had promised so much, seemed to dissolve into nothing, making the party look like a novice overwhelmed by the enormous scale and complexity of the task at hand.

This lack of a strategy was in part a function of the poverty of An-Nahda's political and economic thought. As Sheikh Khamis Majeri commented, 'It came to ruling without anything. No strategy, nothing.'[59] Salehedinne Jourchi observed that Tunisians had come to discover that An-Nahda 'suffered from a complete absence of political thought about how to run the transition',[60] and, even more damningly, that the party 'doesn't have a political programme. It dealt with state affairs as if they were a hobby.'[61] Such a comment may be excessively harsh, but An-Nahda certainly appeared to have no real vision. This was perhaps unsurprising. Like the Brotherhood, An-Nahda was founded on an ideology that focused on reforming society and the individual, rather than on reforming or recalibrating the state. This was the inevitable preoccupation of an opposition movement whose focus was on winning over a critical mass of support. An-Nahda's explicit commitment to 'Islamic democracy' appeared more like an ideological justification for working within the existing framework of governance rather than a genuine commitment to a new or unique political idea.

Moreover, despite its avowed commitment to democracy,

when it came to the practicalities of rule, it seems that, like the Brotherhood in Egypt, the bottom line of An-Nahda's political thinking relied on the idea that, if more pious individuals ran the show, then good would prevail and the country's problems would be solved. As Ed Webb has noted in relation to An-Nahda's economic policy, 'The main tool they offer to ameliorate Tunisia's economic hardships is *homo islamicus* ('Islamic man'), a more virtuous economic actor who will be disciplined enough to refrain from corrupt practices, and who will inspire workers to greater productivity by engaging them in culturally appropriate ways.'[62] The same could be said of its political vision, entailing the idea that the virtuous man was the key to saving the country and putting Tunisia back on the right path, from which it had deviated under successive secular rulers. In other words, An-Nahda's political vision relied almost exclusively on morality and a belief Islam as a universal solution. In fact, it was on precisely this basis that An-Nahda had been elected.

This lack of political vision meant that An-Nahda's policymaking was largely reactive, driven more by trial and error than by any plan. Like its Brotherhood counterparts, An-Nahda soon found itself doing little more than firefighting as the crises piled up, and it seemed to lack the stomach or strength to implement any of the policies included in its programme – not that implementing such policies would have been easy. Aside from the huge scale of the task at hand, An-Nahda quickly found itself up against a ferociously hostile opposition that was intent on tripping it up at every turn. Indeed, An-Nahda had underestimated the power of the opposition, seemingly believing that the opposition's poor showing in the polls meant that it could be discarded. But it soon found out that the task of rule was far more complex and difficult than it had anticipated. As senior An-Nahda member Walid Banani explained in 2013, 'We thought things were simple but we quickly realised that our hands were tied. In the old days the state was run by the telephone. Now we have freedom, nothing is moving easily.'[63]

But there was also a discernible reluctance on An-Nahda's part to engage in real reform of the state, or of any of the structures that had underpinned the old regime. An-Nahda's policy towards the security sector was a case in point. While the 2011 revolution may have been driven largely by socio-economic grievances, there was still a strong demand inside Tunisia for an overhaul of a state security apparatus that had engaged in brutal oppression for decades. Although Interior Minister Ali Larayedh, who had spent years in prison, declared that the security sector needed to be brought in line with the requirements of a democratic regime, there was no real attempt to undertake structural reforms, or even to set out a roadmap for such reforms.[64] Instead, An-Nahda tinkered at the edges, with half-hearted gestures that rested on removing senior personnel. In January 2012, Larayedh attempted to expel the head of the Intervention Brigades, Moncef Laajimi, who had been accused of issuing orders to fire on protestors during the revolution, and also during social unrest that had erupted in previous years. But the minister soon backtracked, after several hundred Laajimi supporters staged a protest in front of the Interior Ministry. Larayedh's willingness to backpedal – and, worse, the fact that he went on to promote Laajimi to the post of deputy chief of the cabinet of the Interior Ministry – gave rise to suspicions that An-Nahda had no real backbone, and that it had entered into a de facto alliance with remnants of the old regime, to the advantage of both parties.[65]

Such moves caused An-Nahda to lose credibility. So too did the harsh way in which the administration dealt with protests, which were occurring with increasing frequency. On 9 April 2012, when thousands of Tunisians gathered in the centre of Tunis to commemorate those killed or wounded during the 2011 uprisings, security forces used excessive and unnecessary force to disperse the protestors, while there were complaints that men in plain clothes had assaulted protestors while the police looked on.[66] The absence of any real effort to bring the perpetrators to justice, with investigations into the violence going nowhere, only fuelled the perception that An-Nahda was acting little different to the former regime.

It therefore came to seem as though, rather than prioritising working with other political actors to push for reforms, An-Nahda preferred to rely on the state in its existing form – as if controlling the state was the key to everything. As Ourghi has observed, during his time in opposition Ghannouchi talked repeatedly about the need to strengthen society, but once An-Nahda came to power it focused entirely on the state, betting on it 'as a tool to achieve everything'. He noted that, by its actions An-Nahda proved that the 'culture of venerating the state ... is at the heart of Islamic thought, exactly as it is at the heart of secular, liberal and nationalist thought'.[67]

Within a few months of coming to power, therefore, An-Nahda had gone from being regarded as a party that could save the country to one whose politics were empty, that had no appetite for genuine reform of the institutions of the past, and that was unequipped to deal with the challenges it faced. But if An-Nahda's political vision turned out to be a façade, its economic vision was a complete mirage. An-Nahda continued to pursue the previous regime's neoliberal, pro-business agenda while trying not to alienate the poorer segments of society, whose grievances had powered the revolution.[68] But, for all its promises of jobs and regional development, An-Nahda struggled to deliver, prompting those in the impoverished regions of the interior to turn against it. As well as repeated strikes across the country in August 2012, angry protests erupted in Sidi Buzid at the government's failure to alleviate economic hardships. Thus, the cradle of the revolution had turned against An-Nahda. Four months later, the town of Siliana erupted in anger at the lack of jobs and investment. The heavy-handed response of the police, which left at least 300 young people wounded – many of them blinded – prompted protestors to accuse An-Nahda of 'reproducing the behaviour of the Ben Ali regime', one of them declaring: 'It's an arrogant government that thinks its election victory means it can use tear gas and birdshot on people instead of giving them jobs and investment.'[69]

It looked as if things were unravelling, and An-Nahda had no idea how to respond – not least because it simply lacked the finances to deal with pressing socio-economic issues. The situation was exacerbated by the fact that, when it had drawn up its ambitious programme, An-Nahda had been banking on receiving assistance from both the Gulf and Libya. The party had fully expected, that once it reached power, Gulf investors would flood into the country to support it. More importantly, it also expected Islamist parties, especially the Libyan Muslim Brotherhood, to come to power in Libya, enabling it to purchase oil at preferential rates, offering the prospect of the creation of thousands of jobs for Tunisians.[70] But, as Alaya Allani commented, 'An-Nahda built its economic programme on expectations rather than reality.'[71] The folly of having done so soon became apparent, as the Islamists failed to win the 2012 elections and Libya spiralled into ever deeper chaos, while Gulf money was not forthcoming in the way An-Nahda had expected. Worse, the deteriorating security situation in Libya meant that money earmarked for development had to be diverted to finance an unexpectedly high security bill.

But the lack of government revenue did not stop An-Nahda from trying to spend its way out of trouble. Its response to its failure to create jobs was to intensify its policy of appeasement, employing thousands of individuals in the already overflowing public sector, with many posts going to An-Nahda members.[72] This favouritism created hostility, as did the introduction of a public-sector recruitment law in June 2014 mandating the direct recruitment of one member of the family of each martyr of the 2011 revolution, as well as of all beneficiaries of the general amnesty that had been accorded to all political prisoners after the revolution.[73] Most of the political prisoners released under this amnesty were Islamists, many of them An-Nahda members. In cases where these former political prisoners were unable to take up such a post, the privilege was transferred to another family member. An-Nahda was to create further scandal when it opted to pay financial compensation to some 20,000 former political prisoners, most of whom were Islamists – a move that drove the finance minister, Hussein Dimassi, an independent, to resign in July 2012.[74]

Despite the promises of economic regeneration and prosperity that had accompanied An-Nahda's election campaign, therefore, it soon became apparent that the economic arena was a complete shambles, and that the party could not work miracles. Indeed, An-Nahda could do nothing more than dispense a few painkillers, largely to its own members, while the country's economic situation went from bad to worse.

All in all, An-Nahda's hold on power was starting to look very precarious. The party stood accused of sharing some of the traits of the Egyptian Muslim Brotherhood. Although An-Nahda was somehow saved by the fact that it was working in a coalition, it still misjudged the political and economic environment, failing to understand the complexity both of the transition and of the society in which it was operating. For all the hype surrounding political Islam and Islamic democracy, therefore, An-Nahda's politics turned out to be an empty shell. After a year and a half in power, it had lost the confidence of whole swathes of the population. But things were about to get much worse.

SEVEN

COMPROMISE, CRISIS AND DECLINE

If An-Nahda's first year and a half in power left it on shaky ground, the toppling of President Mohamed Morsi in Egypt in July 2013 was a thunderbolt that struck right at the core of the movement. Although An-Nahda had always made a point of distinguishing itself from the Muslim Brotherhood, the collapse of the Morsi government could only come as a serious blow. The fall of what represented the heart of the Islamist political project was bound to have both institutional and ideological repercussions for the movement. With the largest and most influential Islamist power in the region gone, the new Islamist dawn that emerged out of the Arab Spring was suddenly cut dead. Morsi's collapse left An-Nahda more isolated and vulnerable than ever. With counterrevolutionary forces back at the helm in Egypt, chaos prevailing in Libya, and Algeria still proving staunchly immune to the Arab Spring, the movement suddenly found itself surrounded by a combination of hostile forces and chaos.

These developments had powerful domestic ramifications. While the situation in Tunisia was clearly not the same as in Egypt – not least because the Tunisian army did not constitute a force comparable to its Egyptian counterpart – Morsi's fall galvanised the Tunisian opposition, which came together with renewed vigour and determination to bring down the An-Nahda-led government. Secular groups in Tunisia even went as far as to establish their own Tamarod movement, emulating the organisation of that name in Egypt, through which they called for the dissolution of the Constituent Assembly and the scrapping of the draft constitution.

Even more troublingly, the Brotherhood's collapse in Egypt raised a number of existential questions about the future and viability of political Islam as a concept. The failure of the Egyptian experience gave rise to loud proclamations, both inside Tunisia and elsewhere, that political Islam had met its end. It seemed as though the tide was turning against both political Islam and An-Nahda, and that the latter's future hung in the balance more precariously than ever. While Ghannouchi proclaimed in October 2013 that what had happened in Egypt was not a setback for political Islam, which he claimed was still moving at unprecedented speed on the 'widest carpet in the world',[1] such bravado belied the very real crisis that An-Nahda was experiencing. Indeed, Morsi's fall shook the very foundations upon which the movement was standing.

The situation was made worse because the Brotherhood's toppling in Egypt came at a time when An-Nahda was already on the back foot. In addition to the rising dissatisfaction over An-Nahda's poor political and economic performance, the assassination of secular opposition activist Chokri Belaid on 6 February 2013 prompted a major crisis, An-Nahda standing accused, if not of direct involvement, then at least of having enabled an environment in which such an atrocity could have taken place. Meanwhile, the presence and growing boldness of Tunisian Salafist currents, including those of a violent bent, was proving increasingly troublesome for An-Nahda. Although the movement tried at first to co-opt the various Salafist factions – believing that, with some 'guidance', they could be brought under its wing – An-Nahda soon found that the Salafists were a beast it could not tame. An-Nahda thus found itself sandwiched between the secular opposition, who were baying for its blood, and the Salafists, who, with their rigid interpretation of Islam, accused An-Nahda of having sold out.

An-Nahda's efforts to forge a middle path between these two opposing currents created a whole new set of problems for the movement. An-Nahda found it increasingly difficult to square its own political ambitions with the desires of its grass roots. An-Nahda's political leadership came to power with the aim of projecting the movement as the ideal example of progressive political Islam, and of proving that a movement with a religious character could also mould itself successfully to the demands of modern governance. An-Nahda's experience in power would represent the culmination of the reformist Islamist project in the contemporary era, and would offer living proof that Ghannouchi's scholarship could be put into practice, going beyond even the Turkish example.

In reality, however, this translated into An-Nahda's being compelled to sacrifice many of its core religious principles in order to stay in the political game. An-Nahda found itself making compromise after compromise, with the result that it started to look like an Islamist party that was ruling without Islam. This caused the movement's political leadership to become somewhat untethered from its base, which was always more conservative than the leadership, and which had supported An-Nahda precisely because of its Islamic credentials.

Although An-Nahda's leadership succeeded in pulling the movement's grass roots along behind it, this fundamental mismatch between the elite and the base – between politics and ideology – posed further difficult questions inside the movement, questions that would acquire greater urgency once An-Nahda left power and began to reflect on its experience. By virtue of its pragmatism, An-Nahda had succeeded in escaping the cataclysmic fate of its Egyptian counterpart; but the movement's time in power nonetheless represented a moment of shattering disappointment, characterised not only by failed politics but also by compromise and crisis, in which its final months in office amounted to little more than the management of its own decline.

Compromises, Compromises...

Despite having come to power partly on an Islamic ticket, An-Nahda struggled from the start to spell out any coherent religious or ideological strategy. This was hardly surprising. While An-Nahda was well aware that its core supporters wanted and fully expected to see it enshrine Islamic principles and values in the state, it also knew that, if it wanted to stay in the political game, it had to meet the demands of other constituencies that were equally determined to preserve the secular nature of the state. Indeed, An-Nahda knew that focusing on religious or ideological issues would ignite a touch-paper that would provoke panicked accusations that it was intent on Islamicising Tunisian society, and that this would undermine its efforts to be seen as a purveyor of consensus and moderate political Islam.

An-Nahda's leadership therefore chose politics over religion. The head of its bloc in the Constituent Assembly, Amer Larayedh, explained: 'We avoided ideology because it is very controversial. We concentrated on what is political. For example, we could have formed a government with our religious ideological allies. They are the closest to us. But we chose politics rather than ideology.'[2] But this choice was to force An-Nahda to make a series of compromises, including over core principles and issues that had been at the heart of what the movement had stood for since its inception.

Arguably the most important compromise that An-Nahda had to make was over the hugely controversial issue of what role Sharia should play in the Tunisian state. There was little doubt that An-Nahda aspired to include Sharia in the constitution. As Ghannouchi's biographer, the Islamist Azzam Tamimi, commented, 'What is best, in [Ghannouchi's] conviction, would be an Islamic democratic state, one in which the sources of legitimacy are Sharia and the Ummah.'[3] In fact, one senior An-Nahda member confided in 2010: 'Ghannouchi thinks democracy is one stage, but not the final stage.'[4] But, given the political environment in Tunisia, it was clear that any attempt to include a reference to Sharia was likely to be explosive. From early on, therefore, An-Nahda's leaders indicated that they had no intention of doing any such thing. Ghannouchi himself had promised before the election that the party would be satisfied with retaining Article 1 of the constitution, which stipulates: 'Tunisia is a free, independent, sovereign state; Islam is its religion; Arabic is its language; and the Republic is its form of government.' Moreover, referencing Sharia in the constitution was not included in the party's political programme, which largely shied away from tackling issues of identity directly.

But when the Constituent Assembly came to debate the issue in March 2012, the An-Nahda bloc surprised everybody by proposing that Sharia should be included as one source of legislation, among others. The proposal was partly a response to the demands of the party's grass roots and supporters; but it was also a result of pressure coming from Islamist groups on An-Nahda's political right – namely the Salafists, who were also pressing hard for Islamic law. In addition, a significant number on An-Nahda's Shura Council, as well as key figures in its leadership, wanted to see Sharia cited in the constitution as a source of legislation, at the very least, and felt that it was only natural for the party to make such a demand. These included figures on the more conservative wing of the party, such as Habib Ellouze and Sadiq Chourou – the latter of whom told a Tunisian radio station at the beginning of March 2012: 'The preamble must mention Sharia as the main source of legislation.'[5] Chourou also asserted: 'Legislators must refer to three essential pillars: the Qur'an, the Sunnah and a Council of Ulemas [religious scholars].'[6] Chourou also told the media: 'The centrality of man is relative, and has to be secondary to the absolute centrality of God.'[7] Such comments, and indeed the proposal itself, were clearly a million miles away from the image of the party that Ghannouchi had worked so hard to foster. While operating as a movement encompassing strongly divergent ideological trends was never a serious problem when An-Nahda had been an underground opposition movement, these differences became more difficult to manage once it had come to power.

Not that all members of the An-Nahda bloc in the Constituent Assembly were in favour of the proposal. Souad Abdelraheem, who stood on An-Nahda's platform, explained: 'Like me, certain members of the An-Nahda bloc objected to Sharia being included in the constitution.' But although she debated with them and reminded them that the proposal had not been in their political programme, she remarked, 'they could not go against the party'.[8]

Predictably enough, An-Nahda's attempt to include Sharia provoked uproar not only among the opposition and civil society, but also inside the troika. Ettkatol leader Mustafa Ben Jafaar threatened to resign unless the proposal was rescinded.[9] Meanwhile, pressure was also coming from the other direction in the form of the Salafists, who staged mass protests in Tunis demanding the application of Islamic law and rejecting any constitution that did not cite Sharia as the main or sole source of legislation. An-Nahda was thus thrown into a quandary. As Islamist progressive and former An-Nahda member Salehedinne Jourchi commented, 'An-Nahda didn't know what to do. Its supporters and leaders differed over this main issue.'[10] As Walid Bannani explained, 'The demand to include [a reference to Sharia] in the constitution is problematic, because Tunisians differ about the concept of Sharia. We in An-Nahda didn't want any commotion about the concept of Sharia.'[11] Indeed, despite the centrality of this question to the constitution and to the future orientation of the Tunisian state, it seems that An-Nahda had not given proper attention to how it would square this inescapable circle, hoping that it could be somehow glossed over.

In the end, the party opted for pragmatic politics. After long and heated debates, the Shura Council voted against including Sharia, while, according to Souad Abdelraheem, Ghannouchi stepped in personally to convince the An-Nahda bloc in the Constituent Assembly to drop its demands. As An-Nahda member and rapporteur of the Constitution Committee, Habib Khodor, explained, 'As for Sharia, we went beyond this problem through a political decision of the An-Nahda leadership that demanded its members refrain from demanding inclusion of a reference to Sharia in return for keeping the first chapter of the 1959 constitution without change.'[12]

On 25 March 2012, therefore, Ghannouchi held a press conference where he announced that An-Nahda supported retaining Article 1 of the constitution. The party's executive bureau, meanwhile, issued a statement confirming that it had voted against including Sharia in the constitution, in the interests of uniting rather than further dividing Tunisians. The statement asserted: 'The recognition of Tunisia as an Arab-Muslim state is more than enough to reinforce the country's identity.' An-Nahda justified its stance on Sharia by crafting an argument holding that Sharia equated to freedom and social justice, and that if the constitution upheld these things then it would by extension be upholding Islam. It also argued that Islam was bigger than Sharia, and that keeping Article 1 as it stood was sufficient. As Constituent Assembly member Hadi Ben Brahem explained, 'We didn't bring Sharia in the way that people wanted. That was impossible for us ... but stipulating Sharia wouldn't bring anything more than stipulating Islam ... We brought something bigger than Sharia. We put Islam in the constitution. Our Islam encourages freedoms.'[13] Meanwhile, Walid Bannani commented, 'We believe that there should be freedom of religion, freedom of possessions, freedom to work, and we think all these freedoms are part of Sharia. Freedoms are the origin of Sharia ... So the constitution upholds religion by upholding freedom. That is enough for a Muslim country, as almost all our people are Muslim.'[14]

It was through such arguments that An-Nahda tried to convince its grass roots of the validity of its stance. Amar Larayedh, who insists that An-Nahda did not make any concessions in relation to Sharia because it had not been included in its election programme, recalled,

> We debated long with those youth who demanded Sharia. There are two types of such youth. The first have a certain image of Sharia and believe the constitution is meaningless without stipulating it. We cannot convince that type. The second type, which are the majority ... were tricked by the idea that stipulating Sharia in the constitution would mean that freedom of worship would be protected. I met a lot of them and I told them that religious freedom is part of other

> freedoms like freedom of expression, freedom to move, and that we have to protect these freedoms in all their types.[15]

But, while An-Nahda's internal PR campaign seemed to work, there was still a deep sense of unease among some of the movement's constituents at the ease with which it had abandoned such a core religious principle. As Larayedh also confirmed, 'At the grass roots of An-Nahda there is a concern that An-Nahda is compromising more than it should. But on the level of the leadership and the elite of the movement, we believe that compromise is in the interests of the country. We are very keen not to behave in a partisan way.'[16] Abdelhamid Jelassi, An-Nahda's deputy leader, noted: 'We managed to solve the Sharia problem and to dismantle this mine by sending reassurance to the Tunisians, to regional and international bodies as well as to businessmen. This opened the way for us to move away from ideological debates to debates about programmes.'[17]

But other ideological debates were to ensue, in which An-Nahda ended up again compromising its religious principles in the name of politics. In June 2012, An-Nahda members of the Committee for Rights and Freedoms in the Constituent Assembly proposed inserting a clause into Article 3 of the draft constitution criminalising blasphemy. The cause stipulated: 'the state guarantees the freedom of religious belief and practice and criminalises all attacks on that which is sacred'. It went on to specify the three Abrahamic faiths – Islam, Judaism, and Christianity – as those religions that would be protected under the legislation.

An-Nahda was prompted to propose this clause partly in response to the riots that erupted in the same month in the upmarket La Marsa suburb of Tunis against an art exhibition that was deemed to have insulted Islam. This was not the first time that Islamist activists had taken to the streets in the name of protecting their religion. Just prior to the elections, in October 2011, huge protests took place against the screening of the film *Persepolis*, an animated film based on a memoir by Marjane Satrapi about her coming of age in revolutionary Iran. Several such incidents were clearly enough to make An-Nahda feel that it needed not only to protect Islam from such 'provocations', but also to be seen to be doing so. As a party with an Islamic basis, An-Nahda could not ignore its own constituents when Islam was under attack in such a direct fashion. Furthermore, An-Nahda felt it had lost something over the Sharia debacle, not least because its decision to back down prompted angry condemnations by Salafist groups that accused the movement of selling out. Through the blasphemy clause, therefore, An-Nahda was hoping to win back some credibility among both its own grass roots and the Islamist groups to its right.

When it made the proposal, An-Nahda must have been fairly confident that other political parties, including those inside the troika, would not stand publicly against it. If secular parties had tried to defend the right to insult Islam in the name of upholding civil liberties, they would have found themselves in a very unpopular position, given deeply cherished cultural and religious traditions that render attacks against religion distasteful, if not reprehensible, to most Tunisians.[18] Thus, introducing this clause was a convenient way for An-Nahda to try to win back some of the religious legitimacy it had lost by its retreat over Sharia.

But An-Nahda went further than just proposing the constitutional clause. At its July exceptional conference, the movement agreed on a series of principles to be included in an updated political programme. These included not only proposals such as opting for a parliamentary over a presidential political system, but also a demand for the criminalisation of blasphemy. This was followed on 1 August 2012 by An-Nahda's proposal of a blasphemy law to the Constituent Assembly. This draft law was somewhat draconian in tone, making 'insults, profanity, derision and representation of Allah and Mohamed' illegal, and stipulating that violators would be liable to up to two years in prison, with repeat offenders liable to up to four-year terms.[19] Quite how this sat alongside An-Nahda's talk of the sanctity of freedom of expression was not clear. Moreover, much of the wording of the draft was vague, leaving much space for interpretation over exactly what constituted blasphemy. With this law, however, An-Nahda was clearly intending to present itself as the defender and protector of Islam and Islamic values.

But, by October 2012, An-Nahda had backed down over the law. The bill's draconian tone had elicited angry condemnation from parts of the opposition and civil society, but also from international human rights groups. Human Rights Watch, for example, called the bill a 'step back for freedom of expression in Tunisia'.[20] Suddenly, An-Nahda's role as proponent of moderate, progressive Islam looked as though it was being called into question. Furthermore, it was looking increasingly unlikely that An-Nahda would be able to get the bill passed inside the Constituent Assembly, especially as it could not rely on its troika partners to give their full backing to the law. In addition, by October An-Nahda was facing growing accusations of complicity with Salafist groups, including those that espoused violence and were wreaking ever greater havoc inside the country. Once again, therefore, An-Nahda chose to prioritise its political fortunes over religious principles.

An-Nahda also ended up rescinding wording it had proposed in the constitution relating to the role of women – an issue that the movement's leadership had made a point of highlighting prior to its election as proof of its enlightened and progressive stance. In 2012, An-Nahda members of the Constituent Assembly's Rights and Liberties Committee proposed the inclusion of a clause in Article 28 stating that men's and women's roles 'complement one another within the family'. To many An-Nahda members, this clause reflected their belief that men and women are equal but have different biological and family roles. Predictably, however, the clause provoked uproar, especially among women's rights groups. This prompted An-Nahda to make a speedy retreat, agreeing to a reformulated wording that guaranteed equality between men and women. Although this issue was not nearly as controversial as the debates over Sharia and blasphemy, An-Nahda's backtracking only fuelled the impression that the movement was not only engaged in reactive policymaking, but abandoning key religious principles that were at the basis of much of the party's grass-roots support. Indeed, it was becoming increasingly difficult to identify what made An-Nahda a specifically Islamist movement, or how it could be differentiated from other actors in the political arena. In short, An-Nahda was facing the challenge of being an Islamist party forced to rule without Islam.

The Salafist Challenge

An-Nahda's willingness to drop some of its core religious tenets may have gone some way towards calming its secular opponents, but it brought a whole new raft of problems, in the form of the Salafist current, which was far less open to the movement's justifications for its doing so.

An-Nahda's relationship to the Salafists, in their various facets and forms, was already complex.[21] Prior to the revolution, An-Nahda eyed the growth of Salafism in Tunisia with a certain disquiet. The former regime had opened space for some apolitical Salafist currents, partly because their teachings argued that it was prohibited to rise up against one's rulers. The obvious attraction that many Tunisian youth had for such currents clearly made An-Nahda uncomfortable, not least because they represented a form of competition to its own dominance of the religious landscape. Despite these concerns, however, An-Nahda's leadership, and Ghannouchi in particular, believed that these young Salafists could be dealt with easily enough. Ghannouchi told a close associate in London in 2010 that, if he returned to Tunisia, he could soon win over these Salafist youths.[22]

Ghannouchi's lack of understanding of the reality of the Salafist trend was also evident in a conversation he had with Salehedinne Jourchi in a Geneva hotel in 2007. The An-Nahda leader told Jourchi that the religious awakening in Tunisia at that time was being driven by guilt: Tunisians had failed to defend the Islamist current when it was being persecuted and were now atoning for their sins. Jourchi commented,

> I was shocked by that explanation, especially from such an important figure in the Islamic movement. I found myself forced to explain the issue from a different angle, so I told him that from the end of the 1990s the country had been going through a tangible psychological and cultural transformation. These youth who are going into religion or moving towards religiosity don't know a lot about An-Nahda. They haven't read its literature. They don't know its leaders. In fact some of them are critical of the movement, rejecting its discourse and refusing to accept that it has any legitimacy to talk in the name of Islam.[23]

Ghannouchi's underestimation of the Salafist phenomenon was partly a result of the fact that he had been outside the country for so long. But it was also driven by a conviction, shared by many in An-Nahda's leadership, that the emergence and growth of Salafism was a direct result of repression. In other words, the Ben Ali regime's repression of An-Nahda had opened up an ideological vacuum that the Salafists, with their imported, foreign ideas, had been able to fill. As An-Nahda member Mohamed Ben Salim explained in 2006, the Salafist influence was spreading 'because mosques are closed to the real preachers and the real sheikhs ... And when thousands of moderate Islamists were arrested the field was left as a vacuum for whoever comes with strange ideas.'[24] These same An-Nahda leaders also believed that, if proper space was given to those with the 'correct' interpretation of Islam, such aberrations would not occur. In other words, if An-Nahda was allowed the freedom to operate, it could impart its proper understanding of the faith, and such currents would soon disappear. An-Nahda Shura Council member Rida Idris commented in 2010 that 'the Salafists are just a fashionable trend that emerged in a vacuum because of the absence of enlightened thinking, and because of moral lapses in society ... An-Nahda is the most qualified to deal with them. We have the intellectual tools, and we can debate with them in order to make them understand.'[25] There was a kind of arrogance, therefore, in An-Nahda's attitude towards the Salafists, as if they were little more than errant youth who, with a little guidance, could be brought back to the straight path.

It was just this attitude that persuaded An-Nahda that, once the revolution had taken place, it could win the Salafists over and turn them into allies and supporters. To this end, it set about courting them in a bid to convince them to become political actors. More conservative elements inside the leadership, such as Habib Ellouze and Sadiq Chourou, tried in particular to convince various Salafist groups to establish political parties, offering them support and facilities for the purpose.[26] As Walid Bannani recalled, 'Habib Ellouze and Sadiq Chourou tried very hard to encourage the Salafists to get engaged in politics ... We told the Salafists: recognise the state and the law, and then do whatever you like. That right has been guaranteed.'[27] An-Nahda also invited Egyptian Salafists who had formed political parties to come to Tunisia, arranging meetings for them with Tunisian Salafists. Meanwhile, before the 2011 elections An-Nahda and the Salafists held a joint meeting in the Tunis suburb of Soukra, attended by some 7,000 people, which resulted in a number of agreements, including one stipulating that the Salafists would support An-Nahda candidates in the elections.[28]

At first, therefore, it appeared that this strategy might be paying off. But An-Nahda soon came to realise that its hopes of taming and winning over the Salafists were grossly misplaced. Instead of serving as useful supporters, the Salafists came to represent an increasingly potent force that An-Nahda could not contain, whose members were quick to condemn its concessions to political realities. As the Salafists moved out of the shadows and into the streets and mosques, many of which they took over, they began calling loudly for the application of Sharia, denouncing secularism, and rushing to defend Islam whenever they believed it to be under threat. They were thus very quickly able to outstrip An-Nahda in positing themselves as the real protectors of Islam against the secular elite.

Some of these Salafist currents became so emboldened that they took to attacking bars and hotels that served alcohol; during Ramadan they used threats to dissuade restaurant owners from opening during the day. This prompted the Jebali government to order the closure of restaurants and cafes during daytime hours in Ramadan – although, strikingly such restrictions went unenforced in more upmarket areas. More worryingly, some Salafist groups took over areas of certain towns, in which they declared emirates and acted like a local police force, imposing strict Islamic codes on the local population.

Rather than being contained or persuaded by An-Nahda's more pragmatic approach, therefore, these Salafist currents used the new freedoms delivered by the revolution to assert themselves and their rigid ideology. Contrary to An-Nahda's arguments, it was not repression that created these Salafist currents, including those of an extremist bent. Rather, as in Egypt, these groups flourished even more strongly once the lid of repression was lifted, and when moderate Islamist forces took power.

But An-Nahda stuck to its approach of maintaining a dialogue with the Salafists and trying to bring them, or at least those not directly involved in violence, to its side. As Amar Larayedh explained, 'Those who didn't raise weapons and who weren't involved in serious violence but who only committed some irregularities or verbal violence, whether from the left or from the religious side, we are keen to have a dialogue with all of them and to bring them to middle ground.'[29] Indeed, there was a strong reluctance within An-Nahda to replicate the behaviour of the former regime by clamping down on people because of their beliefs.

It became increasingly difficult, however, for An-Nahda to uphold this stance after September 2012, when militant Salafists attacked the US embassy in Tunis in protest against a film denigrating the Prophet Mohammed. The ensuing clashes left two dead and twenty-nine injured. With the world watching, An-Nahda had no choice but to get tough. The police arrested 144 Salafists after the incident, including Hassan Brik, a prominent leader of Ansar al-Sharia. Ghannouchi also publicly denounced what had happened, declaring: 'Each time that parties or groups overstep our freedoms in a flagrant manner, we have to be tough, clamp down and insist on public order … These people pose a threat not only to An-Nahda but to the country's freedoms and security.'[30]

Yet this tougher action did not dispel the general perception that An-Nahda was overly lenient towards the Salafists, and had no strategy to deal with them other than appeasement. An-Nahda certainly did not help itself in this respect. In October 2012 a video was circulated on the internet showing Ghannouchi holding a meeting with a group of Salafist leaders that had taken place in April 2012, in which he advised them to be patient, to consolidate what they had gained, and to 'create television channels, radio stations, schools and universities'. Ghannouchi also told these Salafists that An-Nahda wanted to add articles to the constitution stipulating that Sharia should be the main or sole source of legislation, because, despite the inclusion of Article 1, 'the evils are still out there'.[31] But he explained that Tunisia was not yet ready for such a step: 'You and us, we don't differ on religion. We differ on how to deal with reality … We differ on how much medicine this patient can take.'[32] Revealingly, Ghannouchi asserted: 'The Islamic politician is a doctor who prescribes the appropriate medicine.'[33]

Despite the patronising tone that Ghannouchi employed with these Salafist leaders, his comments provoked uproar in the secular camp. On top of the fact that Ghannouchi had compared Tunisian society to a sick patient who needed to be cured, his having advised the Salafists in this way only fuelled the belief that An-Nahda was complicit with the them, and shared their fundamental ultimate aims and objectives. Such accusations are somewhat exaggerated. The recording of this meeting seems to indicate that Ghannouchi was more concerned to try to contain what he believed were hot-headed and misguided youth by convincing them of the wisdom of An-Nahda's more pragmatic approach. But with secular opposition currents already believing that An-Nahda was too close to the Salafists, as well as having a heightened alertness to anything that smacked of double-speak, in this leaked video Ghannouchi confirmed all the worst suspicions of his political opponents.

An-Nahda's failure to distinguish itself more sharply from the Salafist current therefore further eroded trust in the party – among its political opponents, of course, but also within society at large. As social unrest and violence spread, An-Nahda was accused of having spawned a monster it could not control.

But the Salafists also represented an internal challenge for An-Nahda. The Salafists' insistence on holding so tightly to Islamic principles resonated strongly inside An-Nahda – particularly among its grass roots, many of whom had a real sense of unease about the direction the movement was taking. As Walid Bannani commented, 'Our grass roots are more radical than the leadership. They lived under Ben Ali for twenty-five years in prison, without jobs, with difficulties in life. And therefore there are ramifications ... An-Nahda is open, but [the grass roots] insist on their views ... They see that, in our dialogue, we gave away a lot of political concessions to the opposition.'[34] Furthermore, according to several former An-Nahda members, a significant proportion of these grass roots are themselves ideologically closer to the Salafists than to the movement's more progressive political leadership. As former An-Nadha Shura Council member Riyadh Chaibi observed, for example, 'There is a strong Salafist current within the party's own base.'[35] Former culture minister in Jebali's government, Mehdi Mabrouk, meanwhile described how many An-Nahda youth had a 'Salafist mentality', remarking on how, at An-Nahda's 2012 conference, the hall was full of young people holding up banners carrying slogans such as 'Islam is the solution!', and 'Allah you are the great protector!'[36]

In Mabrouk's words, 'The elite of An-Nahda are secularised but those below are not. The discourse may give the impression that the party has moved on, but its base has not.'[37] Amer Larayedh likewise observed that 'at the grass roots of An-Nahda there is a concern that An-Nahda is compromising more than it should. But on the level of the leadership and the elite of the movement, we believe that compromise is in the interests of the country. We are very keen not to behave in a partisan way.'[38] Despite the fact that, as a movement, it has thrived off populism, as its experience in power unfolded, An-Nahda's leadership became increasingly embroiled in the kind of elitist politics that many of the other political parties had been accused of indulging in.

This misalignment between the elite and the base was to create serious tensions, raising further questions about An-Nahda's own identity. Jourchi noted that An-Nadha

> still doesn't understand if it is a political or a religious movement. Its leadership wants to be both. Whenever it gets closer to its religious nature the grass roots are reassured ... Whenever it tries to confirm its political nature, it [finds] itself getting closer to political activists but moving away from a very important part of its grass roots. This is An-Nahda's main problem.[39]

An-Nahda thus found itself in the near-impossible position of being sandwiched between the secular opposition and the Salafists, while simultaneously trying to hold its base together. It could not have imagined before coming to power just how difficult this task would be.

Deepening Crisis

While An-Nahda was grappling with these thorny issues, it was hit by a major crisis. On 6 February 2013, Tunisia was rocked by the assassination of opposition activist Chokri Belaid, who was shot in the head and chest in front of his home in the capital. Belaid had been an outspoken critic of An-Nahda, and of the Islamist current more widely, and his killing unleashed a wave of anger against the government, and An-Nahda specifically. Accusations that An-Nahda was responsible for Belaid's death came, among others, from his widow: 'I can't accuse anyone of doing the crime, but still, [the] An-Nahda ruling coalition holds the responsibility. Let's say for now they are politically accountable.'[40] Tunisians flooded into the streets in response to the assassination, both in the capital and in other towns and cities, including Sidi Bouzid, Sfax, and Gafsa, where An-Nahda's party headquarters were burned down. For many Tunisians, Belaid's death was the last straw in a series of abuses. A real fear developed that the country was unravelling, and that the An-Nahda-led government was wholly incapable of addressing the chaos.

In the face of such ferocious antagonism, Hamadi Jebali announced to the media that his government should be dissolved and a government of technocrats appointed in its place. His announcement provoked fury inside An-Nahda, not least because Jebali had not consulted the party over his intentions. According to a close confidante of Jebali, who stepped in at Jebali's request to try to convince Ghannouchi of the merits of the prime minister's proposal, the An-Nahda leader lashed out and accused Jebali of being a 'traitor', and of trying to stage a bloodless coup against the movement.[41] Indeed, An-Nahda had absolutely no intention of relinquishing power, despite the fury on the streets and the fact that the CPR was threatening to withdraw from the government. On 18 February 2013, An-Nahda's vice president, Abdelhamid Jelassi, told the media: 'The prime minister did not ask the opinion of his party ... We in An-Nahda believe Tunisia needs a political government now. We will continue discussions with other parties about forming a coalition government.'[42] Ghannouchi also told his supporters, who had gathered at a rally in Tunis to reject Jebali's proposal: 'An-Nahda ... will never give up power, as long as it benefits from the confidence of the people and the legitimacy of the ballot.'[43] It was clear that, despite the disaster that was unfolding around it, An-Nahda continued to cling to the belief that its victory at the polls entitled it to stay at the helm whatever occurred. For An-Nahda, it seemed that the ballot box had conferred a legitimacy on its continued incumbency that no amount of failure on its own part could contradict.

In the face of his party's intransigence and hostility, Jebali resigned at the end of February. Interior minister and senior An-

Nahda member Ali Larayedh was appointed as prime minister, and tasked with forming a new government. Although An-Nahda made some concessions to its opponents, relinquishing the Foreign Affairs and Interior Ministries, it was unwilling to give much more ground than that. In fact, the Larayedh government was not fundamentally different from its predecessor: sixteen of twenty-one ministers in the Jebali government retained their posts. As one Tunisian journalist remarked, the Larayedh government was a 'reproduction of the troika that has demonstrated its failure in leading the country during the last period'.[44] It seemed as though An-Nahda had learned nothing from its experiences in power, and that it was bent on continuing on the same path regardless of the circumstances, in the name of electoral legitimacy.

But it was not long before An-Nahda was dealt another blow. Mohamed Morsi's toppling, on 3 July 2013, came as a bombshell for the party, which appeared stunned in its wake. An-Nahda members I met around this time were clearly shaken by what had unfolded. Walid Bannani frankly confessed: 'I am frightened about what is happening in Egypt.'[45] A member of An-Nahda's political bureau likewise commented, 'What happened in Egypt is a real threat to democracy, because we saw the overthrow of a legitimate president ... I don't think any country is secure now from what happened in Egypt.'[46] Although An-Nahda had made a point of distinguishing itself from the Muslim Brotherhood – particularly from its Egyptian branch – signalling its distinctiveness to the media by working in consensus with other parties – the fall of the largest Islamist power in the region could only spell danger. Given Tunisia's limited size and economic vulnerability, An-Nahda had relied from the start on being part of a wider Islamist region with which it shared a sense of political direction. As Ghannouchi had proclaimed in a 2011 interview:

> The Islamist movements are operating within territorial countries, not within the framework of a caliphate state ... At the same time, these countries are working to increase the overall level of relations

> with their fraternal countries, to a level greater than cooperation and interdependence and mutual interests, and to reach progressive levels of Maghreb, Arab, Gulf, and Islamic unity. There are organizations of unity that remind us that we are one Ummah.[47]

Morsi's fall not only shattered An-Nahda's dreams of greater regional interdependence – it left the movement exposed in what was a particularly unenviable geostrategic position. Already wedged between Algeria – which still loomed large in the minds of An-Nahda members for the way it had repressed its own Islamist movements after they were poised to take power in elections in 1991 – and Libya – which was looking more like a failed state by the week – Tunisia's Islamists were now further exposed by the return of the forces of repression and counter-revolution in Egypt. An-Nahda suddenly felt isolated in what had become a decidedly hostile environment.

Many detected the hand of the West in the unfolding events. As Jebali was to reflect in 2014, after Khalifa Haftar had launched his campaign to liquidate Islamists including the Muslim Brotherhood in Libya, 'They [Europe] found Sissi in Egypt and Haftar in Libya, and I don't know who they will find in Tunisia on the pretext of stopping political Islam.'[48] While such comments reflected a conspiratorial mindset, the movement clearly felt as though the world was turning against it, and that the honeymoon period of the Arab Spring had been brought decisively to a close.

Worse still, the events in Egypt spurred on the Tunisian opposition, and calls for An-Nahda to step down became louder and louder. As Hedi Ben Brahim remarked, 'The events in Egypt affected Tunisia a lot. What Sissi did in Egypt attracted some members of the extreme left [in Tunisia]. From July 2013 the drum started beating for the troika to leave.'[49] Members of the Tunisian opposition formed their own Tamarod movement and started collecting signatures across the country in a call to disband the Constituent Assembly and all the institutions it had spawned. Tamarod also condemned the draft constitution on the grounds that it was 'exclusionist'. Although the Tunisian Tamarod movement, which Ghannouchi was quick to dismiss, was not able to achieve anywhere near the same impetus as its counterpart in Egypt, what was important was that Morsi's removal set a precedent for a democratically elected government to be brought down by public pressure and street protests. If it had happened in Egypt, it could just as easily happen in Tunisia, despite the different characteristics of the two countries. An-Nahda therefore feared that the demonstrations and calls for it to go might gather momentum, and spell its end. The movement also feared that the army, which until now had remained neutral, might be harnessed by the opposition in the effort to bring it down. All of a sudden, therefore, An-Nahda's fears that this historic opportunity to rule was going to be snatched away from it suddenly looked as though they were about to be realised.

In this midst of this panic, An-Nahda was faced with a further crisis. On 25 July 2013, leftist opposition politician Mohamed Brahimi was assassinated. Like Belaid before him, Brahimi was shot dead outside his home by unidentified gunmen – allegedly with the same gun. Once again, Tunisians exploded in fury, and the situation in the county ran further out of control. Thousands of protestors took to the streets following Brahimi's killing to demand the dissolution of the government, while in Sidi Bouzid protestors set fire to An-Nahda's offices.

Brahimi's killing galvanised the opposition. The day after his death, secular and leftist opposition parties convened under the banner of the National Salvation Front. Brought together by their antipathy towards An-Nahda, this front called for the dissolution of the Constituent Assembly and the troika government and the establishment of a government of national salvation. The front also demanded that the constitution process be completed and put to a referendum, in order for elections to be held. Meanwhile, some sixty members of the Constituent Assembly suspended their membership of the legislative body and staged a sit-in outside its headquarters.

Yet still An-Nahda would not yield. A few days after Brahimi's killing, Larayedh told the media that his government had every intention of remaining in place until the holding of elections, which he announced were to take place in December. Larayedh declared: 'We are not clinging to power, but we have a duty and a responsibility that we will exercise to the end.'[50] An-Nahda continued to hold to its electoral mandate as though it trumped all other considerations. It was at this time that An-Nahda also turned to mobilisation. In stark contrast to the Brotherhood in Egypt, during its time in power An-Nahda had largely refrained from calling its supporters out into the streets. But by this point the depth of the crisis was such that during August the movement mobilised its members and supporters to rally en masse in large demonstrations in support of its 'legitimacy to govern'. By the summer of 2013, the streets were therefore boiling, and Tunisia was more polarised than ever.

However, in the hope of appeasing some of its opponents, An-Nahda also made a number of concessions. In August 2013, as huge protests against the An-Nahda-led government continued to grip the country, Ghannouchi announced that the proposed political isolation law, barring former ruling party members or anyone who had called for Ben Ali's re-election in 2014 from running for office, would not be implemented. Although this law had been proposed and drafted by the CPR in 2012, An-Nahda, initially at least, had been a strong advocate of its implementation. The party shifted its stance on this law during its time in office – partly because Ghannouchi believed that lustration would create further division, but also because the party had gradually come to the realisation that it would alienate the elite, particularly businessmen, who had been associated with the former regime and might potentially be useful allies.[51] But it was only when the situation in the country was at breaking point and when the opposition was becoming stronger, that the law was formally abandoned. In the same month, the Larayedh government declared Ansar Al-Sharia to be a terrorist organisation, claiming it had proof that the group had been behind the killings of both Belaid and Brahimi and asserting that anyone belonging to the group 'must face judicial consequences'.[52]

But such moves were not enough to save An-Nahda, and the power its claim to electoral legitimacy was now exhausted. At the end of August, Amer Larayedh told the Tunisian media that An-Nahda would accept the formation of a technocratic government. But the movement was still not willing simply to step aside, making clear that it would only do so once an agreement had been reached on the constitution, the election law, and a timetable for elections. It maintained this stance when it signed an agreement with the opposition at the end of September, agreeing that power would be handed to a caretaker government. It also continued to insist that the constitution process must continue alongside the formation of a caretaker government of technocrats when, under increasing pressure, it accepted the mediation of the National Dialogue Quartet – consisting of the Tunisian General Labour Union, the Tunisian Confederation of Industry, Trade and Handicrafts, the Tunisian Human Rights League, and the Tunisian Order of Lawyers.

This quartet proposed a roadmap according to which the government would resign within three weeks of the first session of talks, to be replaced by a technocratic government that would be chosen during the dialogue. It also articulated provisions for the formation of an independent election commission and the modification and approval of a draft constitution. At a ceremony on 5 October, An-Nahda and the opposition parties came together to sign this roadmap agreement. The ceremony was not without its drama. After realising that they were expected to sign the document in front of television cameras – and, more importantly, that it would be binding – some politicians baulked. They included Ghannouchi, who was only persuaded to sign after three hours of heated debate, and who – to the exasperation of the quartet – added a caveat to his signature, stating that the roadmap was only 'a basis for discussion'.[53] This prompted accusations that An-Nahda was not committed to the plans, forcing other parties to extract a written promise from Prime Minister Ali Larayedh that he would abide by the terms of the roadmap and resign.

Some of Ghannouchi's reluctance to sign up to a binding agreement may have been related to the fact that he had taken the decision to agree to the roadmap in the face of opposition from within his own movement. As he recounted,

> Signing the roadmap was a personal stance on my part. I took the decision alone. And when I went to the dialogue I was accompanied by Hamid Jelassi [head of the Shura Council] and Hamadi Jebali [former prime minister] ... I took the decision alone, and when I went to the Shura Council I faced severe criticism. It is true that the choice wasn't favourable to them, but they didn't refuse it either.[54]

Ghannouchi also revealed that he had threatened to resign from the leadership of An-Nahda if the Shura Council did not agree with him.

The signing of the roadmap agreement was followed by more than two months of bitter wrangling, which Jalal Ouerghli has described as 'surrender talks', in which the two sides thrashed out a deal. In December 2013 they agreed on the formation of a technocratic government to be led by Mehdi Juma, the industry minister in the Larayedh government. On 9 January, An-Nahda finally relinquished power – and it was all over.

An-Nahda tried to put a positive spin on these events, strenuously signalling that it had stepped down of its own accord for the sake of the country. Ghannouchi told the *Asharq Al-Awsat* newspaper in June 2014 that '[t]he only way to stabilise the situation was for the An-Nahda movement to give up its place within the government and allow for a transition to a neutral government. We sacrificed our government positions for something more valuable – Tunisia, and in particular, the country's stability and the continuation of a democratic transition.'[55] An-Nahda portrayed its stepping down as a gift it had graciously bestowed upon Tunisia.

But the reality was that An-Nahda had had no choice, and was effectively forced out of office – though in a less brutal fashion than the Brotherhood had been forced out in Egypt. It was a sorry end for a movement whose future had looked so bright. After the 2011 elections, Ghannouchi had repeatedly told his supporters: 'We will rule for long years.'[56] Such confidence was clearly misplaced. An-Nahda had failed to deliver on almost every level. As Riyadh Chaibi commented, 'An-Nahda should have adapted itself to the new reality. But it didn't succeed in coming up with a political programme, or in ruling with other political parties. It wasn't even able to protect its symbolic presence in society.'[57] More importantly, while its progressive and pragmatic approach may have helped save its skin, it was not sufficient to turn An-Nahda into a truly national movement. For all its talk of authenticity, and of bringing Tunisia back to its natural state, once it had assumed power An-Nahda could not convince Tunisians that it was working in the country's interests, rather than its own. Moreover, as the movement struggled to move beyond its own narrow conception of the world, it steadily lost the goodwill of those outside its core base who had been willing to give it a chance.

Not that one should deny or dismiss the enormous scale of the challenges An-Nahda had faced. The secular opposition was ferocious from the start, while the country confronted a catalogue of trials, particularly on the economic front, that were almost impossible to solve. But in its rush to achieve power, An-Nahda took on more than it could cope with. In the words of Jourchi, An-Nahda 'had a historical chance, so they seized it. But they failed to distinguish between what was a chance and what was a trap.'[58]

In this process, An-Nahda compromised its own identity, surrendering its Islamist priorities one by one, until it was hardly recognisable even to its own grass-roots members. Luckily for An-Nahda, these grass roots did not abandon it completely – not least because of the charismatic figure of Ghannouchi, who still functions as a kind of glue holding the movement together. The party's faithful, along with some Salafist elements, turned out to support it in the October 2014 parliamentary elections, in which An-Nahda still won sixty-nine seats, representing just over 31 per cent of the vote. Nevertheless, as Ghannouchi himself acknowledged,

'The Tunisian people gave us a chance to rule but in 2014 sent us a warning because our performance wasn't at the required standard.'[59]

While An-Nahda might have managed to come through the experience with its core base intact, it was still left heavily bruised by the experience. Furthermore, its time in power generated some serious internal questions about the movement's identity, and exactly what it stood for. As Jourchi explained, 'When you talk to the leadership you feel there is a moral crisis between their discourse and their practice. The advanced cadres of the movement started asking questions: Where is our identity as an Islamic movement? We came to implement Islam, but what happened to us?'[60] Indeed, old debates about whether the movement should separate out its religious activities from its political work re-emerged with added urgency as An-Nahda tried to reconcile the difficulties of being both a religious movement and a political party. For a movement that had come to power confidently promising to reconnect Tunisia with its Islamic identity, An-Nahda's experience ultimately posed the fundamental question of what it meant to be an Islamist political party in contemporary Tunisia.

CONCLUSION

Right from the start, there was never any real doubt about who would reap the benefits of the Arab Spring. Although the international media were quick to laud the fact that the protests were non-ideological in character, and appeared to be driven mainly by secular youth – the so-called 'Facebook Generation' – it was always clear that it was the Islamists who would come to political prominence. The regimes of the region had been warning for decades that, were they to be overthrown, they would be replaced by Islamists (or, in their own terminology, 'terrorists') using this threat as a means of justifying the authoritarian nature of their rule. President Hosni Mubarak had repeatedly emphasised the prospect of the Islamist bogeyman, while Qadhafi's son, Saif Al-Islam, once cautioned that, if there were to be free and fair elections across the Arab world, Islamists would sweep to power. Indeed, there was never any real alternative to the Brotherhood and its counterparts, which were the largest and most organised forces on the scene. But it was not only the Islamists' superior organisational and mobilising power, or even their ability to present themselves as untainted successors to the toppled regimes, that made their rise to power inevitable. It was also a result of the fact that the societies of the region had been unable to produce any real alternative whose influence reached out beyond a narrow urban elite. Furthermore, for all that the Arab Spring was a truly momentous and moving set of events in which the fear of decades was finally broken as people took to the streets, it always promised more than it could ever deliver. In reality the Arab Spring was not built on any intellectual or ideological foundation, nor driven by any revolutionary movement equipped with a new way of conceiving of the state and its relationship to society. Rather, the uprisings were a collective expression of frustration with the status quo and a demand for a better, more dignified life. These loose aspirations could not translate into anything more concrete – least of all a new political force powerful enough to fill the vacuum that opened up when the regimes were brought down. Thus, regardless of the fact that the Islamist organisations may have been ailing bodies ground down by years of repression, they still came to dominate the subsequent transitions in the region – in Egypt and Tunisia, gaining power; in Libya, punching well above their true electoral weight.

So it was, therefore, that the first free elections to be held in the region for decades brought to power some of the most reactionary and undemocratic of forces, who had long prized obedience and loyalty above all else, and whose primary preoccupation over the years had been with their own survival. For all the freshness of the Arab Spring, its societies still ended up opting for what were anachronistic forces that had struggled to reform themselves, and that had undergone little in the way of genuine ideological transformation since their inception. While Ghannouchi may have been putting forward more progressive ideas, especially during his time in exile in the UK, An-Nahda had not been able to update its ideological platform since the mid 1980s, both because of sincere differences of approach and because it feared a backlash from its grass roots. The Egyptian Brotherhood, meanwhile, may have issued a series of reform platforms in the 2000s, but these turned out to be vague and limited texts that seemed to have been produced primarily for an international audience. The Egyptian Brotherhood was always a large, unwieldly body that had proved unable to reform itself effectively. One of the greatest ironies of the Arab Spring was surely the second round of the Egyptian presidential elections, which saw Egyptians having to choose between Mohamed Morsi and Ahmed Shafiq – both of whom represented forces of the past that had been battling it out for decades.

The challenge to the Brotherhood and An-Nahda, therefore, was how to turn themselves into movements that could represent both the present and the future. As senior An-Nahda member Said Ferjani told the *New York Times* in February 2012, 'This is our test', explaining that history would judge his generation not on its ability to take power, but rather on what it did with power after four decades of activism.[1] But when they gained power, these Islamist movements, which had so boldly promised to save the societies of the region by reconnecting them to their authentic selves, seemed almost lost. It was as if they had been so carried along by their own sense of importance and mission that they failed to fully comprehend the enormous scale of the task ahead, and their own lack of preparedness for it. Indeed, they seemed like novices. As senior An-Nahda leader Sheikh Abdelfatah Mourou has argued, 'The Islamists had a partial understanding of the reality they were living in. They had no idea about economics or about the international scene. And most importantly they didn't know why our people are backward.'[2]

Moreover, these movements arrived in power seemingly believing that bringing Islam to the centre of things really would on its own be a solution. For all their political programmes, some of which were more elaborate than others, none of these movements attempted to change any of the fundamental aspects of the states they inherited. That is not to overlook the very real difficulties and constraints they were forced to work under – not least the resistance within the state, as well as parts of the opposition and media that were bent on undermining them at every turn. But it is striking nonetheless that none of these movements proposed any roadmap or serious plan to alter the underpinnings of the state, or even to reform state institutions in any meaningful way. Instead, they opted to try to work through the existing structures of the state, either heaping praise upon them in the hope of winning them over, or trusting that, by clearing out some senior personnel and replacing them with more 'morally righteous' individuals that things would improve. Other than in Libya, where Qadhafi had left no state behind to reform, these movements still viewed the state as the only meaningful locus of power. As An-Nahda Shura Council member Jalal Ouerghli has observed, the Islamists' time in power demonstrated that the 'culture of veneration of the state and its historical role as vanguard is at the heart of Islamist thought', just as it sits at the heart of the thinking of the secular, liberal and nationalist forces in the region.[3]

The paramount concern for the Brotherhood and its counterparts, therefore, became who controlled the state. This partly explains why they were so reluctant to share power or genuinely to co-operate with other political forces. Their authoritarian tendencies also prevented them from accepting the need to bring in others during this time of transition, or to try to create a common platform that could better confront the challenges they were facing. Even An-Nahda, which was more open, and was prepared to form a troika government, ended up alienating its partners by its unwillingness to work in the spirit of true partnership. These movements also alienated others by their failure to break free from the mentality of underground or semi-underground opposition forces, trusting only their own and sensing danger at every turn. They repeatedly fell back on conspiracy theories, as if they explained every negative twist and turn in the political road. The Egyptian Brotherhood also justified its increased reliance on the street through the idea that mobilisation was the only way to counter the danger of being swallowed up by hostile forces, failing to see that this only served to polarise society further.

These movements also fuelled polarisation by their attempts to enact political isolation laws that would bar those with links to the former regimes from holding public office. In the Egyptian case, the Brotherhood backed down early on in the face of objections from the judiciary. But An-Nahda, which was divided over whether to back such legislation (which was first proposed by the CPR), only retreated in 2013, when it was coming under growing pressure and feared alienating the elite any further. In the Libyan case, by contrast, the Brotherhood pushed hard, along with the revolutionary elements on the ground, to ensure that this draconian law went all the way, viewing it as the culmination of the revolution. But in Libya it had another important purpose – that of pushing back against the Brotherhood's political opponents, cutting out key figures and leaders from the liberal current who had links to the Qadhafi regime.

Indeed, despite the Brotherhood's pronouncements of support for democracy, or at least democracy within an Islamic framework, democracy turned out to be little more than a process for these Islamist movements. They understood democracy in procedural rather than cultural terms, meaning that while they were happy to come to power through elections and to signal their electoral legitimacy at every turn, they were less open to democratic values such as tolerance, respect for institutions, and individual dissent. It is notable that the Egyptian Brotherhood legalised its political party, the FJP, but never bothered to legalise itself as a movement. It thus remained an illegal entity in the state its party had been elected to lead. The situation was muddied further by the Brotherhood's failure effectively to distinguish the FJP from the movement, raising all sorts of questions about who was really pulling the strings behind the scenes. In fact, this was an issue faced by all three parties, whose inability to convince others that their parties or political representatives were operating independently of unelected leaders or bodies did further damage to their credibility. Meanwhile, the tendency within parts of these movements to equate democracy with majority rule only added to negative perceptions about them.. All this led many to conclude that these movements were working in their own interests, rather than those of the people they claimed to represent.

If the Islamists had no tangible political vision or strategy, their economic policies were equally thin. Both the Brotherhood and An-Nahda proved content largely to follow the neoliberal policies of the previous regimes, and to refrain from challenging the socio-economic structures of the countries they came to rule.[4] It is true that they adopted a number of populist measures, such as Morsi's raising of public-sector wages and pensions by 15 per cent and An-Nahda's creation of thousands of jobs in the state sector; but this was no different from the policies of the nationalist regimes that had preceded them, which had always relied on the state as a means of buying legitimacy and absorbing popular discontent. As their countries struggled through one economic crisis after another, they had no radical solutions to offer. Even their hopes of investment from the Gulf failed to be realised in the way they had envisaged – and in the Libyan case the link with Qatar, which took on the guise of sponsorship more than investment, proved counterproductive, prompting a major backlash against external interference. Like their political policies, therefore, the Islamists' economic policies boiled down to little more than an attempt to change elites within the existing system, as if this by itself would be a panacea for the economic crises that all three states were experiencing...

In the international arena, meanwhile, the Islamists proved unable to distinguish themselves in any meaningful way. Their foreign policy was largely reactive and lacking in vision. While they spoke of reorientating their international relations more towards the Islamic world, there was little tangible shift, aside from a handful of gestures such as Morsi's attempt to deepen relations with Iran. Morsi also made efforts to visit China and Russia, as a way of demonstrating his independence from the West and his determination to enable Egypt to regain its independence and dignity. These efforts turned out to be futile, as the Brotherhood found itself consistently unable to shatter the popular belief that it was the stooge of the United States. Tellingly, after Morsi's toppling, posters of President Obama sporting a short beard and tarboush (fez) appeared in the streets of Cairo, reflecting the general perception that Washington had backed the Brotherhood's assumption of power, and favoured its continuation.

Such perceptions were clearly overplayed, and chiefly a product of the ideological propaganda of the Brotherhood's detractors. The ascent to power of the Brotherhood and An-Nahda in Egypt and Tunisia, respectively, placed the United States in a serious dilemma.

Although Washington had maintained tentative contacts with the Brotherhood prior to the Arab Spring, and while after coming to power President Obama had signalled a more open policy towards Islamists providing they shunned extremism and terrorism, the White House remained apprehensive about the evolving situation, and was left scrambling to come up with an appropriate response.[5] Once these movements had come to power in democratic elections, however, Washington had little choice but to accommodate to the reality on the ground.

But what was striking about the Brotherhood and its counterparts was that, despite the fact that anti-Westernism had long been the mainstay of their rhetoric, when in power their foreign policy seemed to revolve around making themselves acceptable to Western powers. As Nabil Fahmy, Egypt's former ambassador to Washington and a member of the Al-Dustour party, observed, 'Morsi's foreign policy moves seek to send a message to the world that the Islamist current is moderate and could be dealt with.'[6] This was a position that some members struggled with. In the words of Saad Kattatni's brother, Islam Kattatni, 'They brought us up on a hatred for the West and suddenly we were now part of that camp that we used to hate because [the Brotherhood] relied on the US and Western powers. I couldn't square it.'[7] Similarly, while An-Nahda tried to refocus Tunisia's foreign policy more in the direction of Turkey and Qatar, its main preoccupation seemed to be providing a model of progressive Islamism. It pursued no major reorientation or rethinking of foreign policy. For all their talk of reconstituting the Ummah, which was always a pipe dream, these parties very quickly became bogged down in their own national crises and problems.

The movements therefore struggled to convince their own societies that they were capable of ruling, and could break free from their historical moulds to become leaders for all. Even more striking, however, was that these harbingers of Islamism proved unable to deliver anything tangible in the Islamic sphere itself. For all the scaremongering of the secular elites that the Brotherhood and An-Nahda would turn their countries into the Kandahars of North Africa, in fact these movements made few efforts to Islamicise their societies. While this was partly a result of the desire to present a moderate face to the world, it was also because, when they arrived in power, they discovered that there was very little left for them to do on this front, at least socially. Societies in the region had undergone profound changes over the previous decades, as the creeping power of Islamism that had taken hold since the late 1970s had put secularism firmly on the back foot. Aside from some parts of the elite, societies in all three countries (although to lesser extent in Tunisia) were already deeply socially conservative. Religiosity had taken hold to such an extent that it permeated almost every aspect of life, going far beyond what the founders of these Islamist movements could ever have dreamed of. The promises contained in these movements' political programmes to safeguard the family and protect the sanctity of marriage, for example, seemed almost moot given prevailing social norms. Even An-Nahda's efforts to introduce anti-blasphemy legislation did not cause much of a stir beyond the secular elite, as the spirit behind the proposed law did not sit uncomfortably with large parts of Tunisian society.

As a result, the battle over religion centred on attempts to tie legislation more directly to Sharia. Yet here the Brotherhood and An-Nahda proved unwilling to risk their political gains for such an objective. In the interests of getting the constitution passed quickly, the Egyptian Brotherhood ended up trying to rein in the Salafists' demands to cite Sharia more overtly in the constitution, while An-Nahda dropped its calls for Sharia to be cited as a source of legislation, fudging the issue by arguing that Islam was broader than Sharia. The movements thus ended up compromising on their Islamist priorities to the point where it was difficult to ascertain what they actually stood. In Tunisia, this put the party at odds with its grass roots.

In the Libyan case, by contrast, the Brotherhood supported the principle of Sharia being cited in the constitution as the main source of legislation. Given the extreme conservatism of Libyan society, however, in which there were no truly secular parties, there was no political force arguing against such a principle. Even the so-called liberal parties included the demand for the citing of Sharia as the main source of legislation in their election platforms, prompting the Libyan Brotherhood to accuse them of having stolen their clothes. As a result, the Libyan Brotherhood was not forced to make the same kinds of compromises as its counterparts in Egypt and Tunisia; but this only made it harder for it to distinguish itself from other political forces on the scene, including the Islamist players who were already outflanking it.

These three Islamist movements, which had promised salvation itself, spectacularly failed to deliver. For all their claims to authenticity, they failed to understand the complexity of the societies they were intent on saving. Furthermore, their time in power revealed the flimsiness of their vision, including their conception of political Islam. All three came to seem like movements that had lost their way, and no longer knew what they stood for.

What Future for the Brotherhood?

The speed and crushing nature of the Egyptian Brotherhood's demise, as well as the backlash that accompanied it, plunged the movement into turmoil and disarray. With most of its senior leadership in prison or forced abroad, and those left inside the country on the run, the Egyptian Brotherhood was left fighting for its very survival – all the more so after it was designated as a terrorist organisation by the Egyptian authorities in December 2013. Worse still, other countries followed suit, Saudi Arabia labelling it a terrorist group in March 2014 and the UAE in November 2014. Even the UK, traditionally a refuge for persecuted Brotherhood members, embarked in April 2014 upon a controversial review of the movement that was widely believed, to have been initiated as a result of pressure from the UAE. The results of this review, published in December 2015, held that, while the Egyptian Brotherhood had preferred incremental non-violent change, it was 'prepared to countenance violence – including, from time to time, terrorism – where gradualism is ineffective'.[8] It suddenly appeared, therefore, as if the world was closing ranks against the Brotherhood, largely as a result of its political failings.

Although the Egyptian Brotherhood has tried to hold itself together in the face of such challenges, its desperate situation is clear. It is most obvious in the squabbles that have emerged between those brothers who are inside the country and the old leadership outside. Tellingly, these quarrels have focused not on ideology or the issue of reforming the Brotherhood, but on who has control over what is left of the movement. During 2015 a series of statements and rebuttals appeared in the media, as the old historical leadership abroad, comprising General Secretary Mahmoud Hussein (who resides in Doha and Istanbul), the head of the Brotherhood's International Organisation, Ibrahim Mounir (based in London), and Brotherhood powerhouse Mahmoud Izzat, whose whereabouts are still unknown, clashed with members inside Egypt who, in February 2014, had formed part of a Supreme Administrative Committee to run the movement during the crisis. The spat was mainly over who had the power to issue decisions and appoint leaders, including the Murshid. The historical leadership in exile insisted that, in line with the movement's bylaws, Izzat should take over as Murshid; while those in Egypt maintained that, despite his being incarcerated, Mohamed Badie should remain at the helm.

There appears to have been some disagreement, too, over what stance the movement should take towards the Sissi regime. In their frustration at the ongoing repression, some youth elements from the Brotherhood have advocated a more combative and conflictual approach towards the forces that are repressing them. But, against this, the overall direction of the movement continues to be one of peaceful political action, including demonstrations and protests where possible. While it is possible, as scholar Stephen Brooke has argued, that certain elements could turn to violence, given that these demonstrations will fail to achieve their objectives, there is no indication that there will be a wider shift in the direction of more violent action. As Ammar Fayed has observed, 'The adoption of violence clearly contradicts the reigning cultural model within the Brotherhood. It is of course true that, theoretically, any dominant culture can undergo change, but this requires a conducive environment for doing so.'[9]

As this book has shown, the Brotherhood has never been a revolutionary movement given to sudden or violent action. While it may have contained a handful of more radical thinkers, such as Sayid Qutb, it never promoted radical politics or transformation within the political arena, let alone in the social sphere. The UK government's 2015 review reproduced a total mischaracterisation of the movement when it concluded that the Brotherhood 'promoted a radical, transformative politics, at odds with a millennium of Islamic jurisprudence and statecraft, in which the reconstruction of individual identity is the first step towards a revolutionary challenge to established states and a secularised, if socially conservative, order'.[10] The Brotherhood's focus on individual transformation was never about revolution but always about gradual reform. It is highly unlikely, therefore, that the Brotherhood will determine that its interests lie in shifting towards violent resistance. An added deterrent from taking this course exists in the form of the Brotherhood's close ties to both Qatar and Turkey.

The Brotherhood continues to be committed to playing the long game, sitting it out and clinging to constitutional legitimacy – and, by extension, to the moral high ground – while it awaits the failure of the Sissi regime. The Brotherhood has seemingly retreated into a conviction that its primary strength lies in its patience and capacity to endure, almost as if this were an end in itself. Indeed, there are few indications that the Brotherhood has any intention of embarking on any serious process of reform or review. This is partly because a movement cannot reform while in the depths of crisis, but also because of the nature of the Brotherhood, which has never been open to serious internal review and continues to lay the blame for the trajectory of its experience on external forces.

In fact, waiting it out may not be such a bad policy. Despite the very real backlash that its time in power provoked, as well as the brutal repression that has been meted out to its members, the Brotherhood has not been quashed. It still has a considerable constituency inside Egypt, and, more importantly there is still no other force capable of filling the gap that it left, or able to serve as a counterbalance to the current regime. Moreover, Egypt cannot continue to marginalise a whole swathe of its own society indefinitely. All this suggests, therefore, that Egypt will continue to be locked into the same stale conflict between the Brotherhood and the regime – the two creaking forces of the past.

As for the Libyan Brotherhood, it was certainly deeply shaken by Morsi's fall. But the extreme circumstances in Libya, which became increasingly embroiled in chaos and conflict during 2014 and beyond, somehow subsumed the Brotherhood. That is not to suggest that the movement did not play a part in the conflict. It took sides when the country split into two competing authorities in August 2014, forming part of the reconstituted General National Congress in Tripoli and supporting the forces of Operation Libya Dawn against those of Khalifa Haftar. Like many other political players, the Libyan Brotherhood also resisted the UN-brokered peace process launched in 2014. However, by late 2015 the situation inside the country had reached such a point of calamity that the Libyan Brotherhood changed tack and gave its backing to the UN-sponsored roadmap and the National Accord Government this peace process had produced. This turn put the movement directly at odds with some of the more extreme elements it had been partnered with before, including Libya's ultra-conservative grand mufti, Sheikh Sadiq Al-Ghirianni, who criticised the movement for selling out.

While the Brotherhood's political approach may have damaged its reputation and standing among some constituencies in Libya, the movement is unlikely to disappear. It remains the only force that has a genuinely national reach across Libya's various regions. While some of the liberal parties may claim such reach, for the most part they remain localised and linked to individuals, tribes or towns. Even the National Forces Alliance – the largest and most influential liberal alliance – is more of an umbrella body for various localised groups than a national political entity. This suggests that, once conditions inside Libya settle down, the Brotherhood may well succeed in implanting itself inside the society in a more meaningful way. But it will always be restricted by other forces, such as tribalism and the newly emergent local power centres, which will work as constraining influences.

An-Nahda, meanwhile, continues to absorb the crisis of the Egyptian experience, and, in contrast to the Egyptian Brotherhood, has embarked upon what appears to be a serious process of reflection and review. The movement has at long last expressed its intention to review its ideological platform, and there are strong indications that it is going to separate out its political work from its religious activities. As Ghannouchi himself declared in 2016, 'We set up a movement that is as comprehensive as Islam itself. But times have changed. We are moving towards being a modern party that is specialised in the affairs of state.'[11] More explicitly, senior An-Nahda member Said Ferjani explained:

> The dynamics of *dawa* that belong to the sphere of faith is very different from the dynamics of politics and the sphere of party politics ... In An-Nahda, after wide-ranging debate, there is already consensus among all of the movement's intellectual trends that *dawa* and the party must be fully separated because *dawa* is not in tune with the nature of a modern political party as An-Nahda should be.[12]

Ferjani went further: 'We came to the conclusion that Islamism could be moulded to defend the identity of Muslims both intellectually and philosophically, yet might not be very useful in terms of building a flourishing state and prosperous society ... Therefore, Islamism has become irrelevant for us, and one could say we are living in the "post-Islamist" era.'[13]

An-Nahda has therefore clearly determined that – for all that it may dislike the term – secularism is the only route to political survival. In fact, An-Nahda seems to be undertaking a process of self-reinvention, Ghannouchi touting the idea that it should refer to itself as a Muslim democrat party. While such moves are likely to bring continued praise in the international arena, it is not clear how they will sit with the movement's grass roots. It is this base that provides An-Nahda with its strength, and distinguishes it from the other political parties on the scene who struggle to reach out beyond a narrow elite. Thus, while An-Nahda will continue to be a powerful force inside Tunisia, its central challenge will be simply to hold itself together. This challenge will be all the more pressing once Ghannouchi, who has always been both the movement's driving force and its glue, is no longer on the scene.

Meanwhile, An-Nahda has also adopted a much more strident approach towards condemning extremism, including Daesh, or ISIS. This is something of a departure for the Islamist camp. That is not to suggest that An-Nahda or the Brotherhood have not castigated militancy before; they have long condemned terrorism, and sought to distance themselves from it. Furthermore, despite being labelled as a terrorist organisation, there is still no direct evidence that the Egyptian Brotherhood has been directly or indirectly involved in any of the terrorist attacks that have taken place in Egypt since Morsi's fall. But the Brotherhood in general has traditionally upheld the stance that the best way to deal with Islamist militants is to understand them as hot-headed youths who have become carried away with their religion, who could be brought back to the straight path by being shown the 'correct' way of interpreting Islam. This was also the approach advocated by Ghannouchi towards the Salafists prior to his return to Tunis, and in the early period of An-Nahda's rule.

These Islamist movements have always presented themselves as a bulwark against militancy – a proposition that some Western states have also bought into since the 9/11 attacks, and again during the Arab Spring. As the *New York Times* put it in April 2012, when there were fears that Salafist leader Hazem Salah Abu Ismail was gaining ground in his bid for the presidency, 'American policy makers who once feared a Brotherhood takeover now appear to see the group as an indispensable ally against Egypt's ultraconservatives.'[14] Yet such assumptions turned out to be misplaced. Once they achieved power, these Islamist movements proved simply unable contain the more militant elements that flourished under their noses. Rather than acting as a bulwark against extremism, therefore, moderate Islamism found itself increasingly challenged by these more militant groups, which to some appeared to offer the purity and authenticity that the Brotherhood had promised but failed to deliver. For all its misplaced confidence in its ability to bring its hot-headed youth into line, the Brotherhood ended up being outdone by ISIS. As the Brotherhood brand suffered setback after setback, ISIS seemed to go from strength to strength.

This does not mean that the Brotherhood's time is over, or that it is a spent force. Political Islam may have been dealt a serious blow, but it is certainly not dead, and will continue to be a major feature of the region. The Brotherhood and An-Nahda are mass social movements that have always gone beyond the narrow realm of politics, and cannot be quickly or easily dismissed. More importantly, the conditions that spawned and sustained groups such as the Brotherhood have not fundamentally altered. Although there may be more space for political expression today, at least in Tunisia and Libya, the region is still caught up in the same old dilemma it has been facing for decades – namely, how to confront modernisation and Westernisation, and how to map out a sense of itself and its identity. . The region has also been locked for generations in a vicious cycle of authoritarianism and repression, while the lack of political culture has created a zero-sum politics that is reliant on slogans. Indeed, the Brotherhood and An-Nahda are products of their own societies, and probably behaved no better or worse than would other political forces have done, or indeed are now doing. The Brotherhood's failure and ignominious return to the shadows, therefore, is not only a reflection of the failings of political Islam, but also of the tragedy of a region unable to translate its own revolutions into a better, more confident future.

NOTES

Introduction

1. 'A Talk with the Ennahda Movement's Rachid Ghannouchi', *Asharq Al-Awsat*, 26 December 2011, at english.aawsat.com/2011/12/article55243841/a-talk-with-the-ennahda-movements-rachid-ghannouchi.
2. Tarek Osman, 'Failings of Political Islam', *Cairo Review of Global Affairs*, Fall 2015, at www.thecairoreview.com/uncategorized/failings-of-political-islam.
3. 'Islamism is No Longer the Answer', *Economist*, 20 December 2014, at www.economist.com/news/middle-east-and-africa/21636776-political-islam-under-pressure-generals-monarchs-jihadistsand.
4. 'The Brotherhood's Fall and What It Means for Political Islam', Al-Monitor, 21 July 2013, at www.al-monitor.com/pulse/politics/2013/07/egypt-brotherhood-fall-political-islam-implications.html#ixzz453hlbJ4F.
5. See, for example, Olivier Roy, *The Failure of Political Islam*, Cambridge, MA, Harvard University Press, 1996.
6. Jacob Resneck and Jabeen Bhatti, 'Does Morsi Ouster Signal End of "Political Islam"?', *USA Today*, 7 July 2013, at www.usatoday.com/story/news/world/2013/07/07/egypt-middle-east/2496403/.
7. Jocelyne Cesari, 'Egypt Post Morsi: Why There Is No Reason to Hope for a Real Democratic Transition', Huffington Post, 26 July 2013, at www.huffingtonpost.com/jocelyne-cesari/egypt-post-morsi_b_3658288.html.
8. Ibid.
9. Khalil Al Anani, 'The Muslim Brotherhood After Morsi', 2 October 2013, The Arab Center for Research and Policy Studies, at english.dohainstitute.org/release/eca3b305-1038-473b-a67e-b2a63af9ef21.
10. Ashraf El-Sherif, 'The Egyptian Muslim Brotherhood's Failures', Carnegie Endowment, 1 July 2014, at carnegieendowment.org/2014/07/01/egyptian-muslim-brotherhood-s-failure.
11. Eric Trager, 'How Morsi Came Undone', *New York Daily News*, 5 July 2013, at www.washingtoninstitute.org/policy-analysis/view/how-morsi-came-undone.
12. Hani Sabra, 'The New Egypt at (Almost) Two', *Foreign Policy*, 14 January 2013, at foreignpolicy.com/2013/01/14/the-new-egypt-at-almost-two.
13. Carrie Rosefsky Wickham, 2004, 'The Path to Moderation: Strategy and

Learning in the Formation of Egypt's Wasat Party', *Comparative Politics* 36: 2 (2004), pp. 205–28.

Chapter One

1. Sa'ad Al-Qursh, *Althawra Alan: Youmiat min Midan al-Tahrir* ('Revolution Now: Diaries from Tahrir Square'), Cairo, Kotob Khan, 2012.
2. 'Kerry: Muslim Brotherhood "Stole" Egypt's Revolution', *Associated Press*, 21 November 2013.
3. Francois Burgat and William Dowell, *The Islamic Movement in North Africa*, Austin, TX, Center for Middle Eastern Studies at The University of Texas, 1993, pp. 34–35.
4. Carrie Rosefsky Wickham, *The Muslim Brotherhood: Evolution of an Islamist Movement*, Princeton, NJ, Princeton University Press, 2013, p. 23.
5. Facebook page, 'Iinjazat al-Ikhwan al-Muslimin' ('The Achievements of the Muslim Brotherhood'), 24 April 2015, in Arabic at ar-ar.facebook.com/Achievements.Of.Ikhwans.
6. 'Al-Ikhwan al-Muslimoun Kama Yrahm Farid Abdel Khaliq' ('A Witness in Time: The Muslim Brotherhood as Seen by Farid Abdel Khaliq'), Episode 1, Shahid Alla Aser, Al-Jazeera, 7 December 2003, at www.aljazeera.net.
7. Al-Qursh, *Althawra Alan*.
8. Nathan Brown, *When Victory is Not an Option: Islamist Movements in Arab Politics*, Ithaca, NY, Cornell University Press, 2012, p. 181.
9. Ibid., p. 208.
10. '60 Alf Nasha Aiftiradi Yusharikun fi Muzahara Beid al-Sharta' ('60,000 Virtual Activists Take Part in The Demonstration on Police Day'), *Shorouk News*, 20 January 2011, in Arabic at www.masress.com/shorouk/380000.
11. Al-Qursh, *Althawra Alan*.
12. Hicham Al-Wadi, *al-Islamioun fi alssulta: Halat Misr* ('Islamists in Power: The Case of Egypt'), *Mustaqbal al-Araby* 413, July 2013, in Arabic at www.caus.org.lb/PDF/EmagazineArticles/mustaqbal_413_mustaqbal_413_hicham%20al3wadi.pdf.
13. *Al-Qursh, Sa'ad, Althawra Alan: Youmiat min Midan al-Tahrir* ('Revolution Now: Diaries from Tahrir Square'), Cairo, Kotob Khan, 2012.
14. 'Rafiq Alrais Bialssjin: Ikhwan Wadi Alnatrun Akhrjuna ... Hamas bariyat min Aiqtihamih' (*'A Com*rade of the President in Prison: The Brothers Got Us Out of Natrun Valley ... Hamas is Innocent of Storming It'), *Shorouk News*, 15 May 2013, in Arabic at www.shorouknews.com/news/view.aspx?cdate=15052013&id=890876bb-334a-43c7-aa5d-a4154332d3ed.
15. 'Elwatan Tanshur Ness Mudhakirat Shabab Al-Ikhwan ean Kawalees Adm Musharakat Aljama'at Youm 25 Yanayir 2011' ('Elwatan Publishes the Memoirs of Brotherhood Youth Regarding the Non-Participation of the Group on 25 January 2011'), *Elwatan*, Cairo, 24 January 2013, in Arabic at www.elwatannews.com/news/details/118898.

16. 'Muslim Brotherhood's Rashad al-Bayoumi, "The Revolution Will Continue Until Our Demands Are Met"', *Spiegal Online*, 7 February 2011, at www.spiegel.de/international/world/muslim-brotherhood-s-rashad-al-bayoumi-the-revolution-will-continue-until-our-demands-are-met-a-743919.html.
17. Aladdin Abdelmonem, 'Shuhud Eian ala Hajm Wadawr al-Ikhwan fi Althawra Almisria' ('Witnesses on the Size and Role of the Muslim Brotherhood in the Egyptian Revolution'), *Al-Masry Al-Youm*, Cairo, 13 November 2011, in Arabic at www.almasryalyoum.com.
18. Charles Sennott, 'Inside the Muslim Brotherhood: Part 1' *Global Post*, 21 February 2011, at www.globalpost.com/dispatch/egypt/110220/inside-the-muslim-brotherhood.
19. Ibid.
20. Ibid.
21. Mariz Tadros, *The Muslim Brotherhood in Contemporary Egypt: Democracy Redefined or Confined?*, London, Routledge, 2012, p. 35.
22. 'Wikileaks Takshif Wathiqat Qarar Insihab al-Ikhwan min Almaydan ba'ad Mouqa'at Aljamal' ('Wikileaks Reveals a Document on the Decision to Withdraw the Brotherhood from the Square after the Battle of the Camels'), *Masrawy*, 20 June 2015, in Arabic at www.masrawy.com.
23. Author interview with Abdelmonem Abul Futuh, Cairo, December 2013.
24. Ibid.
25. Amer Chamakh, *Al-Ikhwan Al-Muslimun Wathwrat 25 Yanayir* ('The Muslim Brotherhood and the Revolution of 25 January'), Dar al-Tawzie Walnashr, Egypt, 2013, in Arabic at ketab4pdf.blogspot.co.uk/2015/10/pdf-Download-book-Muslim-Brotherhood-revolution-January-25.html.
26. Ibid.
27. Ibid.
28. 'Wikileaks Takshif Wathiqat Qarar Insihab al-Ikhwan min Almaydan ba'ad Mouqa'at Aljamal' ('Wikileaks Reveals A Document On The Decision To Withdraw The Brotherhood From The Square After The Battle of the Camel'), *Masrawy*, 20 June 2015, in Arabic at www.masrawy.com.
29. 'Egypt: Islamist Muslim Brotherhood to Join Second Round of Talks with Govt', *Adnkronos International*, 10 February 2011, at www1.adnkronos.com/IGN/Aki/English/Security/Egypt-Islamist-Muslim-Brotherhood-to-join-second-round-of-talks-with-govt_311664031177.html.
30. Al-Qursh, *Althawra Alan*.
31. Mohammed Habib, *Al-Ikhwan Al-Muslimun: Bayn Alsueud Walriasa Watakul Alsheria* ('The Muslim Brotherhood, the Rising, the Presidency and the Erosion of Legitimacy'), Cairo, Sama Nashar, 2013.
32. 'Egypt Protests: Muslim Brotherhood's Concessions Prompt Anger', *Christian Science Monitor*, 7 February 2011, at www.csmonitor.com/World/Middle-East/2011/0207/Egypt-protests-Muslim-Brotherhood-s-concessions-prompt-anger.
33. Quoted in Tadros, *Muslim Brotherhood in Contemporary Egypt*, p. 37.

34. 'Egypt: Islamist Muslim Brotherhood to Join Second Round of Talks with Govt', *Adnkronos International*, 10 February 2011, at www1.adnkronos.com/IGN/Aki/English/Security/Egypt-Islamist-Muslim-Brotherhood-to-join-second-round-of-talks-with-govt_311664031177.html.
35. Author interview with Mohamed Soudan, London, January 2014.
36. Habib, *Al-Ikhwan Al-Muslimun.*
37. Author interview with Mohamed Soudan, London, 2014.
38. 'Egypt: Military Pledges to Stop Forced "Virginity Tests"', Amnesty International, 27 June 2011, at www.amnesty.org/en/press-releases/2011/06/egypt-military-pledges-stop-forced-virginity-tests.
39. International Crisis Group, 'Lost in Transition: The World According to Egypt's SCAF', Middle East/North Africa Report 121, 24 April 2012, at www.crisisgroup.org/~/media/Files/Middle%20East%20North%20Africa/North%20Africa/Egypt/121-lost-in-transition-the-world-according-to-egypts-scaf.pdf.
40. Ibid.
41. Habib, *Al-Ikhwan Al-Muslimun.*
42. Author interview with Dr Abdelmawgoudd Dardery via Skype, July 2014.
43. Ibid.
44. For a full discussion of the proposed amendments, see Nathan J. Brown and Michele Dunne, 'Egypt's Draft Constitutional Amendments Answer Some Questions and Raise Others', Carnegie Endowment for International Peace, 1 March 2011, at carnegieendowment.org/2011/03/01/egypt-s-draft-constitutional-amendments-answer-some-questions-and-raise-others#.
45. International Crisis Group, 'Lost in Transition'.
46. 'Khairat Al-Shater on "The Nahda Project" (Complete Translation)', *Current Trends in Islamist Ideology*, 10 April 2012, Hudson Institute, at www.hudson.org/research/9820-khairat-al-shater-on-the-nahda-project-complete-translation-.
47. Ibid.
48. 'A Talk with Muslim Brotherhood's Rashad al-Bayoumi', *Asharq Al-Awsat*, 27 February 2011.
49. 'Freedom and Justice Party', *Jadaliyya*, 22 November 2011, at www.jadaliyya.com/pages/index/3154/freedom-and-justice-party.
50. Nathan J. Brown, 'The Muslim Brotherhood as Helicopter Parent', *Foreign Policy*, 27 May 2011, at foreignpolicy.com/2011/05/27/the-muslim-brotherhood-as-helicopter-parent.
51. Khalil Al-Anani, 'Egypt's Freedom & Justice Party: To Be or Not to Be Independent', Carnegie Endowment for International Peace, 1 June 2011, at carnegieendowment.org/sada/?fa=44324.
52. Author interview with Mahmoud Hussein, Doha, April 2014.
53. Hicham Al-Wadi, 'Al-Islamiuwn fi alssulta: Halat Misr' ('Islamists in Power: The Case of Egypt'), *Mustaqbal Al-Araby*, Beirut, 413 (July 2013), at www.caus.org.lb/PDF/EmagazineArticles/mustaqbal_413_mustaqbal_413_hicham%20

al3wadi.pdf.

54. Author interview with Amr Darrag, Doha, April 2014.
55. Jihad Awda, *Suqut Dawlat Al-Ikhwan* ('The Fall of the Ikhwan's State'), Cairo, Kenouz, 2014.
56. 'Senior Judges in Egypt: Field Marshal Not Entitled to Dissolve Parliament', Ikhwanweb, 29 March 2012, in Arabic at www.ikhwanweb.com/article.php?id=29823.
57. Author interview with Mohamed Soudan, London, January 2014.
58. 'Muslim Brotherhood Says Won't Bid for Presidency in Egypt, *RIA Novosti*, 4 February 2011, at sputniknews.com/world/20110204/162449780.html.
59. Author interview with Abdelmonem Abul Futuh, Cairo, June 2014.
60. Habib, *Al-Ikhwan Al-Muslimun*.
61. Ibid.
62. David D. Kirkpatrick, 'Egypt Elections Expose Divisions in Muslim Brotherhood', *New York Times*, 19 June 2011, at www.nytimes.com/2011/06/20/world/middleeast/20egypt.html?_r=0.
63. Kristen Chick, 'In Major Reversal, Muslim Brotherhood Will Vie for Egypt's Presidency', *Christian Science Monitor*, 1 April 2012, at www.csmonitor.com/World/Middle-East/2012/0401/In-major-reversal-Muslim-Brotherhood-will-vie-for-Egypt-s-presidency.
64. 'Egypt's Brotherhood Defends Presidential Bid', Al-Jazeera, 3 April 2012, at www.aljazeera.com/news/middleeast/2012/04/2012431364626861 7.html.
65. Habib, *Al-IkhwanAl-Muslimun*.
66. Author interview with Abdulmonem Abul Futuh, Cairo, June 2014.
67. Ibid.
68. Katherine Jane O'Neill, 'Exclusive: How Mursi's English "Destroyed" his American Students', *Al-Arabiya*, 10 April 2013, at english.alarabiya.net/en/perspective/features/2013/04/10/-Exclusive-How-Mursi-s-English-destroyed-his-American-students-.html.
69. Habib, *Al-Ikhwan Al-Muslimun*.
70. Ibid.
71. Ashrif Eid Antably, 'Ikhwan Wiki, Jwanib min Injazat Aldduktur Muhammad Morsi' ('Aspects of the Achievements of Dr Mohamed Morsi'), in Arabic at www.ikhwanwiki.com.
72. Author interview with Abdelmonem Abul Futuh, Cairo, June 2014.
73. Facebook page, 'Iinjazat Al-Ikhwan Al-Muslimin'.

Chapter Two

1. Mohamed Elsayed Saleem, 'Al'da Alsiasi Liltayarat Al'islamia fi Misr Mundh Thawrat 25 Yanayir' ('The Political Performance of the Islamic Currents in Egypt since the Revolution of 25 January) in *Al-Islamiyoun wa Nizam al-Hukum al-Democrati* ('The Islamists and The Democratic System: Trends and Experiences'), Beirut, Arab Centre for Research and Policy Studies,

September 2013, p. 432.

2. Author interview with Amr Mousa, Cairo, June 2014.
3. 'Al-Ikhwan al-Muslimoun Kama Yrahm Farid Abdel Khaliq' ('A Witness in Time: The Muslim Brotherhood as Seen by Farid Abdel Khaliq.'), Al-Jazeera, Shahid Alla Aser, Episode 1, 7 December 2003, in Arabic at www.aljazeera.net.
4. Mahmoud Abdelhalim, *Al-Ikhwan Almuslimoun, Ahdath Sunat Altareeq, Ru'iah Min Aldakhil* ('The Muslim Brotherhood: The Events that Made History – An Insider Vision'), Alexanderia, Dar al-Dawa, 2004, vol. 2, p. 360.
5. For an analysis of these platforms, see Alison Pargeter, *The Muslim Brotherhood: The Burden of Tradition*, London, Saqi Books, 2010.
6. 'Dr Morsi's Electoral Program – General Features of Nahda (Renaissance) Project', Ikhwanweb, 28 April 2012, at www.ikhwanweb.com/article.php?id=29932.
7. 'Khairat Al-Shater on "The Nahda Project"', *Current Trends in Islamist Ideology*, 10 April 2012, Hudson Institute, at www.hudson.org/research/9820-khairat-al-shater-on-the-nahda-project-complete-translation-.
8. 'Mustaqbel Al-Ikhwan wa ila Qatihim bi Muassasat Al-Riyasa' ('The Future of the Brotherhood and its Relationship with the Presidency.'), Al-Jazeera, Bila Hadoud, 8 July 2012, in Arabic at www.aljazeera.net.
9. 'Dr Morsi's Electoral Program', Ikhwanweb.
10. 'Ikhwan Alfyum: Mashrue Alnnahda hua Mashrue Alnabi Muhammad' ('Brothers of Fayoum: The Renaissance Project is a Project of the Prophet Muhammad'), *Shorouk News*, 15 May 2012, in Arabic at www.shorouknews.com/news/view.aspx?cdate=15052012&id=0f5a36a4-49a6-4e8a-9ce8-6abec1e2fbbb.
11. 'Clarification from Dr Morsi Campaign Regarding Slogan', Ikhwanweb, 23 April 2012, at www.ikhwanweb.com/article.php?id=29918.
12. 'Awa: Min Yadaei Tanfidh Mashrue An-Nahda fi Arbe Sanawat la Yahtarim A'aKoulina' ('Awa: Those who Claim that An-Nahda Project Can Be Implemented in Four Years Don't Respect our Minds'), *Ahram*, 20 May 2012, in Arabic at www.ahram.org.eg/archive/Al-Mashhad-Al-Syiassy/News/150293.aspx.
13. Dr Mohammed Habib, *Al-Ikhwan Al-Muslimun: Bayn Alsueud Walriasa Watakul Alsheria* ('The Muslim Brotherhood: The Rising, the Presidency and the Erosion of Legitimacy'), Cairo, Sama Nashar, 2013.
14. Twitterfeed, at twitter.com/hashtag/ReplaceAMovieNameWithNahda?src=hash.
15. Saad Eddine Ibrahim, 'Mashrue Nahda Alshatir Yahtaj Shebaan Mustwrdaan' ('Shater's Renaissance Project Needs an Imported Population'), *Al-Masry Al-Youm*, 6 October 2012, in Arabic at today.almasryalyoum.com/article2.aspx?ArticleID=355763.
16. Alexa Cerf, 'Mona Makram-Ebei on Egypt's Political Future', Middle East Institute, 11 July 2013, at www.mei.edu/events/mona-makram-ebeid-egypts-political-future.
17. Author interview with former state security official who wished to remain anonymous, Cairo, June 2014.

18. Ibid.
19. Author interview with Alaa Abu Al-Nasser, Cairo, December 2013.
20. Habib, *Al-Ikhwan Al-Muslimun*.
21. Ibid.
22. 'Abdelmonem Abul Futuh li *Watan*: Morsi Yuhdth Alnas Waezaan Bi'akthar min Hadith Rayiys Dawla' ('Abdelmonem Abulfutuh to *Watan*: Morsi Speaks to People More as a Preacher than the Head of State'), *Al-Watan*, 12 November 2012, in Arabic at alwatan.kuwait.tt/articledetails.aspx?id=232993.
23. The court made this ruling on the grounds that some of the seats reserved for political parties had been won by political parties.
24. Borzou Daragahi, 'Morsi Swears Presidential Oath to Tahrir Crowd', *Financial Times*, 29 June 2012, at www.ft.com.
25. Ibid.
26. Mustafa Bakri, *Suqut Al-Ikhwan: Lahazat Alakhira bayn Morsi wa Sisi* ('The Fall of the Ikhwan: The Final Moments between Morsi and Sisi'), Cairo, Al-Dar al-Misria al-Lubnania, 2013, p. 34.
27. 'Inqisam Ikhwani Hawl Ada Morsi Alqism Amam "Aldostoria"' ('Split among the Brothers about Morsi Performing the Oath in Front of the "Constitutional"'), *El-Watan News*, 29 June 2012, in Arabic at www.elwatan-news.com/news/details/21995.
28. Bakri, *Suqut Al-Ikhwan*, p. 34.
29. Ibid.
30. 'President Mohamed Morsi's Speech at Cairo University, Saturday, June 30, after Taking Oath of Office', Ikhwanweb, 1 July 2012, at www.ikhwanweb.com/article.php?id=30156.
31. Bakri, *Suqut Al-Ikhwan*.
32. Author interview with Abdelmonem Abul Futuh, Cairo, June 2014.
33. Abdel-Rahman Hussein, 'Egypt Swears in First Post-Revolution Cabinet with Plenty of Old Guard', *Guardian*, 2 August 2012, at www.theguardian.com/world/2012/aug/02/egypt-middleeast.
34. Author interview with Abdelmonem Abul Futuh, Cairo, June 2014.
35. Author interview with Amr Darrag, Doha, April 2014.
36. Ibid.
37. Bakri, *Suqut Al-Ikhwan*.
38. 'Once Election Allies, Egypt's "Fairmont" Opposition turn against Morsi', Ahram Online, 27 June 2013, at english.ahram.org.eg/NewsContent/1/152/74485/Egypt/Morsi,-one-year-on/-Once-election-allies,-Egypts-Fairmont-opposition-.aspx
39. Heba Saleh, 'Egypt: A Revolution Betrayed', *Financial Times*, 27 June 2013, at www.ft.com.
40. Author interview with Mahmoud Hussein, Doha, April 2014.
41. 'Abdelmonem Abul Futuh ... Almasar Alsiassi fi Misr' ('Abdelmonem Abul Futuh ... Egypt's Political Path'), Today's Interview, Al-Jazeera, 24 July 2012, in Arabic at www.aljazeera.net.

42. Author interview with Abdelmonem Abul Futuh, Cairo, June 2014.
43. Mahmoud Hamdy Abulqassem, 'Daftar Alkhta ... 10 Ashuhur min Hakam al-Ikhwan al-Muslimin li Misr' ('The Notebook of Mistakes ... Ten Months of the Muslim Brotherhood's Rule in Egypt'), Al-Arabiya Institute, 22 March 2013, in Arabic at www.alarabiya.net.
44. Author interview with Islam Al-Katatni, Cairo, June 2014.
45. Other appointees included Khalid Kazzaz, Ayman Hudhud and Abdul-Mageed Al-Mishali.
46. Author interview with Dr Kamel Helbawy, Cairo, December 2013.
47. 'All The President's Men', *Al-Ahram Weekly*, 17 June 2013, at weekly.ahram.org.eg/News/3158/17/All-the-president%E2%80%99s-men.aspx.
48. Author interview with anonymous Egyptian journalist, April 2014.
49. Author interview with Dr Kamel Helbawy, Cairo, December 2013.
50. 'Al-Hurria Waladala Yutliq Hamla Bitilfizoun Turki Lijadhb Alssiaha' ('Freedom and Justice Launches a Campaign on Turkish TV to Attract Tourism'), Islam Memo, 12 December 2011, in Arabic at islammemo.cc/print.aspx?id=139785.
51. Alaa Bayoumi, 'The Many Faces of Mohamed Morsi', Al-Jazeera, 13 December 2012, at www.aljazeera.com/indepth/features/2012/12/20121213713329207 40.html.
52. Ibid.
53. Bahi Al-Deen Hassan (ed), *Rowaq*, No. 65–66, Cairo Institute for Human Rights Studies, 2013, at www.cihrs.org/wp-content/uploads/2014/04/rowaq65-66.pdf.
54. Habib, *Al-Ikhwan Al-Muslimun*.
55. Author interview with Abdelmonem Abul Futuh, Cairo, May 2014.
56. Ibid.
57. Author interview with Mohamed Soudan, London, January 2014.
58. Author interview with Abdelmonem Abul Futuh, Cairo, May 2014.
59. Author interview with Amr Mousa, Cairo, June 2014.
60. Author interview with Gamal Heshmat, Istanbul, February 2014.
61. Author interview with state security official who wished to remain anonymous, Cairo, June 2014.
62. Heba Saleh, 'Egypt's "Deep State" Accused of Whipping Up Anti-Morsi Feeling', *Financial Times*, 3 July 2013 at www.ft.com.
63. Yezid Sayigh, 'Above the State: The Officers' Republic in Egypt', Carnegie Middle East Center, 1 August 2012, at carnegie-mec.org/publications/?fa=48972#.
64. Author interview with Ashraf Abdel Ghaffar, Istanbul, February 2014.
65. Author interview with Gamal Abdelsattar, Doha, April 2014.
66. Ibid.
67. Yezid Sayigh, 'Missed Opportunity: The Politics of Police Reform in Egypt and Tunisia', Carnegie Middle East Center, March 2015, at carnegieendowment.org/files/missed_opportunity.pdf.

68. Author interview with Gamal Heshmat, Istanbul, February 2014.
69. Author interview with Mahmoud Hussein, Doha, April 2014.
70. Ibid.
71. Author interview with Gamal Heshmat, Istanbul, February 2014.
72. Author interview with Ashraf Abdel Gaffar, Istanbul, February 2014.
73. Author interview with Dr Abdelmawgud Dardery via Skype, July 2014.
74. 'Morsi, Tantawi Return to Cairo from Sinai after Flying Visit', Ahram Online, 6 August 2012, at www.masress.com/en/ahramonline/49785.
75. Bakri, *Suqut Al-Ikhwan*.
76. 'Morsi Misses Military Funeral for Soldiers Killed in Sinai', Middle East Online, 7 August 2012, at www.middle-east-online.com/english/?id=53792.
77. Author interview with Mohamed Soudan, London, January 2014.
78. Bakri, *Suqut Al-Ikhwan*.
79. Ibid.
80. Ibid.
81. 'Morsi Yuqil Rayis al-Mukhabarat Wamuhafiz shamal Sayna ala Khelfia Majzara Rafah' ('Morsi Sacks Intelligence Chief and the Governor of North Sinai on the Back of Rafah Massacre'), *Al-Sharq Al-Awast*, 9 August 2012, in Arabic at aawsat.com.
82. 'Mudhakirat al-Mustashar al-Qanuni Lilmaezul Turwi Qissat Itaha Betntawy Wananan' ('Legal Advisor's Memoir Relates the Story of Tantawi and Annan's Expulsion'), *Shorouk News*, 23 November 2013, in Arabic at www.shorouknews.com/news/view.aspx?cdate=23112013&id=29e6b622-acca-4279-b120-68f4dc1bcba8.
83. Kareem Fahim, 'In Upheaval for Egypt, Morsi Forces Out Military Chiefs', *New York Times*, 12 August 2012, at www.nytimes.com/2012/08/13/world/middleeast/egyptian-leader-ousts-military-chiefs.html.
84. Abdel-Rahman Hussein, 'Egypt Defence Chief Tantawi Ousted in Surprise Shakeup', *Guardian*, 13 August 2012, at www.theguardian.com/world/2012/aug/12/egyptian-defence-chief-ousted-shakeup.
85. 'Asrar Alelaqalat Alghamida Bayn Almushir Tantawi Walfariq AbdulFattah al-Sissi' ('Secrets of the Mysterious Relationship between Field Marshal Tantawi and Lieutenant-General Abdul Fattah al-Sissi'), *Sout Almaldaien*, n.d., in Arabic at www.soutalmalaien.com/products15.php?id=490#.VgAjC_lViko. See also 'Abdullah Sanaw: Nesf Inqilab … Nesf Itifaq' ('Abdullah Sanaw: Half Coup … Half Agreement'), *Shorouk News*, 20 August 2012, at www.masress.com/shorouk/598058.
86. Notably, Al-Sissi did not take over Tantawi's office when he was appointed defence minister but continued, out of respect to his predecessor, to operate from his own office. 'Asrar Alelaqalat Alghamida Bayn Almushir Tantawi Walfariq Abdul Fattah al-Sissi' ('Secrets of Thethe Mysterious Relationship between Field Marshal Tantawi and Lieutenant-General Abdul Fattah al-Sissi'), *Sout Almaldaien*, n.d., in Arabic at www.soutalmalaien.com/products15.php?id=490#.V3YfYDXENzV.

87. Ernesto Londoño, 'Egypt's Morsi Defies Predictions', *Washington Post*, 13 August 2012, at www.washingtonpost.com/world/middle_east/egypts-morsi-defies-predictions/2012/08/13/da795aaa-e579-11e1-9739-eef99c5fb285_story.html.
88. 'Sanawi: Tantawi Tahul Ala Rahina fi Alqasr Aljumhuri ... Waistaqbal Qarar Iqalitah Mutamasikan' ('Sanawi: Tantawi Became a Hostage at the Presidential Palace ... and Met His Dismissal with Composure'), *Dostor*, 8 September 2012.
89. Dan Murphy, 'Egypt's President Morsi Fires Senior General Tantawi, Asserting his Power', *Christian Science Monitor*, 12 August 2012, at www.csmonitor.com/World/Security-Watch/Backchannels/2012/0812/Egypt-s-President-Morsi-fires-senior-general-Tantawi-asserting-his-power.
90. Author interview with Mahmoud Hussein, Doha, April 2014.
91. 'Tafasil Alkhira Lihukm Morsi' ('The Last Moments of Morsi's Rule'), Al-Jazeera, Bila Hadoud, Episode 1, 11 December 2013, in Arabic at www.aljazeera.net.
92. Author interview with Gamal Heshmat, Istanbul, February 2014.
93. '"Battle of the Camels" Acquittals Shock Egypt', BBC Online, 11 October 2012, at www.bbc.co.uk/news/world-middle-east-19910446.
94. Ibid.
95. 'Abdel Megid Mahmoud ... Limansib Waliqala' ('Abdel Megid Mahmoud ... The Post and the Dismissal'), Al-Jazeera, 13 October 2012, in Arabic at www.aljazeera.net.
96. 'Al-Arian Lilnayib Alam: Alkhiar Alafdil lak Qabul Mansib Alssafir Bilfatikan' ('Al-Arian to the Attorney General: The Best Option for You Is to Accept the Post of Ambassador to the Vatican'), *Ahram*, 12 October 2012, in Arabic at gate.ahram.org.eg/News/260754.aspx.
97. 'Egypt Prosecutor-General to Remain in Office', Al-Jazeera, 13 October 2012, at www.aljazeera.com/news/middleeast/2012/10/2012101313562637I129.html.
98. Author interview with Saleh Abdelmaqsoud, Doha, April 2014.
99. Bakri, *Suqut Al-Ikhwan*.
100. 'Mahsoub: Alfulul Najahu Bizhar Morsi Dhaefan' ('Mahsoub: Remnants Succeeded in Portraying Morsi as Weak'), Al-Jazeera, Shahid Alla Aser, Episode 12, in Arabic at www.aljazeera.net.
101. 'Al-Bishri Lalshrouk: Qarar Morsi Idwan Ala Alssulta Alqadayia' (Al-Bishri to *Shorouk*: Morsi's Decision is an Aggression Against the Judiciary), *Shorouk News*, 12 October 2012, in Arabic at www.shorouknews.com/news/view.aspx?cdate=12102012&id=5c0c219d-9fa2-41ee-acc9-bb4367cefbfd.
102. 'Muslim Brotherhood to Join Protests against Acquittal of Revolution's Camel Battle Defendants', Ikhwanweb, 11 October 2012, at ikhwanweb.com/article.php?id=30325.
103. 'Arian Youtalib Shabab Al-Ikhwan Bimuhasarat Maktab Alnnayib Ala'am' ('Arian Asks Young Brothers to Surround the Prosecutor General's Office'), *Shorouk News*, 12 October 2012, at www.shorouknews.com/news/view.

aspx?cdate=12102012&id=d9eb4b9d-f18a-4f62-92db-0c6220164467.

104. 'Ashri: Counter-Revolution Old-Regime Stalwarts Free to Roam Again', Ikhwanweb, 13 October 2012 at www.ikhwanweb.com/article.php?id=30328
105. 'Muslim Brotherhood Statement on Friday 12 October Protests and Clashes', Ikhwanweb, 14 October 2012 at www.ikhwanweb.com/article.php?id=30329.
106. Mostafa Ali, 'Morsi Politely "Asks" Defiant Prosecutor-General to Stay On', Ahram Online, 13 October 2012, at english.ahram.org.eg/NewsContent/1/0/55526/Egypt/0/Morsi-politely-asks-defiant-prosecutorgeneral-to-s.aspx.
107. Ibid.
108. 'Mahsoub: Alfulul Najahu Bizhar Morsi dhaefan', Al-Jazeera.
109. 'Halka Nikashia: Alhrakata Aslamyia fi Watan Alrabi' ('Discussion Forum: Islamic Movement in the Arab Nation'), *Mustaqbal* 416 (October 2013), at www.caus.org.lb/PDF/EmagazineArticles/mustaqbal_416_halkanikashia(alhrakatalaslamya).pdf.
110. Gamal Essam El-Din, 'Salafists Battle for a Religious State in Egypt', Ahram Online, 12 July 2012, at english.ahram.org.eg/WriterArticles/NewsContentP/1/47554/Egypt/Salafists-battle-for-a-religious-state-in-Egypt.aspx.
111. 'Mohamed Morsi: Qate Yed Alsariq Lays min Alshria Inama Hakam Fuqahi' ('Mohamed Morsi: Cutting Off the Hand of a Thief Is Not from Sharia, Rather It Is a Rule of Jurisprudence'), YouTube, 10 November 2012, at www.youtube.com/watch?v=nqvf1HffCus.

Chapter Three

1. Heba Saleh, 'Egypt's "Deep State" Accused of Whipping Up Anti-Morsi Feeling, *Financial Times*, 3 July 2013 at www.ft.com.
2. 'Egypt Voices: Protesters See Failed Revolution', BBC Online, 25 January 2013, at www.bbc.co.uk/news/world-middle-east-21206156.
3. 'Have Morsi's First 100 Days Been a Success?', Al-Jazeera, 9 Oct 2012, at www.aljazeera.com/programmes/insidestory/2012/10/201210952026585832.html.
4. Facebook page, 'Injazat Al-Ikhwan al-Muslimin' ('The Achievements of the Muslim Brotherhood'), 24 April 2015, at ar-ar.facebook.com/Achievements.Of.Ikhwans.
5. Mohammed Habib, *Al-Ikhwan Al-Muslimun: Bayn Alsueud Walriasa Watakul Alsheria* ('The Muslim Brotherhood: The Rising, the Presidency and the Erosion of Legitimacy'), Cairo, Sama Nashar, 2013.
6. Riad Zaki Qasim, 'A Report on the Future of Political Islam in the Arab World', Arab Unity Studies Centre, *Mustaqabal Alrabi* 419 (November 2013), at www.caus.org.lb/PDF/EmagazineArticles/mustaqbal_419_rayadkassam.pdf.
7. 'Tafasil Alkhira Lihukm Morsi' ('The Last Moments of Morsi's Rule' Episode 1), Al-Jazeera, Bila Hadoud, Episode 1, 11 December 2013, in Arabic at www.aljazeera.net.

8. The investment minister in Morsi's government, Yahyia Hamid, explained that '[a]fter three months of discussions of that project [to create an industrial zone on the banks of the Suez Canal] in the cabinet the representative of the army that was sent by Al-Sissi came to us and said the army has big reservations ... They don't want to give up any land in the Suez Canal ... The project should be done through the army.' He went on, 'They hindered the law ... For four months the law didn't even leave the cabinet to go to the Shura Council to be discussed. For five months the army stood against the project' ('Tafasil Alkhira Lihukm Morsi', Al-Jazeera). When asked about why the army had blocked such projects, the only justification a senior military official could give was that, he claimed, the Brotherhood was intent on 'selling everything off to Qatar' (author interview with anonymous military official, Cairo, June 2014).
9. 'English Text of Morsi's Constitutional Declaration', *Ahram*, 22 November 2012, at english.ahram.org.eg/News/58947.aspx.
10. David D. Kirkpatrick and Mayy El Sheikh, 'Citing Deadlock, Egypt's Leader Seizes New Power and Plans Mubarak Retrial', *New York Times*, 22 November 2012, at www.nytimes.com/2012/11/23/world/middleeast/egypts-president-morsi-gives-himself-new-powers.html.
11. Peter Beaumont, 'Mohamed Morsi Bars Court Challenges and Orders Hosni Mubarak Retrial', *Guardian*, 22 November 2012, at www.theguardian.com/world/2012/nov/22/mohamed-morsi-mubarak-retrial-egypt.
12. 'Freedom and Justice Party Statement on Recent Constitutional Declaration', Ikhwanweb, 25 November 2012, at ikhwanweb.com/article.php?id=30420.
13. 'Ghozlan: Morsi Constitutional Declaration in Line with Popular Will and Revolutionary Demands', Ikhwanweb, 23 November 2012, at ikhwanweb.com/article.php?id=30413.
14. 'Hisham Qandil ... Ruyatuh Limusteqbal Misr' ('Hisham Qandil ... His Vision for Egypt's Future'), Al-Jazeera, Bila Hadoud, Episode 2, 4 December 2012, in Arabic at www.aljazeera.net.
15. 'Mudhakirat al-Mustashar al-Qanuni Lilmaezul Turwi Qissat Itaha Betntawy Wananan' ('Legal Advisor's Memoir Relates the Story of Tantawi and Annan's Expulsion'), *Shorouk News*, 23 November 2013, in Arabic at www.shorouknews.com/news/view.aspx?cdate=23112013&id=29e6b622-acca-4279-b120-68f4dc1bcba8.
16. Habib, *Al-Ikhwan Al-Muslimun*.
17. Alaa Bayoumi, 'The Many Faces of Mohamed Morsi', Al-Jazeera, 13 December 2012, at www.aljazeera.com/indepth/features/2012/12/2012121371332920740.html.
18. 'Lilat Itihadiya' ('Itihadiya Night'), YouTube, 24 April 2014, at www.youtube.com/watch?v=o2-UVLXA7rE.
19. Author interview with Dr Abdelmawgoud Dardery via Skype, July 2014.
20. 'Brotherhood time', Mohammed Mahdi Akef Program – Part II, Al-Kahera Wal-Nas TV, August 11, 2012, www.youtube.com/watch?v=YL6407Lz62Q.

21. 'Muslim Brotherhood Statement on Events of Friday November 23', Ikhwanweb, 25 November 2012, at www.ikhwanweb.com/article.php?id=30419.
22. Habib, *Al-Ikhwan Al-Muslimun*.
23. Mustafa Bakri, *Suqut Al-Ikhwan: Lahazat Alakhira bayn Morsi wa Sisi* ('The Fall of the Ikhwan: The Final Moments between Morsi and Sisi'), Cairo, Al-Dar al-Misria al-Lubnania, 2013.
24. Jihad Awda, *Suqut Dawlat Al-Ikhwan* ('The Fall of the Ikhwan State'), Cairo, Kenouz, 2014.
25. For a more detailed analysis of this issue, see Human Rights Watch, Egypt, 'New Constitution Mixed on Support of Rights', 30 November 2012, at www.hrw.org/news/2012/11/30/egypt-new-constitution-mixed-support-rights.
26. Clark Lombardi and Nathan J. Brown, 'Islam in Egypt's New Constitution', *Foreign Policy*, 13 December 2012, at foreignpolicy.com/2012/12/13/islam-in-egypts-new-constitution/.
27. *Al-Ittihadiyya: 'Presidential Palace' Clashes in Cairo*, special report issued by Cairo Institute for Human Rights Studies, December 2012, at www.cihrs.org/wp-content/uploads/2012/12/Ittihadiyya.rep_.CIHRS_.Eng_.Dec_.pdf.
28. 'Brotherhood Press Release on Pro-Democracy Demonstration Outside Presidential Palace', Ikhwanweb, 5 December 2012, at ikhwanweb.com/article.php?id=30453.
29. *Al-Ittihadiyya: 'Presidential Palace' Clashes in Cairo*, Cairo Institute for Human Rights Studies.
30. 'Novelist Bahaa Taher: Morsi is Waging a War against the People', *al-Masry al-Youm*, at www.almasryalyoum.com/news/details/258916.
31. Peter Hessler, 'Big Brothers', *New Yorker*, 14 January 2013, at www.newyorker.com/magazine/2013/01/14/big-brothers.
32. David D. Kirkpatrick, 'Morsi Turns to His Islamist Backers as Egypt's Crisis Grows', *New York Times*, 7 December 2012, at www.nytimes.com/2012/12/08/world/middleeast/egypt-islamists-dialogue-secular-opponents-clashes.html.
33. 'Qasr Ittihadia ... Kalimat Alser Wara Iqalat Wazir Aldakhilia Almisri' ('Al-Ittihadiyya Palace ... The Password Behind the Sacking of the Egyptian Interior Minister'), *Islam Memo*, 6 January 2013, in Arabic at islammemo.cc/akhbar/arab/2013/01/06/161959.html.
34. Asma Al Sharif and Yasmine Saleh, 'Special Report: The Real Force Behind Egypt's "Revolution of the State"', Reuters, 10 October 2013, at uk.reuters.com/article/uk-egypt-interior-special-report-idUKBRE99908720131010.
35. 'Abu Futuh: Istibdal Alamn Bemuayidi Alrayis Inhiar Lildawla' ('Abul Futuh: Replacing the Security Forces with the President's Supporters Will Bring Down the State'), *Dostor*, 17 February 2014, in Arabic at www.dostor.org/108286.
36. Amirah Ibrahim, 'What Lies Beneath', *Ahram Weekly*, 13 December 2012, at weekly.ahram.org.eg/News/580/17/What-lies-beneath.aspx.

37. Ibid.
38. Ibid.
39. 'Amnesty Urges Morsi to Protect Egypt's Shias', Ahram Online, 25 June 2013, at english.ahram.org.eg/NewsContentPrint/1/0/74899/Egypt/0/Amnesty-urges-Morsi-to-protect-Egypt%E2%80%99s-Shias.aspx.
40. Omar Ashour, 'Collusion to Crackdown: Islamist–Military Relations in Egypt', Brookings Doha Center, March 2015, at www.brookings.edu/~/media/research/files/papers/2015/03/10-islamist-military-relations-in-egypt-ashour/collusion-to-crackdown-english.pdf.
41. 'Mahsoub: Morsi Qabl Fikrat Intikhabat Mubakira' ('Mahsoub: Morsi Accepted the Idea of Early Elections'), Al-Jazeera, Shahid Alla Aser, Episode 15, 11 May 2014, in Arabic at www.aljazeera.net.
42. Tom Perry and Yasmine Saleh, 'Egypt's Mursi Brings More Islamists into Cabinet', Reuters, 7 May 2013, at www.reuters.com/article/us-egypt-reshuffle-idUSBRE9460AL20130507.
43. 'Egyptian Blooper: Politicians, Unaware They Are Live on Air, Threaten Ethiopia over Dam Construction', Memritv, Clip No. 3857, 3 June 2013, at www.memritv.org/clip_transcript/en/3857.htm.
44. Ibid.
45. 'Ahmed Fahmy Yaqshif Asrar Wasata Al-Lahazat Al-Akhira Bayna Morsi wa Sissi Youm 3 Julio 2013 Sabahan' ('Ahmed Fahmy Reveals the Secrets of the Mediation of the Final Moments between Morsi and Sisi on the Morning of 3 July 2013'), *Akhbar Alwadi*, 6 July 2014, in Arabic at akhbaralwadi.com.
46. Bakri, *Suqut Al-Ikhwan*.
47. Yasmine Saleh and Paul Taylor, 'Special Report: Mursi's Downfall', Reuters, 5 July 2013, at www.reuters.com/article/us-egypt-protests-downfall-specialreport-idUSBRE9640SP20130705.
48. Patrick Ventrell, Director, Press Office, Daily Press Briefing, Washington, DC, June 26, 2013, US Department of State, at www.state.gov/r/pa/prs/dpb/2013/06/211168.htm.
49. 'Tafasil Likhira Lihukm Morsi' ('The Final Moments of Morsi's Rule'), Al-Jazeera, Bila Hadoud, Episode 2, 18 December 2013, in Arabic at www.aljazeera.net.
50. Saleh and Taylor, 'Special Report: Mursi's Downfall'.
51. 'Tafasil Likhira Lihukm Morsi', Bila Hadoud.
52. Ibid.
53. Robert Mackey, 'July 2 Updates on Egypt's Political Crisis', *New York Times*, 2 July 2013, at thelede.blogs.nytimes.com/2013/07/02/latest-updates-on-egypts-political-crisis/.
54. Saleh and Taylor, 'Special Report: Mursi's Downfall'.
55. Ibid.
56. 'Egypt: Security Forces Used Excessive Lethal Force', Human Rights Watch, 19 August 2013, at www.hrw.org/news/2013/08/19/egypt-security-forces-used-excessive-lethal-force.

57. Author conversations with Egyptians during 2013 and 2014.
58. Author interview with Saleh Abdelmaqsoud, Doha, April 2014.
59. Author interview with Gamal Abdelsattar, Doha, April 2014.
60. Author interview with Mahmoud Hussein, Doha, April 2014.

Chapter Four

1. Mahmoud Nacua, *Rahlti Mae Alnas Walfikr* ('My Journey with People and Ideas'), Maktabat Wahiba, Cairo, 2007.
2. Author interview with Haj Abu Sen, London, September 2007.
3. Ibid.
4. These personalities, who included Sheikh Fatallah Ihwass, Mohamed Ramadan Al-Huwaisa and Mahmoud Nacua (who became Libya's first post-Qadhafi ambassador to the UK), held a series of meetings in Al-Huwaisa's flat in the Zawiat Dahmani area of Tripoli. They agreed to set up a Tripoli Brotherhood organisation, appointing Ihwass as its head. Around the same time a group of personalities including Abdelkaim Al-Jihani, Idris Ma'adhi and Hamid Salabi came together in Benghazi to establish a similar Brotherhood organisation for the east. Mahmoud Nacua, *Masarat al-Harakat al-Islamiya fi Libya* ('Paths of the Islamic Movement in Libya'), London, Dar al-Hikmah, 2010.
5. Mahmoud Nacua, *Masarat Al-harakat al-Islamiya fi Libya* ('Paths of the Islamic Movement in Libya'), London, Dar al-Hikmah, 2010.
6. Ibid.
7. Ibid.
8. Author interview by telephone with Dr Alamin Belhaj, January 2006. The group's situation was made even harder by the internal struggles that were being played out inside these new Brotherhood groups at the time. One current that was greatly influenced by Sudanese Islamist Hassan Turabi, who had broken away from the tight restrictions of the Brotherhood's international hierarchy, sought to establish its own Libyan organisation that would share the same ideological orientation as the Brotherhood, but that would be independent from the movement in Egypt. This was not well received by the Guidance Office in Cairo, which moved immediately to establish a separate Libyan Brotherhood group comprising those elements who were keen to be wedded more closely to the mother branch. This prompted the leaders of the two factions to start 'competing [with] and fighting each other to attract the young' (author interview with Haj Abu Sen, London, September 2007). But this battle turned out to be short-lived. In 1984, the former group that was now working under the broader platform of the National Front for the Salvation of Libya launched a disastrous attack on Colonel Qadhafi's Bab al-Aziziya barracks in Tripoli. Quite what possessed it to engage in such a reckless operation is still not clear, but in its rush to topple Qadhafi the group completely misjudged the situation. Indeed, the attack resulted in harsh reprisals, and the NFSL was all but finished off as a force.

9. François Burgat, 'Qadhafi's Ideological Framework', in Dirk Vandewalle, ed., *Qadhafi's Libya 1969–1994*, New York, St Martin's Press, 1995, p. 49.
10. Hanspeter Mattes, 'The Rise and Fall of the Revolutionary Committees', in Vandewalle, *Qadhafi's Libya*, p.109
11. 'An Interview with Suleiman Abdelkader', Al-Jazeera, Special Visit Programme, 30 May 2009, at www.aljazeera.net.
12. Author interview with anonymous Libyan journalist and former Brotherhood member, London, November 2015.
13. Author interview with Alamin Belhaj, Manchester, June 2014.
14. 'Suleiman Abdulkadir Baktus Zaeim Al-Ikhwan al-Muslimin fi Liby lil Ahram: Aldawla fi Islam Madania la Dinia' ('Suleiman Abdulkadir Baktus, Leader of the Muslim Brotherhood in Libya, to Al-Ahram: The State Is a Civil, Not Religious One in Islam'), *Alhram*, 9 September 2011, in Arabic at almanaramedia.blogspot.co.uk/2011/09/blog-post_6394.html.
15. Author interview with Mohamed Abdul Malik, Manchester, September 2013.
16. B. Chernitsky, 'Libyan Muslim Brotherhood on the Rise', MEMRI, Inquiry and Analysis Series Report No. 828 (24 April 2012).
17. *Libya Focus*, Menas Associates, March 2006 (subscription-only publication).
18. Alaya Allani, 'Democratic Transformation in Libya: The Path and Horizons', in *Maghrebi Islamists and Democratic Transition: Libya, Tunisia, Algeria, Morocco, Mauritania*, Maghrebi Monitor for Democratic Transition, 2012–13.
19. Ibid.
20. 'Interview with Suleiman Abdelkader', Al-Jazeera.
21. 'Abdelrazzak al-Aradi fi Liqa Khass' ('Special Interview with Abdelrazzak Al-Aradi'), YouTube, 26 April 2013, at www.youtube.com/watch?v=ojMUIrxY34M.
22. Author interview with Alamin Belhaj, Manchester, June 2014.
23. 'Alamin Belhaj: al-Ikhwan Dikhalu Althawra Mundh Alyoum Awal Lakanahum Touqaeu Almutalaba Bislahat Walays Tagheer Alnizam' ('Alamin Belhaj: Brotherhood Joined the Revolution from the First Day but They Expected that the Demands Would Be for Reform Not for a Change of the Regime'), *Alhayat*, 24 September 2011, in Arabic at www.sauress.com/alhayat/310809.
24. Author interview with Alamin Belhaj, Manchester, June 2014.
25. 'Engineer Suleiman AbdelKader, Guide of Libya Brothers, Switzerland Olten', YouTube, 1 May 2012, at www.youtube.com/watch?v=9wBlscxHRNg.
26. 'Salim Al-Sheikhi, Dor Al-Ikhwan fi 17 Fibrayir' ('The Role of the Muslim Brotherhood in 17 February'), Facebook, 14 May 2013, at www.facebook.com/permalink.php?story_fbid=577404982293211&id=131813446852369.
27. 'Ikhwan Libya Yandhamun ala Ihtijajat dhid Qadhafi' ('Libyan Brothers are Joining the Protests Against Qadhafi'), *Alhayat*, 5 February 2011, in Arabic at daharchives.alhayat.com.

28. The four red lines were: Islam and the application of Sharia law; the security and stability of Libya; national unity; and Muammar Qadhafi.
29. 'Salim Al-Sheikhi, Dor Al-Ikhwan fi 17 Fibrayir', Facebook.
30. Salabi was 'rehabilitated' by the regime in the 2000s after he agreed to assist with Saif Al-Islam's de-radicalisation initiative, using his theological and scriptural knowledge to try to persuade the imprisoned militants to renounce violence.
31. Dr Aqeel Hussein Aqeel, 'Asrar Wahaqiq min Zaman al-Qadhafi' ('Secrets and Facts from Qadhafi's Time'), *Dar Almajouat Aldualia*, n.d., at www.dr-aqeel.com/books/asrar/index.html.
32. Ibid.
33. While the two men were talking, Saif Al-Islam happened to telephone Aqeel, who told him that he had to act to stop the bloodshed. Saif Al-Islam responded by switching off his phone (ibid.).
34. Mary Fitzgerald, 'Finding Their Place – Libya's Islamists during and after the 2011 uprising', in Peter Cole and Brian McQuinn, *The Libyan Revolution and Its Aftermath*, Oxford, Oxford University Press, 2015.
35. 'Salim Al-Sheikhi, Dor Al-Ikhwan fi 17 Fibrayir', Facebook.
36. 'Alamin Belhaj: al-Ikhwan Dikhalu Althawra Mundh Alyoum Awal Alnizam', *Alhayat*.
37. Author interview with Mohamed Abdul Malik, Manchester, September, 2014.
38. 'Salim Al-Sheikhi, Dor Al-Ikhwan fi 17 Fibrayir, Facebook.
39. Author interview with Alamin Belhaj, Manchester, June 2014.
40. Author interview with Alamin Belhaj, Manchester, June 2014.
41. Ibid.
42. Ibid.
43. 'The Muslim Brotherhood in Afghanistan', *Islamism Digest*, Centre for the Study of Terrorism (CFSOT) 2: 10 (October 2007).
44. Author interview with Alamin Belhaj, Manchester, June 2014.
45. Alaya Allani, 'Democratic Transformation in Libya'.
46. Author interview with Alamin Belhaj, Manchester, June 2014.
47. 'Fawzi Abu Katif ... Shahid Ala Althawra Libia' ('Fawzi Abu Katif ... Witness to the Libyan Revolution'Episode 1), Al-Jazeera, Shahid Alla Aser, 8 February 2012, in Arabic at www.aljazeera.net.
48. Author interview with Alamin Belhaj, Manchester, June 2014.
49. Ibid.
50. 'Fawzi Abu Katif ... Shahid Ala Althawra Libia', Al-Jazeera, Shahid Alla Aser.
51. 'Laqa Qana Aljazeera Alkamil mae Masoul Jama'at Al-Ikhwan al-Muslimin Libia Muhandis Suleiman Abdulkadir' ('Al-Jazeera Net Full Interview with the Libyan Muslim Brotherhood Leader Engineer Abdulkadir Suleiman'), Almanara Media, 29 September 2011, in Arabic at almanaramedia.blogspot.co.uk/2011/09/blog-post_9243.html.
52. 'Halka Nikashia: Libya ... Ala Ain?' ('Discussion Forum: Libya ... Where

Is It Heading?), *Mustaqbal Alarabi* 399 (May 2012), in Arabic at www.caus.org.lb/PDF/EmagazineArticles/mustaqbal_399_halak%20nikachieh%20 94-125.pdf.

53. 'Salim Al-Sheikhi, Dor Al-Ikhwan fi 17 Fibrayir', Facebook.
54. 'Alsalabi Walshikhi Wakharun Yuqadimoun Mashruean Llimithaq Watani Antiqali' ('Salabi, Sheikhi and Others Come up with a Draft for a Transitional National Charter'), Almanara Media, 28 March 2011, in Arabic at almanaramedia.blogspot.co.uk/2011/03/blog-post_3481.html.
55. 'Halak Nikashia: Libya Ifaq Watahdiat Tahoul Aldemoqrati' ('Discussion Forum: Libyan Horizons and Challenges of Democratic Transformation'), *Mustaqbal Alarabi* 395 (January 2012), in Arabic at www.caus.org.lb/PDF/EmagazineArticles/mustaqbal_395_halak%20nikachieh%207-74.pdf.
56. Mary Fitzgerald 'Finding Their Place – Libya's Islamists during and after the 2011 uprising', in Peter Cole and Brian McQuinn, *The Libyan Revolution and Its Aftermath*, Oxford, Oxford University Press, 2015.
57. Author interview with Alamin Belhaj, Manchester, June 2014.
58. The representatives from each of the currents then went back to their respective movements for consultation, before meeting again in Benghazi, although this second time Salabi did not attend.
59. Author interview with Alamin Belhaj, Manchester, June 2014.
60. Ibid.
61. 'Halka Nikashia: Libya ... Ala Ain?', *Mustaqbal Alarabi.*
62. Author interview with Alamin Belhaj, Manchester, June 2014.
63. International Crisis Group, *Holding Libya Together: Security Challenges After Qadhafi*, 2011, at www.crisisgroup.org/~/media/Files/Middle%20East%20North%20Africa/North%20Africa/115%20Holding%20Libya%20Together%20--%20Security%20Challenges%20after%20Qadhafi.pdf.
64. *Libya Focus*, Menas Associates, June 2011.
65. Ibid.
66. 'Libya's Muslim Brotherhood snubs Gaddafi', *Asharq Al-Awsat*, 20 June 2015, at english.aawsat.com/2011/06/article55246088/libyas-muslim-brotherhood-snubs-gaddafi.
67. Ibid.
68. Aqeel, 'Asrar Wahaqiq min Zaman al-Qadhafi'.
69. Ibid.
70. Ibid.
71. Jibril states that he had suggested to Abdeljalil that he counter his obvious sympathy for the Brotherhood by appointing Abdelrahman Shalgam as deputy of the NTC. While Abdeljalil was open to the suggestion, Shalgam refused it. 'Jibril fi Hewar mae al-Wasat Gate: Fujiat Bighurfat Amaliat Sirriat fi Tunis Yudiruha Abduljalil wa Belhaj – 3' ('Jibril in His Interview with al-Wasat Gate: I Was Surprised by the Presence of a Covert Operation Chamber in Tunisia Run by Abdul Jalil and Belhaj – Part 3'), *Al-Wasat Gate*, 13 January 2015, at www.alwasat.ly/ar/news/discussion/56310/#sthash.aW1kerRS.dpuf.

Chpater Five

1. 'Muslim Brotherhood Goes Public with Libya Summit', Reuters, 17 November 2011, at www.reuters.com/article/us-libya-muslim-brotherhood-idUSTRE7AG2OY20111117.
2. Ibid.
3. Author interview with Alamin Belhaj, Manchester, June 2014.
4. B. Chernitsky, 'Libyan Muslim Brotherhood on the Rise', MEMRI, 24 April 2012, at www.memri.org/report/en/print6301.htm#_edn12.
5. Ibid.
6. Ibid.
7. 'Al-Islamyoun fi Libya' ('Islamist in Libya'), Al-Jazeera, 22 February 2012, in Arabic at www.aljazeera.net.
8. Ibid.
9. Author interview with Alamin Belhaj, Manchester, June 2014.
10. Author interview with Noman Ben Othman, London, July 2012.
11. Author interview with Alamin Belhaj, Manchester, June 2014.
12. Justice and Construction Party. 'Justice and Construction Political Programme, Libya', 2012, at kurzman.unc.edu/files/2011/06/LBY-2012-al-Adala-wa-al-Bina-Justice-and-Construction.pdf.
13. 'Libya's New "Leader" Says Sharia Law Will Be Used as Basis to Guide Country after Fall of Gaddafi Regime', *Daily Mail*, 13 September 2011, at www.dailymail.co.uk/news/article-2036885/Libya-New-leader-Mustafa-Abdel-Jalil-says-Sharia-law-used-Gaddafi-regime.html.
14. 'Justice and Construction Political Programme, Libya', 2012.
15. Author interview with Mohamed Abdulmalik, Manchester, September 2013.
16. Ibid.
17. Ibid.
18. Abdelrazzak Al-Aradi, 'Alradi: Sahajim al-Ikhwan WaIdouhum Lildifae ean Anfusihim' ('Alradi: I will Attack the Brothers and Invite Them to Defend Themselves'), *Libya Aljadidah*, 10 March 2013, in Arabic at libyaaljadidah.com.
19. Author interview with Alamin Belhaj, Manchester, June 2014.
20. Muammar Qadhafi, *The Green Book*, The World Centre for the Study and Research of The Green Book, Tripoli, n.d.
21. Marty Fitzgerald, 'A Current of Faith', *Foreign Policy*, 6 July 2012, at foreignpolicy.com/2012/07/06/a-current-of-faith.
22. Author interview by telephone with Mohamed Abdulmalik, July 2012.
23. *Libya Focus*, Menas Associates, July 2012.
24. 'Alradi: Sahajim al-Ikhwan WaIdouhum Lildifae ean Anfusihim', *Libya Aljadidah*.
25. Author interview by telephone with civil servant in Tripoli, July 2012.
26. *Libya Focus*, Menas Associates, December 2011.

27. Author interview with Alamin Belhaj, Manchester, June 2014.
28. 'Alradi: Sahajim al-Ikhwan WaIdouhum Lildifae ean Anfusihim', *Libya Aljadidah*.
29. Ibid.
30. 'Halka Nikashia: Libya ... Ala Ain?, *Mustaqbal Alarabi*.
31. Mustafa Abu Shagur's Facebook page, 9 October 2012, at www.facebook.com/Dr.Mustafa.A.G.Abushagur/timeline.
32. Ibid.
33. Absdelrassak Alradi, 'Altarik Lilkartha' ('The Road to Disaster'), *Ean Libya*, 1 March 2015, in Arabic at www.eanlibya.com/archives/31331.
34. Mustafa Abu Shagur's Facebook Page, 9 October 2012.
35. Ibid.
36. Author interview with Mohamed Abdulmalik, Manchester, 2014.
37. Those vetted included NTC and transitional government members, senior security officials, ambassadors, heads of government institutions and companies, heads of universities, and heads of unions, among others.
38. 'A Collective to Isolate a Few', *Correspondents*, 13 April 2013, at www.correspondents.org/node/2370.
39. 'Mohammad Sawan Lalshrq Alawst: Qanoun Aleuzzal Qad Yashmal Rayis Barlaman Wabed Althwar' ('Mohammed Sawan to Alsharq Alwast: Isolation Law Act May Include the Head of Parliament and Some Revolutionaries'), *Alsharq Alwast*, 3 May 2013, in Arabic at aawsat.com.
40. *Libya Focus*, Menas Associates, February 2013.
41. 'A Collective to Isolate a Few', *Correspondents*.
42. Mohamed Magarief, for example, may have headed up one of the most prominent dissident groups, but he had spent several years in the service of the regime as Libya's ambassador to India between 1978 and 1980.
43. 'Ray Sawan fi Aleuzzal Alssiasi' ('Sawan's View on Political Isolation'), YouTube, 21 March 2013, at www.youtube.com/watch?v=hbBozdRGp_M.
44. *Libya Focus*, Menas Associates, February 2013. See also 'Ray Sawan fi Aleuzzal Alssiasi', YouTube.
45. Ibid.
46. Author interview with Mohamed Abdulmalik, Manchester, September 2013.
47. *Libya Focus*, Menas Associates, March 2013.
48. Ibid.
49. Ibid.
50. Ibid.
51. 'Aleuzzal Yutawil Shakhsiat Libyia Kabirah' ('Isolation Law Includes Senior Libyan Figures'), Al-Jazeera, 5 May 2013, in Arabic at www.aljazeera.net.
52. Author interview with Alamin Belhaj, Manchester, June 2014.
53. Ibid. See also 'Al-Hirazi: Hizb al-Adalat Walbina Aldahiat Alqadima Lithawar' ('Justice and Development Party is the Next Victim of the Revolutionaries'), *Libya al-Mostakbal*, 19 March 2015, in Arabic at www.libya-al-mostakbal.org/news/clicked/65610.

54. *Libya Focus*, Menas Associates, June 2013.
55. Ibid.
56. 'Ikhwan Libya: Zidane Lays Rajul Almarhalat Watanzimina Lm Yatakhabat baed Suqut Qiadat Ikhwan Misr' ('Ikhwan Libya: Zidane is Not the Man for This Period and Our Organisations are in Disarray after the Fall of the Muslim Brotherhood's Leaders in Egypt'), *Alquds Alarabi*, 9 September 2013, in Arabic at www.alquds.co.uk/?p=82458.
57. *Libya Focus*, Menas Associates, July 2013.
58. *Libya: Politics and Security*, Menas Associates, 7 August 2013.
59. Ibid.
60. Ibid.
61. 'Ikhwan Libya: Zidane Lays Rajul Almarhalat Misr', *Alquds Alarabi*.
62. *Libya Focus*, Menas Associates, May 2014.
63. Khalid Mahmoud, 'Libyan Muslim Brotherhood Condemns Haftar "Coup"', *Asharq Al-Awsat*, 23 May 2014, at english.aawsat.com/2014/05/article55332524/libyan-muslim-brotherhood-condemns-haftar-coup.
64. 'Libya Muslim Brotherhood Statement on General Haftar's Desperate Coup Attempt', Ikhwanweb, 21 May 2014, at www.ikhwanweb.com/article.php?id=31656&ref=search.php.
65. Facebook page of Mohamed Abdulmalik, 18 May 2014, at www.facebook.com/abusondes
66. Bouazza Ben Bouazza and Maggie Michael, 'Thousands of Libyans Flee to Tunisia to Escape Fighting', Associated Press, 30 July 2014, at www.washingtontimes.com/news/2014/jul/30/thousands-flee-to-tunisia-to-escape-libya-fighting/?page=all.
67. 'Al-Hirazi: Hizb al-Adalat Walbina Aldahiat Alqadima Lithawar' ('Justice and Development Party Is the Next Victim of the Revolutionaries'), *Libya al-Mostakbal*, 19 March 2015, in Arabic at www.libya-al-mostakbal.org/news/clicked/65610.
68. Author interview with Mohamed Abdulmalik, Manchester, September 2013.

Chapter Six

1. Author interview with Sheikh Khamis Majeri, Tunis, July 2014.
2. Lorenzo G. Vidino, *The New Muslim Brotherhood in the West*, New York, Columbia University Press, 2010, p. 60.
3. Author interview with Walid Bannani, Tunis, June 2013.
4. Author interview with Riyadh Chaibi, Tunis, July 2014.
5. Quoted in Mohammed Elhachmi Hamdi, *The Politicisation of Islam*, Boulder, CO, Westview, 1998, p. 22.
6. Emad Eldin Shahin, *Political Ascent: Contemporary Islamic Movements in North Africa*, Boulder, CO, Westview, 1998, p. 70.
7. Moncef Ouanes, *Al-Khitab al-Arabi al-Hudood wa Tanaqudat* ('Arab Discourse: Limits and Contradictions'), Tunis, Al-Dar al-Tunisia Li Nashra, 1992.
8. Francois Burgat and William Dowell, *The Islamic Movement in North Africa*,

Austin, TX, University of Texas Press, 1993, p. 184.
9. Ibid.
10. Ibid., p. 220.
11. Author interview with Hmida Ennaifer, Tunis, March 2010.
12. Burgat and Dowell, *Islamic Movement in North Africa*, p. 218.
13. Author interview with Mehdi Mabrouk, Tunis, February 2008.
14. For example, public institutions were barred from rehiring Islamists who had lost their jobs during the crackdown of 1981–84; veiled women were banned from universities and workplaces; and male Islamist students were expelled from university.
15. A Unique Occasion is Offered to Tunisia. Third Anniversary of the MTI, Tunis, 1984. Cited in Burgat and Dowell, *Islamic Movement in North Africa*, pp. 196–7.
16. Shadi Hamid, 'Ennahda and the Islamic Project in Tunisia', *Muftah*, 9 July 2014, at muftah.org/tunisias-battles/#.VtWROs9WKUk.
17. Ibid.
18. Salehedinne Jourchi, 'Sena ala Iktishaf Muamara' ('A Year after the Discovery of the Conspiracy'), *Majallat Al-Majalla*, 13–19 May 1992.
19. Author interview with Mehdi Mabrouk, Tunis, February 2008.
20. Allaya Allani, *Al-Harakat Al-Islamiya bil Watan Al-Arabi: Tunis Namoudajan 1970–2007* ('Islamic Movements in the Arab Nation: The Tunisian Example 1970–2007'), Rabat, Dar Fater Wichad Natha, 2008, p. 184.
21. Zakya Daoud, 'Chronique Tunisienne', *Annuaire de l'Afrique du Nord* 28 (1989), p. 685.
22. Salehedinne Jourchi, 'Sena ala Iktishaf Muamara'.
23. Author interview with Sheikh Khamis Majeri, Tunis, June 2013.
24. Ibid.
25. Author interview with Rida Idris, Paris, April 2010.
26. Ibid.
27. Author interview with Amar Larayedh, Paris, April 2010.
28. Ibid.
29. Ibid.
30. Al Mouldi Al-Ahmar, *Intikhabat al-Tounsia: Khafia Fashal Alqua Alhadathia Wamashakil Najah Hizb an-Nahda* ('Tunisian Elections: The Reasons behind the Failure of the Modernists and the Problems of An-Nahda's Success'), Arab Centre for Research & Policy Studies, December 2011, in Arabic at www.dohainstitute.org/file/Get/6b4fe295-a935-4153-8e86-d9d1b3177ea9.
31. See, for example, Hamdi Redrissi, 'La Nahdha et la transition democratique' in '*La Transition Democratique en Tunisie Etat des Lieux: Les Acteurs*, L'Observatoire Tunisien de la Transition Democratique, Tunis, L'Observatoire, Tunis, 2012, p. 113.
32. Author interview with Tunisians close to An-Nahda in Tunis and Paris during 2010.
33. An-Nahda Movement Programme For Freedom, Justice & Development in

Tunisia, 2011 at kurzman.unc.edu/files/2011/06/Nahda_2011_summary_in_English.pdf

34. Nazanine Moshiri, 'Interview with Rachid Ghannouchi', Al-Jazeera, 7 Feb 2011, at www.aljazeera.com/news/africa/2011/02/201123346427362 4.html.
35. 'We Won't Ban Bikinis and Beer, Says Islamist Politician', *The Times*, 15 July 2011, at www.thetimes.co.uk/tto/news/world/middleeast/article3094677.ece.
36. Rachid Ghannouchi, 'A Day to Inspire All Tunisians – whether Islamic or Secular', *Guardian*, 17 October 2011, at www.theguardian.com/commentisfree/2011/oct/17/tunisians-islamic-secular-ennahda-election
37. Author interview with Walid Bannani, Tunis, June 2013.
38. Author interviews with Salehedinne Jourchi, Tunis, July 2014, and Alaya Allani, Tunis, June 2013.
39. Author interview with Riyadh Chaibi, Tunis, July 2014.
40. Marc Lynch, 'Tunisia's New al-Nahda', *Foreign Policy*, 29 June 2011, at foreignpolicy.com/2011/06/29/tunisias-new-al-nahda.
41. Author interview with Alaya Allani, Tunis, June 2013.
42. Author interview with Riyadh Chaibi, Tunis, July 2013.
43. Moshiri, 'Interview with Rachid Ghannouchi'.
44. Jamel Dridi, 'Pourquoi Ennahdha rencontre un succès populaire en Tunisie?' *Kapitalis*, 18 October 2011, at kapitalis.com/afkar/68-tribune/6378-pourquoi-ennahdha-rencontre-un-succes-populaire-en-tunisie.html.
45. Author interview with Abu Yaareb Marzouki, Tunis, June 2013.
46. Abou Yaâreb Marzouki, 'Ennahdha est débile, hypocrite et assoiffé de pouvoir', *Kapitalis*, 6 March 2013, at www.kapitalis.com/politique/14860-abou-yaarebmarzouki-Ennahda-est-debile-hypocrite-et-assoiffe-depouvoir.html.
47. Jalal Ouerghi, *Al-Islamiyoun Fi Dawla: Tajribat Harakat An-Nnahda al-Tounsia fi Siaq Aldawla Alhaditha* ('The Islamists in the State: The Experience of the Tunisian An-Nahda Movement in the Context of the Modern State'), Al-Difaf, Beirut 2014.
48. Author interview with Mehdi Mabrouk, Tunis, June 2014.
49. Author interview with Hamadi Jebali, Tunis, July 2014.
50. Author interview with Souhir Dardoui, Tunis, June 2013.
51. Abderrazak Lejri, 'L'extradition de Baghdadi Mahmoudi: une raison d'état commune à trois pays', *Mediapart*, 28 June 2012, blogs.mediapart.fr/abderrazak-lejri/blog/280612/l-extradition-de-baghdadi-mahmoudi-une-raison-d-etat-commune-trois.
52. Lilia Weslaty, 'Les dessous de la crise au sommet de l'Etat selon l'ex Conseiller de la Présidence', *Nawaat*, 16 July 2012, at nawaat.org/portail/2012/07/16/lex-conseiller-principal-a-la-presidence-ennahdha-est-un-parti-anti-revolutionnaire.
53. Author interview with Salehedinne Jourchi, Tunis, 2013.
54. Mohamed Farouk, 'Politique: Rached Ghannouchi dirige-t-il "de fait" la Tunisie?', webmanagercenter, 16 February 2012, at www.

webmanagercenter.com/actualite/societe/2012/02/16/116249/politique-rached-ghannouchi-dirige-t-il-de-fait-la-tunisie.

55. Ibid.
56. Author interview with Hamadi Jebali, Tunis, July 2014.
57. Author interview with Salehedinne Jourchi, Tunis, July 2013.
58. *Sana Ajmi*, 'Ennahdha Discourse: The Sixth Caliphate or a Misunderstanding?', Tunisia Live Net, 16 November 2011, at www.tunisia-live.net/2011/11/16/ennahdha-flipflopping-the-sixth-caliphate-a-misunderstanding/#sthash.9BmTXoqM.dpuf.
59. Author interview with Sheikh Khamis Majberi, Tunis, 2014.
60. Author interview with Salehedinne Jourchi, Tunis, July 2013.
61. Ibid.
62. Ed Webb, 'Economics in Ennahda's Tunisia: Neoliberal Continuity or Redistribution; Liberal Individualism or Nomocentric Communalism?' at www.academia.edu/3236360/Economics_in_Ennahdas_Tunisia_neoliberal_continuity_or_redistribution_liberal_individualism_or_nomocentric_communalism.
63. Author interview with Walid Banani, Tunis, June 2013.
64. Derek Lutterbeck, 'After the Fall: Security Sector Reform in Post-Ben Ali Tunisia', Arab Reform Initiative, September 2012, at www.arab-reform.net/sites/default/files/After%20the%20Fall.%20SSR%20in%20Post-Ben%20Ali.pdf.
65. Ibid.
66. Amnesty International, 'Tunisia: One year on, no accountability for repressed protest', 9 April 2013, at www.amnesty.org/en/documents/MDE30/004/2013/en/.
67. Jalal Ouerghi, *Al-Islamiyoun Fi Dawla: Tajribat Harakat An-Nnahda al-Tounsia fi Siaq Aldawla Alhaditha* ('The Islamists in the State: The Experience of the Tunisian An-Nahda Movement in the Context of the Modern State'), Al-Difaf, Beirut 2014.
68. K. Dalacoura, 'Islamism and Neoliberalism in the Aftermath of the 2011 Uprisings', in Emel Akçali, *Neoliberal Governmentality and the Future of the State in the Middle East and North Africa*, London, Palgrave, 2016.
69. Tarek Amara, 'Protests in Tunisian Town Show Anger at Islamist Government', Reuters, 2 December 2012, at www.reuters.com/article/us-tunisia-protests-idUSBRE8B108620121202.
70. Author interview with Alaya Allani, Tunis, June 2013.
71. Ibid.
72. Ibid.
73. Domenica Preysing, *Transitional Justice in Post-Revolutionary Tunisia 2011–2013*, Berlin, Springer, 2016, p. 144.
74. Tarek Amara, 'UPDATE 2 – Tunisia Finance Minister Quits, Adds to Transition Fears', Reuters, 27 July 2012, www.reuters.com/article/tunisia-finance-resignation-idUSL6E8IRM2V20120727.

Chapter Seven

1. Rachid Ghannouchi, 'Madaa Misdaq Daewaa Fashal Al'islam Alsyasi?' ('How Credible Is the Claim that Political Islam Has Failed?'), Al-Jazeera, 24 October 2013, in Arabic at www.aljazeera.net.
2. Author interview with Amer Larayedh, Tunisia, June 2014.
3. A. Tamimi, *Rachid Ghannouchi, A Democrat within Islamism*, Oxford, Oxford University Press, 2001, p. 151.
4. Author interview with anonymous senior An-Nahda leader, Paris, April 2010.
5. Hacen Ouali, 'Débats houleux en Tunisie: Ennahda veut imposer la charia', *El Watan*, 3 March 2012, at forumdesdemocrates.over-blog.com/article-debats-houleux-en-tunisie-ennahda-veut-imposer-la-charia-100665836.html.
6. Camille le Tallec, 'La charia inscrite dans la Constitution?', *La Libre*, 7 March 2012, at www.lalibre.be/actu/international/la-charia-inscrite-dans-la-constitution-51b8e6c8e4b0de6db9c5bb36.
7. 'Harakat An-Nahda Tureed Dustoran Tunisien Min Quran Wa Sunna Wa Sharia' ('The An-Nahda Movement Wants a Tunisian Constitution that is Based on the Quran, the Sunna and Sharia'), *Assda Al-Maghreb*, 19 February 2012, in Arabic at www.assdae.com.
8. Author interview with Souad Abdelraheem, Tunis, June 2013.
9. Sarah J. Feuer, 'Islam and Democracy in Practice: Tunisia's Ennahdha Nine Months In', *Middle East Brief*, September 2012, at www.brandeis.edu/crown/publications/meb/MEB66.pdf.
10. Author interview with Salehedinne Jourchi, Tunis, July 2014.
11. Author interview with Walid Bannani, Tunis, June 2013.
12. Author interview with Habib Khoder, Tunis, June 2013.
13. Author interview with Hedi Ben Brahim, Tunis, June 2014.
14. Author interview with Walid Bannani, Tunis, June 2013.
15. Author interview with Amar Larayedh, Tunis, July 2014.
16. Ibid.
17. 'Qiadi Biharakat An-Nahdat al-Tounisia Yaqul Aanah Tama 'Tfikik Leghm' Tansis eala al-Sharia al-Islamia Bildostor' ('A Leader in the Tunisian An-Nahda Movement Says a Mine was Dismantled by Not Stipulating Islamic Sharia in the Constitution'), in Arabic at www.alqudsalarabi.info/index.asp?fname=data%5C2012%5C03%5C03-28%5C28qpt959.htm.
18. Monica Marks, 'Speaking on the Unspeakable: Blasphemy and the Tunisian Constitution', Carnegie Endowment, 4 September 2012, at carnegieendowment.org/sada/?fa=49259.
19. Pesha Magid 'Newly Proposed Blasphemy Law Raises Concerns about Freedom of Expression', Genocide Watch, 2 August 2012, at www.genocidewatch.org/images/Tunisia,_12_08_02,_Newly_Proposed_Blasphemy_Law_Raises_Concerns_About_Freedom_of_Expression.pdf.
20. Ibid.

21. A discussion of the various Salafist currents, ranging from apolitical Salafism at one end to Salafist jihadism at the other, is beyond the scope of this book. However, the Salafists did not represent one monolithic block.
22. Author interview with anonymous former An-Nahda member, Tunis, July 2014.
23. Salah Jourchi, 'Hadha Ma jinah al-Silfioun al-Radikalioun eala harakat An-Nahda' ('This is What the Radical Salafists Brought Upon An-Nahda'), Mominoun Without Borders For Studies and Research, January 2014, in Arabic at www.mominoun.com.
24. 'Majalat Kalima Tuhawir Qiadat min Maktab Alsiasi Liharakat An-nahda' ('Kalima Magazine Interviews Some Politburo Members of the An-Nahda Movement'), *Kalima Magazine*, 24 December 2005, in Arabic at tunisie.over-blog.org/article-1458532.html.
25. Author interview with Rida Idriss, Paris, April 2010.
26. Author interview with Alaya Allani, Tunis, June 2013.
27. Author interview with Walid Bannani, Tunis, July 2013.
28. Alaya Allani, *Islaymioun al-Tunisounon min Marada ala Hukem: Anasha, Tatour, Afaq* ('The Tunisian Islamists from Opposition to Rule: Formation, Development, Horizons'), Tunis, Hans Zidal, 2014, p. 241.
29. Author interview with Amer Larayedh, Tunis, July 2014.
30. Kaouther Larbi, 'Under-Pressure Ghannouchi Vows Crackdown on Hardline Salafists', *Middle East Online*, 22 September 2012, at www.middle-east-online.com/english/?id=54505.
31. 'Dr Ghannouchi & Mr Blunder', 25 October 2013, video clip at www.freearabs.com/index.php/politics/73-video-gallery/771-jb-span-leaked-video-jb-span-dr-ghannouchi-and-mr-blunder.
32. Ibid.
33. Ibid.
34. Author interview with Walid Bannani, Tunis, July 2013.
35. Author interview with Riyadh Chaibi, Tunis, July 2014.
36. Author interview with Mehdi Mabrouk, Tunis, July 2014.
37. Ibid.
38. Author interview with Amer Larayedh, Tunis, July 2013.
39. Author interview with Salehedinne Jourchi, Tunis, July 2014.
40. Ali Hashem, 'Chokri Belaid's Widow Holds Ennahda "Politically Accountable"', Al-Monitor, 11 February 2013, at www.al-monitor.com/pulse/originals/2013/02/chokri-belaid-widow-ennahda-responsible-assassination.html#ixzz43MXe2y6r.
41. Author interview with anonymous former cabinet minister in the Jebali government, Tunis, July 2014.
42. Jeffrey Fleishman and Radhouane Addala, 'Tunisia Ruling Party Rejects Prime Minister's Call for New Cabinet', *Los Angeles Times*, 7 February 2013, at articles.latimes.com/2013/feb/07/world/la-fg-tunisia-islamists-20130208.
43. 'Tunisia PM Sees Government Plan Collapse', Al-Jazeera, 18 February 2013,

at www.aljazeera.com/news/middleeast/2013/02/2013218194218416135.html.

44. Noureddine Hlaoui, 'No Major Changes in New Tunisian Government', al-Monitor, 12 March 2013, at www.al-monitor.com/pulse/politics/2013/03/new-tunisian-government-no-change.html#ixzz43MftoVe8.
45. Author interview with Walid Bannani, Tunis, July 2013.
46. Vivienne Walt, 'After Morsi's Ouster in Egypt, Tunisia's Islamists Fear a Similar Fate', *Time*, 16 July 2013
47. 'A Talk with the Ennahda Movement's Rachid Ghannouchi', *Al-Sharq Al-Awsat*, 26 December 2011, at english.aawsat.com/2011/12/article55243841/a-talk-with-the-ennahda-movements-rachid-ghannouchi.
48. Author interview with Hamadi Jebali, Tunis, July 2014.
49. Author interview with Hedi Ben Brahim, Tunis, June 2014.
50. 'Tunisia Government Will Not Quit – PM Ali Larayedh', BBC Online, 29 July 2013, at www.bbc.co.uk/news/world-africa-23496929.
51. Author interview with anonymous former minister in the Jebali government, Tunis, July 2014.
52. 'Tunisia Declares Ansar al-Sharia a Terrorist Group', BBC Online, 27 August 2013, www.bbc.co.uk/news/world-africa-23853241.
53. Sarah Chayes, 'How a Leftist Labor Union Helped Force Tunisia's Political Settlement', Carnegie Endowment, 27 March 2014, at carnegieendowment.org/2014/03/27/how-leftist-labor-union-helped-force-tunisia-s-political-settlement.
54. Walid Al-Talili, 'Tumasik alnuseij al-Tounsie Inqidhna fi Binqrdan' ('Rachid Ghannouchi: The Cohesion of Tunisian Society Saved us in Ben Guerdane'), Alaraby, 17 March 2016, in Arabic at www.alaraby.co.uk.
55. Hatim Betioui, 'Ghannouchi: Ennahda Left the Government, but Not Its Position of Authority', *Al-Sharq Al-Awsat*, 6 June 2014, at english.aawsat.com/2014/06/article55332976/ghannouchi-ennahda-left-the-government-but-not-its-position-of-authority.
56. Jalal Ouerghi, *Al-Islamiyoun Fi Dawla: Tajribat Harakat An-nahda Tounisia fi Siaq Aldawla Alhaditha* ('The Islamists in the State: The Experience of the Tunisian An-Nahda Movement in the Context of the Modern State'), Al-Difaf, Beirut, 2014.
57. Author interview with Riyadh Chaibi, Tunis, July 2014.
58. Author interview with Salehedinne Jourchi, Tunis, July 2014
59. Walid Al-Talili, 'Tumasik alnuseij al-Tounsie Inqidhna fi Binqrdan'
60. Author interview with Salehedinne Jourchi, Tunis, July 2014.

Conclusion

1. Anthony Shadid, 'Islamists' Ideas on Democracy and Faith Face Test in Tunisia', *New York Times*, 17 February 2012, at www.nytimes.com/2012/02/18/world/africa/tunisia-islamists-test-ideas-decades-in-the-making.html?_r=0.
2. 'Abdelfatah Mourou ... Tajribat al-Harakat al-Islamia' ('Abdelfatah Mourou

... The Experience of the Islamic Movement'), Al-Jazeera, Bila Hadoud, 19 March 2014, in Arabic at www.aljazeera.net.

3. Jalal Ouerghi, *Al-Islamiyoun Fi Dawla: Tajribat Harakat An-nahda Tounisia fi Siaq Aldawla Alhaditha* ('The Islamists in the State: The Experience of the Tunisian An-Nahda Movement in the Context of the Modern State), Beirut, Al-Difaf, 2014.
4. K. Dalacoura, 'Islamism and Neo-Liberalism in the Aftermath, in Emel Akçali, ed., *Neoliberal Governmentality and the Future of the State in the Middle East and North Africa*, London, Palgrave Macmillan, 2016.
5. Steven Brooke, 'US Policy and the Muslim Brotherhood', Al-Mesbar Studies and Research Centre, 19 January 2015, at www.fpri.org/docs/chapters/201303.west_and_the_muslim_brotherhood_after_the_arab_spring.chapter1.pdf.
6. Alaa Bayuoumi, 'Morsi's Foreign Policy Record Reviewed', Al-Jazeera, 27 June 2013, at www.aljazeera.com/indepth/features/2013/06/201362511431896 3367.html.
7. Author interview with Islam Kattatni, Cairo, June 2014.
8. 'Muslim Brotherhood Review: Main Findings', UK Government, 2015, at www.gov.uk/government/uploads/system/uploads/attachment_data/file/486932/Muslim_Brotherhood_Review_Main_Findings.pdf.
9. Ammar Fayed, 'Is the Crackdown on the Muslim Brotherhood Pushing the Group Toward Violence?', Brookings, March 2016, at www.brookings.edu/research/papers/2016/03/muslim-brotherhood-crackdown-violence-fayed.
10. 'Muslim Brotherhood Review', UK Government.
11. Mohamed Ben Rajab, 'Harakat An-Nahda al-Tounsia: Makhad Fasl Aldin ean Aldawla' ('The Tunisian An-Nahda Movement ... The Trials of Separating Religion from the State'), Elaph, 10 March 2016, in Arabic at elaph.com/Web/News/2016/3/1075637.html.
12. Said Ferjani, 'The "End of Islamism" and the Future of Tunisia', Hudson Institute, 29 April 2016, at www.hudson.org/research/12349-the-end-of-islamism-and-the-future-of-tunisia.
13. Ibid.
14. David D. Kirkpatrick, 'In Egyptian Hard-Liner's Surge, New Worries for the Muslim Brotherhood', *New York Times*, 1 April 2012, at www.nytimes.com/2012/04/02/world/middleeast/attacking-the-west-islamist-gains-in-egypt-presidential-bid.html.

BIBLIOGRAPHY

Books

Abdelhalim, Mahmoud, *Al-Ikhwan al-Muslimoun, Ahdath Sunat Al-Tareeq, Ru'iah Min al-Dakhil* ('The Muslim Brotherhood, the Events that Made History – an Insider Vision'), vol. 2, Alexandria, Dar al-Dawa, 2004.

Allani, Alaya, *Islaymioun al-Tunisounon min Marada ala Hukem: Anasha, Tatour, Afaq* ('The Tunisian Islamists from Opposition to Rule: Formation, Development, Horizons'), Tunis, Hans Zidal, 2014.

Al-Qursh, Sa'ad, *Althawra Alan: Youmiat min Midan al-Tahrir* ('Revolution Now: Diaries from Tahrir Square'), Cairo, Kotob Khan, 2012.

Hussein, Aqeel, *Asrar Wahaqiq min Zaman al-Qadhafi* ('Secrets and Facts from Qadhafi's Time'), Dar Almajouat Aldualia, n.d.

Awda, Jihad, *Suqut Dawlat al-Ikhwan* ('The Fall of the Ikhwan State'), Cairo, Kenouz, 2014.

Bakri, Mustafa, *Suqut Al-Ikhwan: Lahazat Alakhira bayn Morsi wa Sisi* ('The Fall of the Ikhwan: The Final Moments between Morsi and Sisi'), Cairo, Al-Dar al-Misria al-Lubnania.

Brown, Nathan, *When Victory is Not an Option: Islamist Movements in Arab Politics*, Ithaca, NY, Cornell University Press, 2012.

Burgat, Francois, and William Dowell, *The Islamic Movement in North Africa*, Austin, TX, University of Texas Press, 1993.

Cesari, Jocelyne, *The Awakening of Muslim Democracy*, Cambridge, Cambridge University Press, 2014.

Chamakh Amer, *Al-Ikhwan Al-Muslimoun Wathwrat 25 Janayir* ('The Muslim Brotherhood and the Revolution of 25 January'), Dar Alttawzie Walnnashr, Egypt, 2013.

Cole, Peter, and Brian McQuinn, *The Libyan Revolution and its Aftermath*, Oxford, Oxford University Press, 2015.

Djait, Hichem, *La Personnalité et le Devenir Arabo-Islamiques*, Paris, Editions Du Seuil, 1974.

Habib, Mohammed, *Al-Ikhwan Al-Muslimoun: Bayn Alsueud Walriasa Watakul Alsheria* ('The Muslim Brotherhood: The Rising, the Presidency and the

Erosion of Legitimacy'), Cairo, Sama Nashar, 2013.

Hamdi, Mohammed Elhachmi, *The Politicisation of Islam*, Boulder, CO, Westview Press, 1998.

Joffe, George, ed., *Islamist Radicalisation in North Africa*, London, Routledge, 2012.

Kandil, Hazem, *Inside the Brotherhood*, Cambridge, Polity, 2015.

Labat, Severine, *Les Islamistes Tunisiens: Entre L'etat et la mosque*, Paris, Demopolis, 2013.

Maktouf, Lotfi, *Sauver La Tunisie*, Fayard, Paris, 2013.

Nacua, Mahmoud, *Rahlti Mae Alnas Walfikr* ('My Journey with People and Ideas'), Maktabat Wahiba, Cairo, 2007.

———*Masarat al-Harakat al-Islamiya fi Libya* ('Paths of the Islamic Movement in Libya'), London, Dar al-Hikmah, 2010.

Ouanes, Moncef, *Al-Khitab al-Arabi al-Hudood wa Tanaqudat* ('Arab Discourse: Limits and Contradictions'), Tunis, Al-Dar al-Tunisia Li Nashra, 1992.

Ouerghi, Jalal, *Al-Islamiyoun Fi Dawla: Tajribat Harakat An-Nnahda al-Tounsia fi Siaq Aldawla Alhaditha* ('The Islamists in the State: The Experience of the Tunisian An-Nahda Movement in the Context of the Modern State'), Al-Difaf, Beirut, 2014.

Pargeter, Alison, *The Muslim Brotherhood: The Burden of Tradition*, London, Saqi Books, 2010.

Preysing, Domenica, *Transitional Justice in Post-Revolutionary Tunisia (2011–2013)*, Springer, Berlin, 2016.

Roy, Olivier, *The Failure of Political Islam*, Harvard, Harvard University Press, 1996.

Rubin, Barry, ed., *The Muslim Brotherhood: The Organisation and Politics of a Global Islamist Movement*, London, Palgrave Macmillan, 2010.

Shahin, Emad Eldin, *Political Ascent: Contemporary Islamic Movements in North Africa*, Boulder, CO, Westview, 1998.

Tamimi, A., *Rachid Ghannouchi: A Democrat within Islamism*, Oxford, Oxford University Press, 2001.

Tadros, Mariz, *The Muslim Brotherhood in Contemporary Egypt: Democracy Redefined or Confined?*, London, Routledge, 2012.

Vidino, Lorenzo G., *The New Muslim Brotherhood in the West*, New York, Columbia University Press, 2010.

Wickham, Carrie Rosefsky, *The Muslim Brotherhood: Evolution of an Islamist Movement*, Princeton, NJ, Princeton University Press, 2013.

Zoubir, Yahia, and Gregory White, eds, *North African Politics: Change and Continuity*, London, Routledge, 2016.

Journal Articles, Papers and Chapters in Edited Volumes

Al Anani, Khalil, 'The Muslim Brotherhood after Morsi', 2 October 2013, Arab Center for Research and Policy Studies (ACRPS), Doha.

———'Egypt's Freedom and Justice Party: To Be or Not to Be Independent',

Carnegie Endowment, 1 June 2011.

Al-Ahmar, Al Mouldi, 'Intikhabat al-Tounsia: Khafia Fashal Alqua Alhadathia Wamashakil Najah Hizb an-Nahda' ('Tunisian Elections: The Reasons Behind the Failure of the Modernists and the Problems of An-Nahda's Success'), Arab Centre for Research and Policy Studies, December 2011.

Allani, Alaya, 'Democratic Transformation in Libya: The Path and Horizons', in *Maghrebi Islamists and Democratic Transition: Libya, Tunisia, Algeria, Morocco, Mauritania*, Maghrebi Monitor for Democratic Transition, 2012–13.

Al-Shater, Khairet, 'The Nahda Project' (Complete Translation), *Current Trends in Islamist Ideology* (Hudson Institute), 10 April 2012.

Alwadi, Hicham, 'Al-Islamiyoun fi alssulta: Halat Misr' ('Islamists in Power: The Case of Egypt'), *Mustqbal al-Alaraby* 413 (July 2013).

Ashour, Omar, 'Collusion to Crackdown: Islamist–Military Relations in Egypt', Brookings Doha Center, March 2015.

Brooke, Steven, 'US Policy and the Muslim Brotherhood', Al-Mesbar Studies and Research Centre, 19 January 2015.

Brown, Nathan J., and Michele Dunne, 'Egypt's Draft Constitutional Amendments Answer Some Questions and Raise Others', Carnegie Endowment, 1 March 2011.

Brown, Nathan J., 'The Muslim Brotherhood as Helicopter Parent', ForeignPolicy.com, 27 May 2011.

Burgat, François, 'Qadhafi's Ideological Framework', in Dirk Vandewalle, ed., *Qadhafi's Libya 1969–1994*, New York, St Martin's Press, 1995.

Chayes, Sarah, 'How a Leftist Labor Union Helped Force Tunisia's Political Settlement', Carnegie Endowment, 27 March 2014.

Chernitsky, B., 'Libyan Muslim Brotherhood on the Rise', MEMRI, 24 April 2012.

Dalacoura, K, 'Islamism and Neoliberalism in the Aftermath of the 2011 Uprisings', in Emel Akçali, ed., *Neoliberal Governmentality and the Future of the State in the Middle East and North Africa*, London, Palgrave, 2016.

Daoud, Zakya, 'Chronique Tunisienne,' *Annuaire de l'Afrique du Nord* 28 (1989).

El-Sherif, Asharf, 'The Egyptian Muslim Brotherhood's Failures', Carnegie Endowment, 1 July 2014.

Fayed, Ammar, 'Is the Crackdown on the Muslim Brotherhood Pushing the Group Toward Violence?', Brookings, March 2016.

Ferjani, Said, 'The "End of Islamism" and the Future of Tunisia', Hudson Institute, 28 March 2016.

Fitzgerald, Mary, 'The Libyan Revolution and its Aftermath', in Peter Cole and Brian McQuinn, *The Libyan Revolution and Its Aftermath*, Oxford, Oxford University Press, 2015.

Lombardi, Clark, and Nathan Brown, 'Islam in Egypt's New Constitution', *Foreign Policy*, 13 December 2012.

Lutterbeck, Derek, 'After the Fall: Security Sector Reform in Post-Ben Ali Tunisia', Arab Reform Initiative, September 2012.

Al-Magariaf, Mohamed Yousef, 'Libya Bayn Al-Madi Wal- Hadir: Safahat min

Al-Tarikh Al-Siyasi ('Libya between the Past and the Present: Chapters in Political History'), part 1, vol. 1, Oxford, Centre for Libyan Studies, 2004.

Mattes, Hanspeter, 'The Rise and Fall of the Revolutionary Committees', in Dirk Vandewalle, ed., *Qadhafi's Libya 1969–1994*, New York, St Martin's Press, 1995.

Osman, Tarek, 'Failings of Political Islam', *Cairo Review of Global Affairs*, Fall 2015.

Redissi, Hamdi, 'La Nahdha et la Transition Democratique' in 'La Transition Democratique en Tunisie. Les Acteurs', *L'Observatoire Tunisien de la Transition Democratique*, 2012.

Saleem, Mohamed Elsayed, 'Al'da Alsiasi Liltayarat Al'islamia fi Misr Mundh Thawrat 25 Yanayir' ('The Political Performance of the Islamic Currents in Egypt since the Revolution of 25 January') in *Al-Islamiyoun wa Nizam al-Hukum al-Democrati* ('The Islamists and the Democratic System: Trends and Experiences'), Beirut, Arab Centre for Research and Policy Studies, September 2013.

Sayigh, Yezid, 'Above the State: The Officers' Republic in Egypt', Carnegie Endowment, 1 August 2012.

———'Missed Opportunity: The Politics of Police Reform in Egypt and Tunisia', Carnegie Endowment, March 2015.

Tamam, Hassan, 'Al-Ikhwan al-Muslioun: Sanwat Ma Kabl Althawra' ('The Muslim Brotherhood: The Years before the Revolution'), 2nd edn, Cairo, Dar al-Shorouk, 2013.

Webb, Ed, 'Economics in Ennahda's Tunisia: Neoliberal Continuity or Redistribution; Liberal Individualism or Nomocentric Communalism?'

Wickham, C., 'The Path to Moderation: Strategy and Learning in the Formation of Egypt's Wasat Party', *Comparative Politics* 36: 2 (2004).

Press and NGO sources

Adnkronos International (AKI), Ahram Online, Akhbar Alwadi, *Al-Arabiya, Alaraby, Al-Hayat,* Al-Jazeera, *Al-Masry al-Youm,* Al-Monitor, *Al-Quds Al-Arabi, Al-Sharq Al-Awsat, Al-Watan (Kuwait),* Amnesty International, Assda Al-Maghreb, *Associated Press,* BBC Online, *Christian Science Monitor,* Correspondents, *Daily Mail, Dostor, Economist, El Watan, Financial Times,* Foreign Policy, *Frontline,* Genocide Watch, *Global Post, Guardian, Ha'aretz,* Huffington Post, Human Rights Watch, Ikhwan Wiki, Ikhwanweb, International Crisis Group, *International Herald Tribune,* Jaddaliya Website, Kalima Magazine, Kapitalis, La Libre, Libya Aljadidah, Libya al-Mostakbal, *Los Angeles Times, Masrawy, Mediapart, MEMRI, Middle East Brief,* Middle East Online, Mominoun without Borders, *Nawaat, New York Daily News, New York Times, New Yorker,* Reuters, *RIA Novosti, Rowaq Magazine,* Shorouk News, Sout al-Malaien, *Spiegel Online, The Times,* Tunisia Live, *Washington Post,* YouTube.

INDEX